Defending Europe

EUROPE IN TRANSITION: THE NYU EUROPEAN STUDIES SERIES

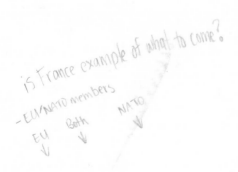

Defending Europe

The EU, NATO and the Quest for European Autonomy

Edited by

Jolyon Howorth
and
John T.S. Keeler

palgrave
macmillan

DEFENDING EUROPE
© Jolyon Howorth and John T.S. Keeler, 2003

First published 2003 by
PALGRAVE MACMILLAN™
175 Fifth Avenue, New York, N.Y. 10010 and
Houndmills, Basingstoke, Hampshire, England RG21 6XS.
Companies and representatives throughout the world.

PALGRAVE MACMILLAN is the global academic imprint of the Palgrave Macmillan division of St. Martin's Press, LLC and of Palgrave Macmillan Ltd. Macmillan® is a registered trademark in the United States, United Kingdom and other countries. Palgrave is a registered trademark in the European Union and other countries.

ISBN 1–40396–114–X hardback

Library of Congress Cataloging-in-Publication Data

Defending Europe: the EU, NATO and the quest for European autonomy/ edited by Jolyon Howorth and John T.S. Keeler.
       p. cm.
    Includes bibliographical references.
    ISBN 1–40396–114–X
       1. National security—Europe—History—20th century. 2. National security—Europe—History—21st century. 3. Security, International. 4. North Atlantic Treaty Organization. 5. Europe—Economic integration. 6. Post-communism—Europe. 7. Europe—Defenses. 8. European Union. I. Howorth, Jolyon. II. Keeler, John T.S.

JZ5930.D44 2003
355'.03304—dc21   2002035593

A catalogue record for this book is available from the British Library.

Design by Newgen Imaging Systems (P) Ltd., Chennai, India.

First edition: April, 2003
10   9   8   7   6   5   4   3   2   1

Printed in the United States of America.

For
Anne Keeler
and
Vivien Schmidt

Contents

Part Three
NATO Enlargement, ESDP and the Discrimination Issue

Two Contrary Conclusions

Acknowledgments

This volume is evidence of the value of grants and their serendipitous effects. The two of us first collaborated when applying for a grant, coadministered by FIPSE (the Fund for the Improvement of Post-Secondary Education within the U.S. Department of Education) and the European Commission, to create a consortial M.A. program in Trans-Atlantic Studies. We were awarded the grant and have become friends in the process of establishing and codirecting one of the resulting programs, *Euromasters with Trans-Atlantic Track* (TAT), which features a core course at the University of Bath and an American module at the University of Washington. The grant also produced the *Trans-Atlantic Masters* (TAM) program, which features a core course at the University of North Carolina, Chapel Hill. Both *Euromasters-TAT* and *TAM*, now completing their fifth year of operation, function as consortia in partnership with the Free University of Berlin/Humboldt University, the University of Madrid (Carlos III), the University of Siena, the Institut d'Etudes Politiques de Paris, and Charles University in Prague. The idea for the conference that generated this volume grew largely out of our many conversations on transatlantic security relations at meetings of the consortia directors from Bath to Berlin and Siena to Seattle.

That conference, "The Transformation of NATO and the Question of European Unity," was held in Seattle, May 5–6, 2000 and was cosponsored by the European Union Center and Center for West European Studies of the University of Washington, the New York University Center for European Studies and the Indiana University Center for West European Studies as well as the European Research Institute at the University of Bath. Most of the chapters in this volume were presented in an earlier form as papers at the conference; chapters 4, 10 and 11 were written subsequently. Gordon Adams, Charles Cogan, Patrick Morgan, Guillaume Parmentier and Michael Smith are not represented in this volume but all also made important contributions to our conference. Cogan's conference paper has been published as a chapter in his new book: *The Third Option: The Emancipation of European Defense 1989–2000* (Praeger, 2001). Parmentier's paper has been published as "NATO: Lost Opportunities," in Michael Brenner and Guillaume Parmentier, eds., *Reconcilable Difference: US–French Relations in the New Era* (Brookings, 2002).

We thank the editor of *Survival* for permission to print chapter 5 by David Yost; an earlier version of that chapter was published as "The NATO Capabilities Gap and the European Union," *Survival*, vol. 42, no. 4 (Winter 2000–2001). We also thank the Centre for European Reform (CER), London, for permission to print chapter 6 by Kori Schake; an earlier version of that chapter was published by the CER as a working paper entitled "Constructive Duplication: Reducing EU Reliance on US Military Assets" (January 2002).

We would like to thank FIPSE, the National Resource Center ("Title VI") program of the U.S. Department of Education, the European Commission, the U.K.'s Economic and Social Research Council (for grant #L213 25 2008, which Howorth coadministers with Stuart Croft, Terry Terriff and Mark Webber under the auspices of the "One Europe or Several?" program), the University of Bath and the University of Washington for the funding that made our collaboration, our conference and this book possible. We thank Katherine Kittel and Phil Shekleton of the UW EU Center/Center for West European Studies staff, and Jill O'Brien and Ann Burge of the University of Bath Department of European Studies, for their contributions to this project and their hospitality to the two of us when we were visiting each others' home bases to collaborate on various pieces of the puzzle. Jolyon Howorth thanks the Institut Français des Relations Internationales, Paris, and the Institute for Security Studies of the Western European Union for repeatedly extending their hospitality and research facilities. John Keeler thanks the Institut d'Etudes Politiques de Paris ("Sciences Po") for access to its library and its invaluable *dossiers de presse*. We thank our editor at Palgrave, Toby Wahl, for his patience when we felt we needed to delay getting the manuscript to press long enough to allow for revisions of the chapters to reflect the impact of the tragic events of September 11, 2001.

We dedicate this book to Anne Keeler and Vivien Schmidt, both of whom have supported us in too many ways to count despite our consortial university-hopping and the many hours devoted to this project.

Jolyon Howorth and John T.S. Keeler

Notes on the Contributors

FRÉDÉRIC BOZO is Professor of History at the University of Nantes and Senior Research Associate at the Institut Français des Relations Internationales, Paris.

JOLYON HOWORTH is Jean Monnet Professor of European Politics at the University of Bath and Senior Research Associate at the Institut Français des Relations Internationales, Paris.

JOHN T.S. KEELER is Professor of Political Science and Director of the European Union Center/Center for West European Studies at the University of Washington, Seattle.

JULIAN LINDLEY-FRENCH is Research Fellow at the European Union Institute for Security Studies, Paris.

ANAND MENON is Professor of Politics and Director of the European Research Institute, University of Birmingham.

ALEXANDER MOENS is Associate Professor of Political Science, Simon Fraser University, Vancouver, Canada.

KORI SCHAKE is Senior Research Professor at the Institute for National Strategic Studies, National Defense University, Washington, D.C.; now serving as a member of the National Security Council staff.

TERRY TERRIFF is Senior Lecturer in the Department of Political Studies at the University of Birmingham.

SUNNIVA TOFTE is Doctoral student in European Studies at the University of Bath.

MARK WEBBER is Senior Lecturer in the Department of European Studies at the University of Loughborough.

DAVID S. YOST is Professor of Security Studies at the Naval Postgraduate School, Monterey, California.

Introduction

CHAPTER 1

The EU, NATO and the Quest for European Autonomy

Jolyon Howorth and John T.S. Keeler

Our title, *Defending Europe*, was chosen because its double meaning reflects the central themes of this book. All of the chapters that follow deal with issues related to the profound transformation of policy for the defense of Europe and the assurance of its security, as formulated within both the North Atlantic Treaty Organization (NATO) and the European Union (EU), since the end of the Cold War. At the same time, all of the chapters address the issue of how new institutional arrangements may be viewed, in part, as devices for defending Europe's interests or enhancing its influence vis-à-vis an increasingly hegemonic United States within the Atlantic Alliance. "Not since Rome has a single power enjoyed such superiority," as Timothy Garton Ash noted recently—"but the Roman colossus only bestrode one part of the world."[1] As figure 1.1 illustrates, the U.S. defense budget is now *five times* that of Russia and is larger than the combined defense budgets of the next nine states on the top ten list.

For allies, the problem with America's dazzling high-tech military power—as manifested from the Gulf War to Kosovo to Afghanistan—is not primarily that it is American, but simply that it is so awesome. Ash's essay implores American readers to understand that it "would be dangerous even for an archangel to wield so much power" and goes on to stress that Americans should understand allied concerns given that the

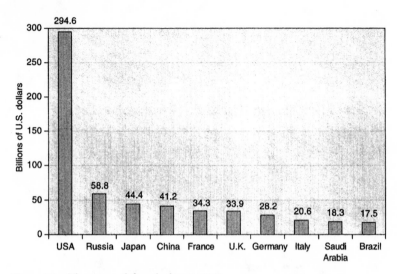

Figure 1.1 The top ten defense budgets in 2000

U.S. constitution, replete with checks and balances, is predicated on the assumption that "no single locus of power, however benign, should predominate; for even the best could be led into temptation."[2] While American defense spending has always exceeded that of its European allies, the gap has increased substantially since the end of the Cold War (see table 1.1) and is now in the process of being widened further by the Bush administration's $40 billion defense-budget hike for 2002 triggered by the events of September 11. It is striking to note that the planned *increase* in the American defense budget for 2002 is substantially more than the *entire* defense budget of the highest-spending EU member state. Moreover, as a number of chapters in this volume will discuss in detail, the growing spending gap *understates* the U.S.–European capability gap, especially in terms of the latest high-tech weaponry. In this context, even many staunchly pro-American Europeans have become concerned about the transatlantic power imbalance. On the other side of the Atlantic, many American commentators have welcomed what they view as a long-overdue recognition by Europeans that the EU should play a larger role in—and shoulder more of the burden for—maintaining the security of the Continent.

Throughout the last decade both European and American officials, for their own reasons, have thus sought to "rebalance" or strengthen NATO through the development of a stronger "European pillar." Thousands of

Table 1.1   EU and US defense expenditures in 2000

Country	Defense expenditures ($ billions)	% change 1985–2000	Per capita expenditures	% GDP for defense
France	34.3	−29	580	2.6
U.K.	33.9	−28	576	2.4
Germany	28.2	−46	343	1.6
Italy	20.6	−19	359	1.9
Spain	7.1	−37	178	1.3
Netherlands	6.3	−28	405	1.9
Greece	5.5	+58	513	4.9
Sweden	5.2	+10	583	2.2
Belgium	3.3	−45	328	1.4
Denmark	2.4	−22	454	1.5
Portugal	2.2	+21	222	2.2
Austria	1.6	−16	196	0.8
Finland	1.5	−32	294	1.3
Ireland	0.7	+44	183	0.7
Luxembourg	0.1	+33	291	0.8
EU-15	152.9	−30	408	2.0
U.S.A.	294.7	−23	1059	3.0

hours have been devoted to drafting and debating alternative means to accomplish this goal: the launch of a Common Foreign and Security Policy (CFSP) for the EU, the revival of the Western European Union (WEU), the establishment of Combined Joint Task Forces (CJTFs), the development of a European Security and Defense Identity (ESDI) within NATO, and finally the creation of a potentially more robust European Security and Defense Policy (ESDP) for the EU. All of these institutional innovations have reflected, at least to some extent, a quest for greater European autonomy. All of them have been officially supported by American leaders—but with increasing misgivings, especially in regard to the possibility that movement toward autonomy could lead to "decoupling." And all of them have been widely supported in Europe—but with growing concerns about both the means and the ends of the enterprise.

This volume thus seeks to analyze the competing ambitions, the contrasting visions and the transatlantic tensions related to the recent quest by Europe for autonomy in the sphere of security and defense. "Autonomy" is a word that has given rise to much misunderstanding. We define it as meaning the political and military capability on the part of the EU to take decisions and to embark on initiatives involving the projection of military power with limited or no assistance from the United States. As the chapters in this book will illustrate, a central challenge facing the ESDP project is to give practical meaning to each element of such an abstract definition.

It should be noted at the outset that today's ESDP may be viewed as a project that has been in gestation for some fifty years. From Ernest Bevin's and Georges Bidault's 1947 scheme for *Western Union* in which "Western Europe should be independent both of the United States and of the Soviet Union,"[3] to the *European Defense Community* of the 1950s that aimed to create an autonomous, "supranational defense capacity with common institutions, common armed forces and a common budget,"[4] to the *Fouchet Plan* of the 1960s that sought to create a politically independent Europe with its own defense policy and capacity (but structured intergovernmentally),[5] to *European Political Cooperation* in the 1970s that attempted to achieve "better mutual understanding, harmonisation of views, coordination of positions and a common approach" to foreign policy,[6] to the revival of *Western European Union* in the 1980s, culminating in a declaration by the nine WEU foreign and defense ministers at the Hague in October 1987 that "the construction of an integrated Europe will remain incomplete as long as it does not include security and defense,"[7] to the project for a *Common Foreign and Security Policy* (CFSP) since 1991, Europe has had many bites at the "ESDP cherry." Some may argue that the reasons why these previous attempts failed are precisely the reasons why the current attempt will fail. But the earlier experiences all arose from different historical impulses—and they failed for different reasons.[8] One of the tasks undertaken in this volume is to demonstrate why the current ESDP project deserves to be taken seriously despite the failure of many previous initiatives.

This introductory chapter will briefly highlight the most significant developments since the end of the Cold War, frame central issues to be addressed throughout the book, and provide an overview of the ten chapters to follow.

The Prelude

With the fall of the Berlin Wall in 1989, traditional principles regarding European security and transatlantic relations seemed to have been rendered irrelevant overnight. The prevailing wisdom among security experts and many actors was that NATO, which had just celebrated its fortieth birthday, would not outlive the demise of the Soviet threat against which it had been forged.[9] Several European leaders, and most notably French president François Mitterrand, assumed that the European Community (EC: soon to be renamed the EU) would now aspire toward some form of autonomous security capacity—albeit within the context of a radically restructured Atlantic Alliance.[10] In March 1991, European Commission President Jacques Delors made what is often regarded as the classic speech in favor of European security autonomy.[11] In June 1991, Luxembourg's foreign minister, Jacques Poos, chairing the Council of Ministers when Serbia engaged in military hostilities against Slovenia, declared (a shade prematurely) that "the hour of Europe" had arrived. These stirrings of independence—bordering on insubordination—were sufficiently irritating to President George Bush (the elder) that, when he met his European colleagues in Rome in November 1991 to discuss a new strategic concept for the Alliance, he bluntly warned them "if what you want is independence, the time to tell us is now."[12]

The 1991 Gulf War had made it abundantly clear to both Washington and the main European capitals that Europe was far from being in a position to move toward anything approaching security autonomy. The subsequent wars of Yugoslav succession in the Balkans drove the point home. Although there were a variety of schemes in circulation for replacing the dominant "NATO narrative"—including a Soviet bid to reestablish the balance of powers, a German/Czech bid to turn the Conference for Security and Cooperation in Europe (CSCE) into a major security actor and the French-led bid to prioritize the WEU—all of those alternative narratives failed to materialize. By 1994, NATO had risen, Phoenix-like, from its own apparent self-immolation and had reemerged as the only show in town.[13] And yet it was a show that could not go on in the same old way. On Washington's Capitol Hill, in particular, the decibel levels were rising around inquiries as to why it was that an EU with a GDP equal to or superior to that of the United States and with a considerably larger population could not do more to organize and above all to fund its own security.[14]

The Movement toward Limited Autonomy: WEU, NATO and ESDI

Since the late 1980s, when European political leaders began to think seriously about enhanced coordination of EC/EU security policy, the solution to the conundrum seemed to be optimally sought via the WEU. Hence, the enormous profusion of policy papers, analytical studies and institutional blueprints that dominated the attention of actors and analysts from 1987 (*Platform of the Hague*) to 1997 (AFSouth crisis and U.K. veto on EU–WEU merger proposals). The potential of WEU to offer the solution to the conundrum seemed self-evident to most experts. WEU had a long (if not glorious) history. It was the only dedicated *European* security and defense institution common to most EC/EU member states. It succeeded, progressively, in associating with its activities most other European states, although this is considered to have exacerbated the awkwardness of its procedures.[15] It had begun to work increasingly effectively with NATO. And it avoided the apparent political minefield of introducing defense and security issues directly into the EU—a proposition to which the U.K. (Europe's most efficient military power), in particular, was unutterably opposed.

The mid-1990s proposals for an ESDI and for the development of CJTFs flowed directly from the WEU logic. The very fact that ESDI was about *identity* (within NATO) rather than about either *policy* or *capacity* indicated its limited ambition. ESDI was unofficially launched at the North Atlantic Council (NAC) meeting in Brussels in January 1994. It was initially conceived largely as a technical-military arrangement that would allow the Europeans to assume a greater share of the burden for security missions—that is, "strengthen the European Pillar of the Alliance"—by providing the WEU with access to those NATO assets and capabilities that European member states did not possess. But it also had a transformative political dimension in that it posited a willingness on the part of NATO as an institution, and on the part of the United States as the foremost NATO member state, to countenance a greater security role for the EU. Ultimately, as we will discuss later, the *political* message of ESDI—that a clearer, bigger European role was both acceptable and desirable—acquired more importance than the technical-military arrangements designed essentially to provide access to NATO/ U.S. assets.[16]

NATO's June 1996 Berlin ministerial meeting may be seen, in retrospect, as the high point of ESDI. In an apparent breakthrough, an agreement was reached involving a U.S. commitment to support a meaningful European military capacity through CJTFs (see later) and a French commitment to move toward full integration of a restructured Atlantic Alliance.[17] ESDI was to entail allowing EU forces to be separated out from the NATO force pool in order to undertake a mission with which the United States or "the Alliance as a whole" did not wish to be involved. ESDI was therefore envisioned as a facilitating mechanism within NATO that hinged around the notion of "separable but not separate" forces. A key feature was the predesignation of a European command chain allowing the Deputy Supreme Commander (DSACEUR), a European officer, to command a WEU-led operation. The CJTFs, as Terry Terriff demonstrates in chapter 3, were conceived as military structuring arrangements allowing given operations to be manned by appropriate forces drawn from a range of services and a number of different countries. This allowed total flexibility in the designation, from within NATO, of air, naval and land elements from a range of European countries, under the predesignated European command chain. These would be drawn up via WEU/NATO consultation procedures. A key feature was the transfer to an EU-led force of certain U.S. military assets and capabilities.

In theory, the political-military potential of the Berlin agreement was substantial. However, the Berlin formula for ESDI proved to be a double illusion. First, what became known as the "Berlin Plus" process—the post-Berlin discussions intended to put ESDI/CJTFs on solid procedural ground by providing assured access to NATO planning facilities, presumed access to NATO assets and capabilities, and the identification of a distinct European chain of command—failed to make much headway, despite repeated official Alliance assurances to the contrary. Most important, the U.S. military produced objections to allowing the Europeans access to crucial but sensitive American assets. Second, at the first real test of "Europeanization" of the Alliance structures—the French bid for NATO's Southern Command (AFSouth)—the whole house of cards came tumbling down.[18]

Despite the mishandling of this crisis by Paris, the AFSouth incident also revealed the real limits of U.S. political flexibility over transatlantic leadership. Tasksharing in the field (risking U.S. equipment and European lives) was one thing. Sharing leadership, especially in an area as sensitive for U.S. policy as the Eastern Mediterranean, was quite another. The Europeans had already experienced the U.S. approach to leadership in the 1995 resolution of the Bosnian War. U.S. bombers and Richard Holbrooke's strong-arm tactics at Dayton achieved in a few weeks what the Europeans had failed to achieve in three years. The European delegations at Dayton were shocked by the brutal unilateralism of the U.S. "negotiators."[19] The final straw seemed to come at the European Council meeting in Amsterdam in June 1997 when, citing NATO primacy, the newly elected Blair government, in its first major security policy decision, vetoed a proposal by nine EU member states to merge the EU with the WEU—as a means of conferring upon the former some of the military attributes of the latter. The explanation offered by London was that the EU–WEU merger proposal would weaken NATO.

Intriguing though it seemed for a time, the WEU "solution" thus proved to be an impasse. By 1997, WEU was perceived by many key analysts as part of (if not *the*) problem rather than as part of (if not *the*) solution. Politically, it perpetuated the unhealthy imbalance between the EU and the United States, the rectification of which was at the heart of the European security conundrum. Institutionally, it still left the EU impotent in terms of decision making. Militarily, it enshrined the EU's dependency on NATO/U.S. assets and capabilities without offering any long-term guarantees that such assets and capabilities would actually be available in the event of a crisis. The crises in the Balkans in the early 1990s—rendered even more dramatic by 1997–1998 with the looming conflict in Kosovo—had demonstrated to the EU the unsatisfactory nature of such a series of handicaps.

The Drive for Autonomy: From Saint-Malo to ESDP

A new approach was urgent. It came with the Franco-British *Declaration* at the Saint-Malo (France) summit orchestrated by British Prime Minister Tony Blair and French President Jacques Chirac in December 1998.[20] By positing the need for "appropriate structures" to be established *within* the EU, for the EU itself to acquire "the capacity for autonomous action backed up by credible military forces," and for an EU contribution to "the vitality of a modernized Atlantic Alliance," the Saint-Malo Declaration went directly to the heart of the European security conundrum.

The immediate logical corollary to Saint-Malo was the construction, within the EU, of a common ESDP.[21] At the European Council in Cologne (June 1999), the EU announced its intention to develop an ESDP and outlined an institutional framework for the new policy that would be put in place by March 2000. The key security and defense institutions included: a High Representative for CFSP (now Javier Solana, former secretary-general of NATO); a Political and Security Committee (usually referred to by its French acronym, COPS), composed of senior officials from each EU member state, whose function is to monitor crisis situations and offer advice to the European Council; a European Military Committee (EUMC), the highest EU military body, composed of the chiefs of the defense staffs of the EU member states; and a European Military Staff (EUMS) to work under the military direction of the EUMC.[22]

The Helsinki European Council meeting of December 1999 formally launched the new institutions of ESDP and also established a military

"Headline Goal" involving the creation of a European armed force capable of significant humanitarian, crisis-management and even peace enforcement operations. The EU pledged that by December 2003 it would have a corps-level force (60,000 troops) capable of rapid deployment within 60 days and sustainable for at least one year. This capability was intended to enable the conduct of effective EU-led military operations, with or without recourse to NATO assets, as well as to provide a full contribution to NATO-led operations.[23]

The Saint-Malo/ESDP initiative responded in many ways to the repeated calls from Capitol Hill for the Europeans to get their act together, yet it produced an ambivalent reaction inside the DC beltway. US Secretary of State Madeleine Albright immediately countered with her famous "3-Ds," giving guarded support to the project on condition that there was no: *d*ecoupling, *d*uplication or *d*iscrimination.[24] Nine months later, these concerns, still dominant in Washington, were articulated in the by now classic warning from Deputy Secretary of State Strobe Talbott: "We would not want to see an ESDI that comes into being first within NATO, but then grows out of NATO and finally grows away from NATO, since that would lead to an ESDI that initially duplicates NATO but that could eventually compete with NATO."[25]

The problem by then was that *ESDI* had already ceased to be the primary focus of European efforts. At the Cologne European Council in June 1999, the ESDP project had been launched and European *autonomy* (at both political and military levels) had become an aspiration widely accepted across the EU as both legitimate and necessary. Moreover, although no EU member state (including France) had any explicit desire to weaken the Atlantic Alliance, still less to enter into competition with NATO or the United States, none could really foretell what the future would hold or what would be the eventual nature of the Atlantic Alliance. From the perspective of Washington, nevertheless, the launch of ESDP could be read as a reckless leap into the dark on the part of an EU that had totally inadequate military capacity, no significant plans to raise military budgets and that appeared obsessed with institutional engineering in Brussels rather than with the more serious business of acquiring the wherewithal to deliver genuine security in the European theater. The Europeans might whine about U.S. hegemony or "hyperpower," but they were manifestly in no position either to challenge it or to replace it.

Strobe Talbott's remark that "NATO, after all, is about the long term" appeared to the Europeans to carry two implications: first, that the alliance should best confront the long term by remaining what it had always been—rather than by embarking on controversial new projects; second, that it was the Europeans who were rocking the boat. But from a European perspective, neither of these implications withstood serious scrutiny. The fact that Saint-Malo had happened could be attributed first and foremost to U.S. pressure over burden sharing, coupled with a clear reluctance in Washington to share leadership. It also reflected growing confidence on the part of an EU intent on becoming a regional military actor. Moreover, far from it being the Europeans who were endangering the future of the alliance,[26] it was widely perceived in Europe—particularly after Dayton, NATO enlargement and Kosovo—that it was the uncompromising and domineering Americans who were undermining the bases of the transatlantic partnership.[27]

As the Clinton administration prepared to hand over the reins to the Bush administration in late 2000, the residual tensions over the ESDP project remained very active. The final speech of outgoing Secretary of Defense William Cohen, to the NATO meeting in Brussels in December 2000,[28] was as uncompromising in its ambivalence toward ESDP as was the first major speech by incoming Secretary Donald Rumsfeld to the *Wehrkunde* in February 2001.[29] But by then, other bones of contention had appeared, which soon had the two sides not merely growling at one another but snapping at one another's heels. The litany of contestation included American plans for a defensive missile shield against so-called "rogue states," dismissive or hostile attitudes toward Russia and China, refusal to sign new—or even retain commitments to traditional— international treaties and conventions (the Kyoto Protocol to the Climate Change Convention, the International Criminal Court, the Biological Weapons Convention, the ABM Treaty), lack of proactivism in the deteriorating Middle East peace process, to which were added a host of cultural factors such as the controversy over the death penalty, or commercial squabbles over hormone-treated beef or bananas. In the summer of 2001, despite an orchestrated Bush charm offensive—which saw the introduction of "chemistry" into international relations as the U.S. president struck up seemingly close personal relations with Tony Blair, Jacques Chirac, German Chancellor Gerhard Schröder, and above all Russian President Vladimir Putin—the balance sheet of EU–U.S. relations seemed about as negative as it had been for a very long time.

The Impact of September 11, 2001

Then along came Osama bin Laden. The September 11 terrorist attacks on New York and Washington rendered even more complex than previously the transatlantic quest for a new, restructured, post–Cold War alliance. Whereas in the initial weeks after the attacks the Bush administration appeared to have abandoned unilateralism in favor of coalition building, consultation and restraint, the European allies appeared to have taken the opposite course, engaging in a *de facto* form of renationalization of their security thinking. National leaders expressed solidarity with the United States—on behalf of their respective countries. Each pledged *national* military assets to the U.S. administration—which Washington, at least initially, ignored. Most European leaders, with the notable exception of Britain's Tony Blair, insisted that the emerging campaign against Al-Quaeda was not a "war," and that attention had to be paid to the root causes of terrorism. Most leaders, with the notable exception of Italian Prime Minister Silvio Berlusconi, also expressed their respect for Islam and Muslim nations. Yet there was something of a cacophony between those insisting that U.S. military retaliation should be tightly "targeted" and those (including, surprisingly, Germany) who offered "unlimited" support to the U.S. military effort. Some managed to articulate both.

This heterogeneity of response was best symbolized by two highly publicized events. The first was the October 2001 European Council meeting in Ghent, which was preceded by a tripartite conclave featuring Chirac/Jospin, Blair and Schröder to discuss the (as yet hypothetical) military involvement of their respective national forces in Afghanistan. This crude attempt to organize a widely resented *Directoire* overshadowed the substantive decisions of the Council itself. The triumvirate planned to meet again on November 5 in London, but this time a cozy *dîner à trois* was gate-crashed by a variety of other European leaders, highlighting once again the disorderly ranks of first, second and third division players, allies and neutrals, "militarists" and "pacifists," and one ESDP opt-out (Denmark). This feature enormously complicated the ESDP work of the Belgian presidency, struggling to impose its authority in the context of high-profile solo diplomacy on the part of Europe's big three.

Above all, it was Tony Blair's crusading leadership style that, while commanding respect, also fostered divisiveness. Acting *as UK prime minister* rather than as spokesperson for the EU (a role that could have been his), Blair threw himself into personal shuttle diplomacy on behalf of the U.S. administration. NATO's September 12 invocation of Article V emanated from a telephone conversation between Blair and the Alliance's secretary-general, Lord Robertson. Did this amount to unconditional EU alignment on U.S. policy?

Paradoxically, NATO's invocation of Article V, high in political symbolism, could prove to be the historical swan song of the Alliance *as a military instrument.* It also helps explain why, despite the short-term disorder of European responses to September 11, the longer-term dynamics of ESDP are likely to be reinforced.[30] Although NATO adopted a series of measures in mid-September 2001 to enhance intelligence sharing, increase security of Alliance facilities, guarantee blanket overflight for allied aircraft, and redeploy certain naval assets to the Eastern Mediterranean, these must be regarded as the bare minimum given the gravity of the crisis. The United States, while reengaging tentatively with a number of multilateral institutions (particularly the United Nations), preferred to discuss *military* cooperation via multiple bilateralisms rather than through the framework of the Alliance itself. Why?

Throughout the 1990s, several U.S. leaders had been calling for NATO to go "out of area or out of business." No longer perceiving Europe to be central to U.S. security interests, they proposed a global deal whereby Europe might acquire regional security autonomy in exchange for political and possibly even military support for U.S. policy across the globe.[31] The Europeans, preoccupied with their own backyard, remained uninterested. On October 7, 2001, in the skies over Afghanistan, the United States went "out of area"—unilaterally. Although Washington eventually associated with its military efforts small numbers of cherry-picked European forces, and although NATO's contribution in terms of logistics and infrastructure was not insignificant, the Afghan War was anything but a NATO operation.

European nations, in proffering their troops, may well have hoped to lock the United States into a multilateral campaign legitimized by the United Nations (UN). The reality was that, despite the coalition-building efforts of the State Department, U.S. instincts remained deeply unilateral. By mid-November, transatlantic tensions were multiplying. The Europeans prioritized the political over the military; humanitarian relief over further escalation of the war on terrorism; the quest for a balanced Middle East settlement over blanket support for Israel; and a long-term commitment to stabilization in Afghanistan over the hunt for Bin Laden. Did the unilateral U.S. shift to "out of area" therefore imply that NATO was destined to go "out of business"? No. NATO will survive. But it will be further transformed from an essentially military organization to an essentially political one.[32] Enlargement from Central and Eastern Europe, announced at the Alliance's Prague summit in November 2002, will accelerate the Alliance's transformation from a collective defense to a collective security agency. The new upgraded relationship with Russia—formalized in May 2002 with the signing of a new partnership agreement between Russia and NATO—will intensify and accelerate that development. In the war against terrorism, in the campaign against weapons of mass destruction and in regional peacekeeping tasks, Russia is likely to share center stage with the United States and the EU. An Alliance with less U.S. military involvement and more participation from former Warsaw Pact members will be a very different actor from the body founded in 1949.

This brings ESDP even more prominently into the spotlight. Despite the immediate phenomenon of *renationalization*, analysts and actors agree that, in the longer term, September 11 made the case for ESDP even more compelling. Beyond the probe of the cameras, significant elements of integration emerged. ESDP institutional turf wars were set aside and the complex EU nexus of agencies and actors worked seamlessly together to develop a coherent political approach to the crisis. Within ten days, the main outlines had been agreed on and were articulated at the extraordinary meeting of the European Council on September 21, 2001. Beyond the expression of "total support" for the *American people* and recognition that UN Security Council resolution 1368 made a U.S. military riposte "legitimate," a relatively distinct EU political agenda suggested a longer-term approach to the global crisis. First, the creation of the "broadest possible global coalition against terrorism *under United Nations aegis*" (emphasis added). Second, major political emphasis on reactivating the Middle East peace process on the basis of the Mitchell and Tenet reports.[33] Third, the "integration of all countries into a fair world system of security, prosperity and improved development." Humanitarian relief for Afghanistan and its neighbors became a number one priority. Europe's ESDP leaders, in various combinations, embarked on an unprecedented round of shuttle diplomacy, repeatedly visiting most countries of Central and South Asia and the Middle East in a relentless quest for dialogue. The EU, despite its obvious shortcomings, was emerging as an international actor.

The EU also intensified overtures toward its neighbors, with heightened diplomatic activity toward Russia, the Mediterranean and Turkey. These coordinated efforts bore fruit. Russia became an increasingly qualitative partner, not only on trade (the move toward a "Common European Economic Area") but also in the field of security. Monthly meetings began between Russia and the EU's COPS. A Euro-Mediterranean Conference of foreign ministers (5–6 November) highlighted a commonality of purpose in the fields of economic development, anti-terrorism, cultural exchanges and security. Above all, an apparent breakthrough was finally announced (early December) in the long-standing impasse over Turkey's refusal to play ball with ESDP.[34]

Military capacity remains the one crucial problem. The war against terrorism may well be more effectively conducted through civilian, police and intelligence instruments than through smart bombs. Checkbook diplomacy and a concentration on development aid and the reconstruction of civil society are appropriate foreign and security priorities for an EU not seeking to become a military superpower. But the carrot without the stick is a less effective instrument than the carrot backed by the stick. At the *Capabilities Improvement Conference* on November 19, 2001, the EU began to make headway toward rectifying the considerable deficiencies in its military "Force Catalogue." But progress was minimal. Despite an optimistically worded report, and despite the controversial declaration of ESDP "operationality" at the December 2001 Laeken European Council meeting, most analysts concur with London's *International Institute for Strategic Studies* that the EU has still "fail[ed] to grasp the severity of the looming crisis" and that "final operating capability" is unlikely to be met before 2012.[35] The EU's military inadequacy, compounded by the likely unavailability of U.S. assets, thus remains the Achilles heel of the ESDP project.

The Organization of the Book

The chapters to follow, written by ten different scholars from Britain, France, Norway, the United States and Canada, will elaborate on the themes highlighted above and provide contrasting perspectives on the development of European policy and its implications for the Atlantic Alliance. The three chapters of Part I will explore more fully, in broad terms, the evolution of NATO and the development of ESDI/ESDP. In chapter 2, Alexander Moens (Simon Fraser University, Canada) explains how the ESDP project has advanced with the support of the three major West European powers and why the United States has supported the initiative despite the objectionable rhetoric of some of its advocates. He also places ESDP in the context of the process of European integration and argues that, like the development of the single currency (the Euro), the creation of a viable EU capacity for military action may take as long as two decades.

In chapter 3, Terry Terriff (University of Birmingham, U.K.) explains how NATO has developed since the mid-1990s the notion of CJTFs as a pivotal part of its commitment to a new ESDI. His major contribution is to clarify how and why the prospect of employing CJTF HQs as command instruments for Europe-led military operations has become less and less attractive, for both political and military reasons, to many

European officials and security experts. In technical-military terms, as Terriff demonstrates, one of the most important and controversial dimensions of the European shift from ESDI to a more autonomous ESDP is the EU's ambition to obviate reliance on a NATO-operated CJTF HQ by developing its own operational HQ.

Chapter 4 by Frédéric Bozo (University of Nantes, France) argues that the Kosovo crisis revealed that a huge gap was threatening to open up between Europe and the United States in regard to capabilities, responsibilities and strategic priorities. In so doing, Kosovo represented a "moment of truth for NATO," exposing structural flaws with the potential to lead to a virtual decoupling of the transatlantic allies. From the Kosovo experience the United States has drawn the lesson that the allies must be required to play a larger military role in the future, while Europeans have tended to deduce that what is required is a greater willingness by the United States to share decision-making power. Yet Kosovo has also served to propel the EU into launching the ESDP project, which Bozo sees as opening the way for a new grand transatlantic bargain: a rebalanced alliance, in which the Europeans play a more assertive, autonomous role and gain acceptance for this by Americans who welcome their unprecedented seriousness of purpose in the defense sphere.

Part II explores in detail the crucial issue of the Euro-American capabilities gap. In chapter 5, David Yost (Naval Postgraduate School, Monterey) begins by noting that "the gap" is properly viewed as the aggregate of many gaps—in technology, investment and procurement—that add up to U.S. superiority, not only quantitative but also qualitative, in military capacity. He then traces the origins of the gap, discusses the importance of the gap in the Kosovo War, and highlights the implications of the gap for the conduct of NATO military operations and transatlantic relations. His conclusion, very sobering for passionate advocates of ESDP, is that a variety of "stubborn facts" will make it extremely difficult for the EU—or even its central players in this sphere, Britain and France—to increase defense spending substantially so as to make significant improvements in European military capabilities.

In chapter 6, Kori Schake (National Defense University, Washington and National Security Council) examines the issue of duplication of NATO's military assets. She demonstrates that while initially there may well have been concern in Washington about the *competitive potential* of ESDP on the military procurement front, it soon became clear that the opposite was, in fact, the case: that the EU ran the risk of failing significantly to procure the weapons systems necessary to engage in high-end

Petersberg missions. Schake examines in some detail the case for "constructive duplication," a course that would ensure that the EU should not be dependent on U.S. systems in a situation where those systems might well be unavailable to putative EU-led missions. Constructive duplication, she demonstrates, would actually benefit both main pillars of the Alliance by creating an adequate pool of military instruments to confront the challenges of the twenty-first century. However, she also notes that the sort of improvements in capability she suggests would require the EU to increase defense spending by 10 percent per year—a figure that Yost and others deem politically impossible to achieve.

Part III examines the complications posed for the development of ESDP by the issue of "discrimination" (by the EU against the six European non-EU NATO members) and the prospect of NATO/EU enlargement. In chapter 7, Sunniva Tofte (University of Bath, U.K.) illuminates the sensitive matter of discrimination by concentrating on the two non-EU allies—Turkey and Norway—most affected by the ESDP project. She argues that both countries, for rather different reasons, have strong incentives to prefer the *status quo ante*, but demonstrates that both have begun to take the measure of ESDP and to adapt their defense and security policies accordingly. Although the asymmetrical relationship between EU/NATO membership carries within it the seeds of multiple tensions for the future, a formula for mutually acceptable non-EU allied involvement in ESDP is likely to be achieved in the not too distant future. All parties involved, as Tofte notes, have too much political capital invested in the process for this not to happen.

In chapter 8, Mark Webber (University of Loughborough, U.K.) focuses on the ways in which the ongoing enlargement of NATO—and the EU—has complicated the development of ESDI/ESDP. He addresses such issues as the concerns of the new post-Communist NATO members (Poland, Hungary and the Czech Republic), the debates over how the EU should involve the thirteen EU accession candidates and the six non-EU NATO states, the problem of "backdoor commitments," the possibility that enlargement may generate a substantial anti-ESDP European caucus within NATO, and the multifaceted effects of September 11. Webber concludes by explaining that the extent to which the NATO–EU/ESDP institutional interface matters will ultimately depend on whether or not ESDP obtains real material substance. Chapter 9 by Julian Lindley-French (European Union Institute for Strategic Studies) covers some of the same ground as chapter 8, but it provides a different perspective by concentrating on dilemmas that NATO enlargement poses for the Atlantic Alliance, by developing a sharp critique of American policy within the Alliance, and by proposing a variety of reforms to rebalance and strengthen NATO.

The final section reflects the intensity of current debates by presenting two contrary conclusions regarding the EU's quest for autonomy within the Atlantic Alliance. Anand Menon (University of Birmingham, U.K.) makes the case for opposing ESDP as misguided and potentially dangerous for the EU and the Alliance. In contrast, Jolyon Howorth (University of Bath, U.K.) argues that ESDP is necessary for the EU and, in the long run, almost certainly in the interests of the Alliance.

Notes

1. Timothy Garton Ash, "The Peril of Too Much Power," *New York Times*, April 9, 2002.
2. Ibid.
3. J.L. Gaddis, "The US and the Question of a Sphere of Influence in Europe," in O. Riste, ed., *Western Security: The Formative Years* (Oslo: Universitetsvorlaget, 1985), p. 78.
4. Edward Fursdon, *The European Defence Community: A History* (London: Macmillan, 1980), p. 153.
5. Georges-Henri Soutou, "Le Général de Gaulle et le plan Fouchet, in *De Gaulle en son siècle: 5. L'Europe* (Paris: Plon, 1992), pp. 126–144.
6. David Allen, R. Rummel and W. Wessels, eds., *European Political Cooperation: Toward a Foreign Policy for Western Europe* (London: Butterworth, 1982), p. 2.
7. Western European Union, *The Reactivation of WEU: Statements and Communications 1984–1987* (London: WEU, 1988), p. 37.
8. In reality, only EDC and Fouchet were clear "failures." The thinking behind "Western Union" was remarkably similar to current ESDP thinking, and EPC led naturally into CFSP, which currently goes from strength to strength.
9. John J. Mearsheimer, "Back to the Future: Instability in Europe after the Cold War," *International Security* 15 (1990); Kenneth Waltz, "The Emerging Structure of International Politics," *International Security* 14 (1990).
10. Jolyon Howorth, "Renegotiating the Marriage Contract: Franco-American Relations since 1981," in Sabrina P. Ramet and Christine Ingebritsen, eds., *Coming in from the Cold War: Changes in US–European Interactions since 1980* (Lanham: Rowman & Littlefield, 2002).
11. Jacques Delors, "European Integration and Security," *Survival* 33 (1991), pp. 99–110.
12. Catherine Kelleher, *The Future of European Security: An Interim Assessment* (Washington: Brookings, 1995).
13. Stuart Croft, "The EU, NATO and Europeanization: The Return of Architectural Debate," *European Security* 9 (Autumn 2000), pp. 1–20.

14. Stanley R. Sloan, "Burdensharing in NATO: The US and Transatlantic Burdensharing," *Les Notes de l'IFRI* 12 (Paris: IFRI, 1999), p. 12.

15. Non-EU NATO members were known as "associate members." Non-NATO EU members were offered "observer" status, and EU/NATO accession candidates from Central and Eastern Europe were offered "associate partnership." Although this involved all possible partners, it did not increase the effectiveness of the WEU as an organization.

16. Jolyon Howorth, *European Integration and Defence: The Ultimate Challenge?* (Paris: WEU-ISS, 2000), Chaillot Paper 43.

17. Ibid., p. 24.

18. Guillaume Parmentier, "NATO: Lost Opportunities," in Michael Brenner and Guillaume Parmentier, eds., *Reconcilable Difference: US–French Relations in the New Era* (Washington, D.C.: Brookings, 2002).

19. See the testimony of a member of the British delegation, Pauline Neville-Jones, "Dayton, IFOR and Alliance Relations in Bosnia," *Survival* 38 (1996/7), pp. 45–65.

20. The text of the Saint-Malo Declaration (as well as most of the key speeches, documents, and texts on European security since 1998) can be found in Maartje Rutten, ed., *From Saint-Malo to Nice: European Defence—Core Documents* (Paris: WEU-ISS, 2001), Cahiers de Chaillot 47; 2001 documents in Maartje Rutten, ed., *From Nice to Laeken. European Defence—Core Documents* 2 (Paris: EU-ISS, 2002), Chaillot Paper 51, 2002.

21. Since the European Council meeting in Helsinki in December 1999, ESDP has often been referred to as CESDP, in part to distinguish it better from ESDI.

22. Howorth, *European Integration and Defence*, pp. 32–33.

23. Ibid., pp. 37–38.

24. Madeleine K. Albright, "The Right Balance will Secure NATO's Future," *Financial Times*, December 7, 1998.

25. Strobe Talbott, "America's Stake in a Strong Europe," Speech to Royal Institute of International Affairs, London, October 7, 1999.

26. From the British perspective, Saint-Malo was largely about saving NATO from imminent demise. See Jolyon Howorth, "Britain, NATO and CESDP: Fixed Strategy, Changing Tactics," *European Foreign Affairs Review* 5 (2000), pp. 1–20.

27. The Dayton Agreement that put an end to the Bosnian War was practically *imposed* both on the Balkan delegations and also on the European delegations that attended the meeting in Dayton, Ohio, in the summer of 1995; in May 1997, it was the United States that unilaterally dictated the designation of the new members of the Alliance. During the Kosovo War, U.S. military leadership was so total that the Europeans vowed "never again" to allow themselves to be reduced to a sideshow. The United States, for its part, vowed "never again" to allow the fractious European allies to retain political oversight over a complex military operation ("war by committee").

Kosovo, as Frédéric Bozo argues in chapter 4, was the real beginning of the end of the Alliance as a predominantly military instrument.

28. Cohen warned that NATO risked becoming "a relic" if ESDP were not kept on a tight leash; cited in Rutten (2001).

29. Rumsfeld argued that ESDP was a very dangerous path to tread; cited in Rutten (2002).

30. Charles Grant, "A Stronger European Foreign and Defense policy," in Edward Bannerman et al., eds., *Europe after September 11th* (London, Centre for European Reform, December 2001), pp. 31–48.

31. F. Stephen Larrabee and David Gompert, *America and Europe: A Partnership for a New Era* (Cambridge: Cambridge University Press, 1997).

32. Anthony Forster and William Wallace, "What is NATO for?" *Survival* 43 (2002), pp. 107–122. See also Anatole Lieven, "The End of NATO," *Prospect*, December 2001, pp. 14–15.

33. Former U.S. Senator George Mitchell presented a plan to end the *intifada* in May 2001 that met with reservations from Israel. George Tenet, director of the CIA, then refined the plan with concrete proposals for a ceasefire and withdrawal to positions held in September 2000.

34. The so-called "Istanbul document" was accepted by Turkey in December 2001, but the terms of the agreement were subsequently refused by Greece. See Sunniva Tofte's account of this in chapter 7.

35. International Institute for Strategic Studies, *The Military Balance 2001–2002* (Oxford: Oxford University Press, 2001), p. 291.

PART ONE

NATO and the Development of ESDI/ESDP

CHAPTER 2

ESDP, the United States and the Atlantic Alliance

Alexander Moens

Introduction

European security ambitions have given rise to debates within the Atlantic Alliance since the launch of the CFSP in the early 1990s. At that time, the Bush (the elder) administration was worried that Franco-German initiatives floated in Europe's intergovernmental conference on political union would undermine NATO's military structure and preempt NATO's function as the essential forum for consultation and the venue for transatlantic decision-making on security and defense. The Clinton administration expressed concerns about a variety of facets of the emerging ESDP, but it generally was quite keen about getting NATO and the new ESDP into a harmonious relationship. In contrast, the administration of George W. Bush has pursued a type of "laissez-faire" policy, stressing the need for real increases in European military capability rather than focusing on rhetoric or organizational diagrams before engaging the Europeans on the subject.

This chapter will assess the political and military dynamics of the ESDP and then trace the development of debates generated by this ambitious initiative within the Atlantic Alliance, with emphasis on the Clinton era. Later chapters (especially those by Kori Schake, Jolyon Howorth and Anand Menon) will highlight the extent to which such transatlantic debates have changed with the onset of the Bush adminis-tration and the impact of September 11.

ESDP: A Combination of European Ambition and Kosovo Momentum

The breakthrough in the development of European defense policy came at the 1998 Anglo-French summit in Saint-Malo, when the British Government confirmed a major change in its position.[1] Tony Blair's agreement to put hard military security and defense squarely inside the EU and to create with other Union members a robust intervention capac-ity was a substantial change from the post–Cold War British position of posing the WEU as the bridge between the Union and the Alliance.

As Bozo discusses at length in chapter 4, the crisis in Kosovo essentially sped up the European initiative. Consensus built quickly that Europe must prepare to undertake such crisis response actions without complete military dependence on the United States. Some have suggested that Britain felt that Europe had to develop a real military capacity to keep the United States interested in NATO.[2] In other words, the British move was not so much an attempt to shift security and defense to Europe for the sake of creating European rather than NATO defense capability as a move to preempt the loss of American interest in the Alliance given the more pressing areas of military concern for the United States in Asia or the Middle East. We cannot assume at this point that there will be no diver-gence in the British and French approach. It is also clear that defense, in contrast to economic or monetary policy, is the key area in Europe where Britain can lead, and where its leadership is a win–win situation.

A European defense entity came a step closer to reality in December 1999 at the conclusion of the European Council in Helsinki, when EU members agreed to set up a decision-making and military planning capacity and to create a joint readiness force for crisis response opera-tions. In the so-called HG, they pledged to construct within three years a European military crisis management force of some 60,000 troops with a rapid response and sustainability capacity, covering the spectrum of operations known as the Petersberg Tasks.

Though European states are already employing military personnel close to that size in the Kosovo Force (KFOR), Europe pledged to make substantial military, budgetary and structural innovations to build a robust corps-level force with a reaction capacity of 60 days and sustain-ability for up to one year. The EU outlined several capabilities as prior-ities to help achieve the HG.[3] The challenge of developing these capabilities such as command and control, interoperability, a reliable logistics chain, air and sea lift and intelligence is complicated by declining defense budgets (see table 1.1) and a great deal of divergence among European capabilities. EU member governments spend approximately half the amount of money on defense and a third of the amount on military R&D as the Americans.[4] Moreover, as David Yost explains in chapter 5, the Europeans get relatively little military and security value for the money they spend.

By and large, European militaries are still overstaffed and underequipped for modern operations, though the British and French, who are leading the initiative, are the most advanced. EU members depend on NATO command and control and American assistance in sophisticated intelligence, air transportation, logistics and power projection capability to undertake crisis response operations, including the more demanding possibilities of peace enforcement. European militaries must rationalize, restructure and specialize, using both the capacity of the larger states and the value-added of smaller member states to prepare a common military crisis-management capacity. Arguably, this will be one of the most difficult tasks the Union has undertaken. European governments briefly considered but then rejected so-called "convergence criteria" in defense spending and common priorities similar to what was used during the formation of the Euro. Instead, individual governments at various conferences are to pledge resources, guided loosely by a sense of peer review and common commitment.

The new initiative will put pressure on rationalizing the defense industry in the EU. EU leaders have expressed their determination "to foster the restructuring of the European defense industries," and "seek further progress in the harmonization of military requirements."[5] The globalization of the armaments market is pushing the European members toward consolidating their arms industry and pooling their military resources. Despite the recent merger announcements between British Aerospace and GEC Marconi, and between DaimlerChrysler Aerospace and Aerospatiale Matra, and the subsequent arrival of the European Aeronautic Defense and Space Company (EADS), consolidation will take time and its effects will not be known for a long time.[6]

Europe's defense industry reform will no doubt be complicated by the "dawning realization" on the part of the Americans that Europe is likely to buy fewer American weapons in the future and may sell more arms as a result of the consolidation of its industry.[7] In terms of specialization and cost savings, transatlantic mergers may be more rational than some intra-European mergers. However, given that American companies will be in a position to dominate such partnerships, political sensitivities will slow down the process. One of the barriers to "industrial bridge-building across the Atlantic" is the continuation of rigid export controls on defense industry products by the United States.[8] Realizing that such controls will increasingly hinder American companies in their attempt to supply European militaries with new equipment proposed both in the Defense Capabilities Initiative (DCI) in NATO and in the HG requirements in the Union, Secretary of State Madeline Albright announced at the Foreign Ministers' meeting in Florence in May 2000 a package of seventeen specific steps to reduce these controls.[9] These steps aim "to streamline the U.S. Defense export control licensing process and forge closer industrial linkages between U.S. and allied defense suppliers."[10]

Despite the high military threshold and political uncertainty, the EU is seriously committed and will find a way to reach the HG. I believe ESDP will emerge as a substantive move forward in the development of more European "say and do" in military affairs, not because all the military pieces of the puzzle are falling into place but because the fundamental conditions for an EU advance in this area are now present.

First, the three major Western European powers appear to agree on it. The British move to merge its European crisis-management plans with the French in Saint-Malo in December 1998 established the beginnings of a trilateral (Britain, France and Germany) approach, bringing London into both "the Atlantic and European houses."[11] In terms of military initiative and capability, the British are leading the EU in close harmony with the French. In the lead-up to Helsinki, the Germans did not take an active role, perhaps because they face the most difficult budgetary and military restructuring questions of the three large states. Yet, they support the initiative and are not insisting on a more federalist approach to a common security and defense capacity.[12]

The Weizsäcker Report on military reform released in late May 2000 initiated a rapid process of change in Germany's defense planning. A *Bundeswehr* paper in June 2000 laid out the ground for renewal, spelling a breakthrough in German military policy by calling for a halt to defense-spending reductions and a fundamental restructuring of the armed forces.[13] Building on Helsinki's consensus for jointly taking on military operations—a necessary context for German military restructuring—German plans now call for large reductions in the overall armed forces (but not the elimination of conscription) to generate savings to be used for a 40,000 all-professional projection force. The new measures aim to put Germany at par with the existing capabilities of Britain and France. While the Schröder government has approved the plans in principle, it is not yet sure how the financing will take place.[14] In preparing for the force pledging conferences scheduled for November 2000, the German Defense Minister Rudolf Scharping, announced that Germany would contribute 18,000 troops to the new EU force.[15] The German commitment to join the Anglo-French initiative will solidify a credible European force. However, German defense spending has thus far not increased, and by some measures has actually continued to decline. As a result, Germany is still a long way off from matching the British level in European defense capability.

Second, regardless of the debate on the EU's political manifest destiny or *finalité politique*—whether the Union will be a looser federation or a more centralized organization—few question that ESDP currently is one of the EU's decisive missions alongside enlargement and the implementation of the Euro.[16] It should not be forgotten that the concept of the economic and monetary integration launched in Dublin in 1979 took twenty years before it produced a very tangible outcome in the form of the Euro. The achievement of a concrete European capacity for military action is likely to take at least as long (see Howorth's elaboration of this theme in chapter 11).

Third, the United States supports the "autonomous capacity project" in its stated objective of improving European military capability, and is committed to explore means whereby it can function effectively with NATO. From Washington's perspective, the DCI launched in NATO in the fall of 1999 and ESDP pursue complementary objectives of strengthening Europe's military role in crisis management. The Bush administration is most interested in seeing an enhancement of European defense capability and has placed no hindrances in the way of ESDP development.

Fourth, since 2000 the EU has been taking concrete steps toward welcoming the participation of non-EU European NATO allies. Plans made by COPS and the military staff for a specific "catalogue of forces" have been adopted by the EU defense ministers. In 2001 these pledges were formalized into national commitments. European public support a European military capacity, probably as long as it does not constitute an excessive financial burden.[17]

As a politico-military objective, the HG of 60,000 troops has considerable flexibility. In March 2000, at the informal EU Council in Lisbon, it was agreed to add a civilian crisis-management component to the ESDP plans. The European Summit in Santa Maria da Feira in June announced a second HG—what could be called "Headline Lite"—in this instance to set up a police capacity for international missions across the range of conflict prevention. It draws on the WEU's agreed set of Civilian Crisis Management procedures articulated again at the WEU ministerial in May 2000. The goal is to create a 5,000 strong force of gendarmerie-style police officers to do peace reconstruction work alongside civil and economic reconstruction.

With only a little progress in three years on some of the categories (civilian or military), the EU could announce a successful outcome. At the European Council in Laeken in December 2001, the European leaders did exactly that. They declared ESDP operational even though all its requirements were not yet in place and its mission still under consideration.

ESDP, the United States and NATO

Along with budgetary, planning and military capability challenges, EU members have faced the crucial task of arranging a constructive, complementary and transparent relationship with the Atlantic Alliance, and especially the United States. When the European Council Conclusions at Cologne in June 1999 accepted and elaborated the Anglo-French plans on the Union's role in defense, there was at least one phrase (author's italics) that caused an American reaction: "the Union must have the capacity for autonomous action, backed up by credible military forces, the means to decide to use them, and a readiness to do so, in order to respond to international crises *without prejudice to actions by NATO.*"[18]

The Clinton administration argued that the phrase "without prejudice to actions by NATO" was unacceptable for it left the impression that crisis management would be the prerogative of the Union and thus by implication boxed NATO into "Article V" operations only.[19] The Saint-Malo Declaration between France and Britain had defined the need for a capacity for autonomous European action as follows: "In order for the EU to take decisions and approve military action where the Alliance as a whole is not engaged."[20] From Washington's point of view, the Cologne Summit had strayed from this wording, which had been carefully repeated in the Washington Summit Communiqué in April 1999.[21]

On the eve of the Helsinki European Council Summit, the Americans intervened "at the highest level" by calling on Prime Minister Blair to persuade President Chirac to put "where the Alliance as a whole is not engaged" into the EU Council Conclusions. With some difficulty, the British were able to persuade the French to include the phrase. Given that the French had already agreed to it at Saint-Malo, there was no convincing reason to keep it out.[22]

This is not a debate about semantics as the phrase cuts to the core of what is meant by "autonomy." Strictly speaking, the question is whether "autonomy" includes EU political will to launch military action in cases when the United States explicitly disagrees with such action. The British do not want the concept of autonomy to mean that, and thus strongly favor the phrase "where NATO as a whole is not engaged" because that would mean, in practice, that the United States has already given its agreement. The French want to be prepared for both contingencies.

The Helsinki Conclusions also implied that the EU was preparing for at least two types of capabilities and operations: its own operations without the use of NATO assets and capabilities, and EU-led operations with NATO assets and capabilities. The apparent dual purpose of this new EU capacity put into question the agreement the Alliance had affirmed in Washington, that is "our commitment to building the ESDI within the Alliance..."[23]

ESDP thus moves beyond ESDI as it has been defined and used since 1994. In the arrangements between the WEU and NATO on CJTFs (see chapter 3), the Alliance not only decides on what assets the WEU can borrow, but will also monitor these assets and can technically recall them. The ESDP definition of "autonomous action" includes a much greater degree of its own mission and control over decision-making and NATO assets once they have been assigned to the EU operation by the Alliance. Therefore, as the European Council Conclusions in Fiera in June of 2000 acknowledge, NATO and the EU modalities may not be the same as WEU and NATO modalities. It is not possible, for example, for NATO simply to replace the references to the WEU with EU. The view that the EU is legally, institutionally and politically much more in the areas of security and defense than the European pillar of NATO is held by many European governments.[24]

Logically, American and other NATO members have been probing the terms used in the new ESDP terminology, such as "autonomous action" (rather than "separable but not separate forces") and "unnecessary duplication" (rather than "no duplication") in the months after the Helsinki Conclusions. As the Union is not simply going to take over the WEU crisis-management functions, which had been defined in the ESDI-in-NATO construct, all the arrangements as well as the overall political relationship have to be renegotiated.

The Europeans have tried to calm the waters but without diminishing or slowing down the momentum for a genuine EU military capacity. Lord Robertson argued that the new European initiative would maintain the "indivisibility" of the transatlantic link, would "improve"

European capabilities, and would be "inclusive of all the allies." German Defense Minister Rudolf Scharping wrote that the problem with NATO was not too much America but too little Europe.[25] The British clarified further that they had no intention of creating an independent European army, or a standing force, and that they did not seek strategic independence for Europe.[26] However, the first half of 2000 has seen a good deal of negotiation inside the EU and NATO to define the new relation between ESDP and NATO.

NATO foreign ministers in Florence in May 2000 called for "means to ensure the development of effective mutual consultation, cooperation and transparency, building on the mechanisms existing between NATO and the WEU; participation of non-EU European Allies; as well as practical arrangements for assured EU access to NATO planning capabilities and for ready EU access to NATO collective assets and capabilities on a case-by-case basis and by consensus."[27] Capping the need for modalities for NATO–EU consultation and cooperation, and practical arrangements for assured EU access to NATO planning and ready access to NATO assets, is the overall need for a "Political Arrangement."[28]

It may be tempting to downplay the political side of ESDP as most EU members are also NATO allies, and as the Western democracies have been through thick and thin together and essentially share the same values and interests. However, in light of the experience in the 1990s, it should be clear that the political relationship between NATO and the EU requires careful thought and management. U.S. Assistant Secretary of State for European Affairs, Marc Grossman, stated before the Senate in March 2000: "Our goal is simple: we want to get ESDI right. That's because we want ESDI to succeed... More European military capacity will make the Alliance stronger, lift some of the burden we now have to act in every crisis, and make the U.S.–European relationship more of a partnership."[29]

ESDP and Non-EU Members

Procedures for EU consultation with European NATO allies that are not EU members were outlined at the European Summit in Portugal in June 2000. The annex of the EU Presidency Conclusions in Fiera discusses the involvement of non-EU European NATO countries and candidate (for EU membership) countries in EU crisis management. During "routine phase" there will be regular consultations. In case of a crisis, the EU will make a decision whether or not to launch a military or civilian operation. Once the decision is made to commit forces, an ad hoc Committee of Contributors is to be set up.[30]

Pending a final agreement with NATO, the EU set up "ad hoc working groups" working on four issue areas of cooperation between the EU and NATO.[31] One group will explore security issues such as information exchange and access between the two. In preparation, Javier Solana recently tightened security considerably in the Secretariat of the European Council on issues pertaining to military affairs in order to make confidential contact with NATO possible.[32] Another group will examine capabilities goals to assure that the DCI in NATO and the preparations for the HG will be "mutually reinforcing." Here, the EU will need to draw on NATO military expertise and may also make use of its defense planning procedures. The third group will tackle the sensitive issue of EU access to NATO assets and capabilities. Presumably it will build on the negotiations and modalities that dealt with WEU-led CJTFs. In these last two groups, the EU anticipates a possible role for the Deputy SACEUR (always a European). The final group will attempt to define a permanent political relationship for EU–NATO consultation.

The principles that are to guide all these groups, and presumably the foundation for the last group, are "full respect of the autonomy of EU decision-making," cooperation based on "shared values, equality, and a spirit of partnership," "mutually reinforcing" "military capabilities, full and effective consultation, cooperation, and transparency." When adapting the procedures that govern WEU–NATO relations, negotiators are to keep in mind that the two organizations are "of a different nature." Finally, in their relations, there is to be "no discrimination against any of the Member States of either organization" (see chapter 7).[33]

The intent was to finalize a political relationship with NATO at the same time that the interim ESDP bodies took on their permanent shape, that is, at the Nice European Council in December 2000. The problem was that Turkey continued to block EU access to NATO assets and no agreement had been reached on a final politico-military agreement between NATO and the ESDP.

Conclusion: What will a Future NATO–EU Framework Look Like?

Until December 2001, Turkey blocked a final agreement between NATO and the ESDP. Just prior to the European Council meeting in that month, Ankara was persuaded to drop its opposition to EU access to NATO's command and control structures and other assets. However, Greece blocked the EU's acceptance of Turkey's agreement with NATO, continuing the standoff. Unless solved during the Spanish presidency of the EU in 2002, the Greek veto is likely to remain in place as Greece takes the presidency and also assumes responsibility for security and defense policy on behalf of the Danish government that has opted out of the ESDP.

Despite this overall impasse, NATO and ESDP member states have made a great deal of progress toward cooperation. Acting on a Dutch initiative, NATO's NAC and the EU's COPS are now meeting in joint session at least six times a year. Several non-EU states, including the United States and Norway (and soon Canada) have liaison staff at the new European Military Staff (EMS) to make planning and cooperation more transparent.

Lord Robertson of NATO and Javier Solana on behalf of the EU often meet informally to coordinate the activities of the two organizations. EU–NATO management of the Macedonia crisis has successfully proceeded and built on "lessons learned" from the various crises in the former Yugoslavia. Their cooperation has given NATO an early and critical crisis management capacity and has produced remarkable EU–NATO cooperation, thus allowing the United States and the European allies to work together constructively, easing some of the early tension between the Bush administration and European states.

The idea proposed by then Secretary of Defense William Cohen in October of 2000 to merge the decision-making and defense planning process of NATO and the ESDP may not be on the table for a long time. However, in practice, NATO members and double-hatted ESDP members are making the planning process as complementary as possible.

Though there is no unified European position on the future EU–NATO security relationship, most EU members want more EU decision-making power, planning capacity and operational capability for military crisis management in Europe. Europe is planning to take on the civilian police function in Bosnia at the end of 2002. It will be the first test of the civilian ESDP capacity or the "Headline Lite." With such a capacity comes more European influence to determine the strategy and means of military crisis management, including in NATO. Soon after, the EU may want to take on the remaining operation in Macedonia. A common military ability will help define stronger shared national priorities in security and defense. ESDP in this view fortifies NATO while strengthening the EU. For most Europeans, these two goals are not contradictory. What is contradictory is the meager amount of money that the Europeans are willing to spend to make their pledges come true. As a result, Britain's Foreign and Commonwealth Office now predicts that a European Rapid Reaction Force (ERRF) will not be able "to undertake combat operations" until, at the earliest, 2012.[34]

Unlike the Clinton administration, most advisers in the new Bush administration share this win–win view of ESDP (see chapter 6). European security is no longer seen as a potential threat to the integrity of NATO. In the age of global terrorism, any capacity is welcome. The Bush administration is holding its nose on the strong ESDP rhetoric and is not getting distracted by institutional tinkering in the EU or even wrangling between the EU and NATO because it is ultimately looking at military capability. There is more concern in the Bush administration with declining European defense budgets than with the potential of an ERRF competing with NATO.

Notes

1. Tim Butcher, "Britain Leads Call for EU Defence Shake-Up," *Daily Telegraph*, November 5, 1998. See also Kori Schake, Amaya Bloch-Lainé and Charles Grant, "Building a European Defence Capability," *Survival* 41 (Spring 1999), pp. 23–24.

2. Jolyon Howorth, "Britain, France and the European Defence Initiative," *Survival* 42 (Summer 2000), p. 33.

3. The "Annex on Strengthening the Common European Policy on Security and Defence" states: "Particular attention will be devoted to the capabilities necessary to ensure effective performance in crisis management: deployability, sustainability, interoperability, flexibility, mobility, survivability and command and control..." Presidency Conclusions, Helsinki European Council, December 10 and 11, 1999, Annex 1 to IV.

4. Craig Whitney, "U.S. Raises Objections to New Force in Europe," *New York Times*, October 11, 1999.

5. See Annex III. European Council Declaration on Strengthening the Common European Policy on Security and Defence, Cologne European Council, June 3 and 4, 1999.

6. Anne Swardson, "French, German Defense Giants Plan Merger," *Washington Post*, October 15, 1999; Page E01.

7. Martin Woollacott, "Europe Sets New Policies with a Clashing of Symbols," *The Guardian*, December 10, 1999.

8. Gordon Adams, "Building Barriers or Building Bridges? Defense Industries in the Transatlantic Framework," Conference Paper, University of Washington, Seattle, May 2000.

9. Statement by Madeline Albright, Ministerial Meeting of the North Atlantic Council, Florence, May 24, 2000, http://www.nato.int/docu/speech/2000/s000524c.html.

10. State Department Press Release on Defense Trade Initiative, May 24, 2000. http://www.usembassycanada.gov/outreach/s0525b.html.

11. Peter Schmidt, "Neuorientierung in der Europäischen Sicherheitspolitik? Britische und Britisch-Französische Initiativen," Ebenhausen: Stiftung Wissenschaft und Politik, January 1999, pp. 5, 6.

12. Confidential interview with Finnish Foreign Ministry official involved in the Helsinki Preparations, May 2000.

13. See Gemeinsame Sicherheit und Zukunft der Bundeswehr: Bericht der Kommission an die Bundesregierung, May 23, 2000. For a commentary on the Weizsäcker Commission, see François Heisbourg, "Germany Points the Way to a Strong Self-Sufficiency," International Herald Tribune, May 24, 2000. The German Defense Ministry Paper is titled "Die Bundeswehrsicher ins 21. Jahrhundert: Eckpfeiler für eine Erneuerung von Grund auf."

14. Interview with senior German Defence Ministry official, June 2000.

15. Allen Nacheman, "EU Ministers Start Work on Rapid Reaction Force," National Post, September 23, 2000.

16. Joschka Fischer, the German foreign minister, in early 2000, called for "the creation of a functioning European government on a federalist model within the next decade." French President Jacques Chirac in his address to the Bundestag in late June, suggested a "pioneer group" of core countries to lead the Union in the direction of deepening integration. John Vinocur, "EU's Future: The Vision and the Slog," International Herald Tribune, July 8, 2000. British prime minister Blair advocates a much looser intergovernmental structure. See, for example, "Blair's Vision," The Economist, September 30, 2000.

17. According to Eurostat, the EU's statistical office, Europeans continue to support the idea of a joint foreign policy (64 percent) as well as a joint security and defense policy (73 percent). EU Info, August 2000, p. 3.

18. Presidency Conclusions, Cologne European Council, June 3, 4, 1999, Annex III, paragraph 1.

19. Charles G. Cogan, "Absorption vs. Autonomy: The Euro-American Security Dilemma," Conference Paper, University of Washington, Seattle, May 5–6, 2000.

20. Franco-British Summit. Joint Declaration on European Defence, Saint-Malo, December 4, 1998, paragraph 3. http://www.info-france.org/news/statmnts/pr/stmalo.html.

21. "An Alliance for the 21st Century," Washington Summit Communiqué, Washington, April 24, 1999, paragraph 9a.

22. Cogan, "Absorption vs. Autonomy"; Confidential interview with Finnish Foreign Ministry official, May 2000.

23. Washington Summit Communiqué Washington D.C., April 23, 24, 1999, paragraph 5.

24. Confidential interview with Finnish Foreign Ministry official, May 2000.

25. Rudolf Scharping, "One Germany in a Unifying Europe Alongside America," International Herald Tribune, November 15, 1999.

26. Peter Norman, "EU: Plan for Peace Force Moves Forward," *Financial Times*, November 16, 1999. See also "Brits voorstel voor Europees legerkorps," *NRC Handelsblad*, November 16, 1999.
27. Final Communiqué, Ministerial Meeting of the North Atlantic Council, Florence, May 24, 2000, paragraph 27.
28. Ibid., the quotations are from paragraph 29.
29. Marc Grossman, Assistant Secretary of State for European Affairs, Testimony. Senate Committee on Foreign Relations. European Affairs Subcommittee, Washington, March 9, 2000. See also: Stephen Larrabee, "The European Security and Defense Identity and American Interests," Hearings. Senate Committee on Foreign Relations. Subcommittee on European Affairs. Washington, March 9, 2000; Franklin D. Kramer, Assistant Secretary of Defense for International Security Affairs, Testimony. Senate Committee on Foreign Relations. European Affairs Subcommittee, Washington, March 9, 2000.
30. Fiera, appendix 2, paragraph 13 and 20, respectively.
31. Fiera, appendix 2.
32. Solana's sudden decision is now challenged before the European Court of Justice. See: Barry James, "Dutch to Take EU to Court over Tough Secrecy Rules," *International Herald Tribune*, October 28, 2000.
33. Feira, appendix 2.
34. James Kitfield, "NATO Metamorphosis," *National Journal*, February 8, 2002.

CHAPTER 3

The CJTF Concept and the Limits of European Autonomy

Terry Terriff

Since the early 1990s, NATO's focus has shifted from being solely prepared for Article V missions to being able to engage as well in crisis response operations in the event of out-of-area crises. At the same time, the Alliance has proceeded with internal military change and adaptation, the most important of which are the three interrelated elements of ESDI, the CJTF concept and the new military command structure.[1] The CJTF initiative is frequently seen as the key internal military innovation undertaken by NATO. The CJTF initiative was initially conceived as a means for NATO to generate an out-of-area military crisis response in circumstances of great uncertainty, but it was quickly recognized that it was also an instrumentality through which the Alliance could effectuate an ESDI. The centrality of the CJTF concept means that it has served as a symbol that NATO knows where it is going and why, that it really does know what it is doing, that it does have a purpose. As a symbol of NATO's purpose and direction, the CJTF concept provided an answer to those who had questioned whether the Alliance did have a role in the post–Cold War era, or whether it was simply an anachronism whose day was done.[2]

An important question regarding the CJTF concept, given its political symbolism as well as its proposed practical utility, is whether *its* day is done. The original idea for the CJTF was first put forward in 1993, in response to the political and military realities of the day. Yet, as NATO enters the new millennium, the political and military circumstances in which it finds itself have changed significantly from that time; indeed the Atlantic Alliance itself has changed and continues to change. Hence, just as NATO is endeavoring to implement the CJTF concept, there are reasons to question whether the Alliance, in fact, requires it to fulfill its aims. The answer to this question depends on the answer to two interrelated questions: first, whether NATO itself needs the CJTF in order to respond effectively to a crisis, and second, whether the EU should rely on the CJTF concept to implement a European-only military operation or instead develop its own autonomous alternative.

Before proceeding it will be useful to provide a definition of NATO's CJTF concept, as the term "combined joint task force" or its acronym, CJTF, has a more general meaning as well. A combined joint task force can generally be defined as a deployable multinational, multi-service formation generated and tailored for specific contingency operations.[3] This definition applies to any military formation in any mission. NATO's particular CJTF concept has been defined, in the words of the head of NATO's Combined Joint Planning Staff (CJPS), as "a flexible, deployable, multinational, multiservice HQ using a building block approach. The build-up of the CJTF HQ would take place by selecting a nucleus (a permanent core staff element) from the parent HQ (one of NATO's standing military HQs) and augmenting it with modules (resources provided by other NATO or national sources) and individuals (personnel). Modular and individual augmentation would take place initially from within the Alliance's military structure before seeking additional augmentation from nations."[4] This operational HQ, with the support of the CJPS, determines the mission requirements needed to meet the political aims specified and then generates and integrates the appropriate military and other capabilities to execute the mission.

This chapter begins by examining what NATO's various military operations in the 1990s suggest about whether the CJTF HQ concept will be used in future. Next, it will address the problems that attend the use of the CJTF HQ concept as a command and control framework for the EU's ESDP, and then whether the CJTF HQ concept could be used as a model for the development of a European military HQ.

NATO and the CJTF HQ Concept

There were a number of factors that underpinned the emergence of the concept of CJTF HQs in 1993–1994. First, it was becoming clear that

NATO would have to respond to out-of-area crises and hence that it needed a command capability that was flexible enough to achieve uncertain political objectives in indeterminate contingencies. Second, the extent of the reduction of NATO's member states' armed forces by 1993 made clear that the Alliance had to move to a capabilities-based approach to generating military operations. Third, the Alliance needed a command arrangement that would permit the inclusion of non-NATO military units. Finally, the Alliance needed a means to provide a command capability to support the emerging ESDI.[5] NATO worked on the idea of the CJTF HQ concept from 1994 onwards, and the NAC authorized its implementation during the Washington summit meeting in 1999.

Despite the original perceived utility of the CJTF HQ concept, there are a number of reasons to suggest that NATO is now unlikely to respond to a crisis situation using a CJTF HQ to serve as the operational HQ for the mission. NATO since 1995 has undertaken a number of different military deployments and missions in the Balkans region, ranging from peacekeeping missions such as the Bosnian Implementation Force (IFOR) in 1995, through humanitarian operations such as Operation Allied Harbor in Albania in 1999, to military combat such Operation Allied Force in Serbia/Kosovo, also in 1999. Supreme Headquarters Allied Powers Europe (SHAPE) has proved itself sufficiently adaptable to generate the forces needed to engage in a range of mission types in responding to out-of-area crises. All of these operations were combined joint military operations in that all were multinational in character, were joint operations with different services working together, and were generated by drawing together the requisite capabilities to provide the best fit to the mission aims and profile. Moreover, these operations were able to incorporate a wide range of non-allied military contingents from Partnership for Peace (PfP) states, including Russian contingents. SHAPE has demonstrated that it has the capacity to generate the forces needed to engage in out-of-area crises in areas adjacent to NATO's perimeter, and to do so utilizing the principles that underpin the idea of CJTFs.

The question that thus arises is whether NATO needs the CJTF HQ in order to generate and command a military response to future crises? The command arrangements for IFOR, NATO's first out-of-area military deployment, are illustrative of how subsequent operations were structured. In the case of IFOR, the deployed force had a unified command, under the political direction and control of the NAC and under the overall military authority of the SACEUR (Supreme Allied Commander-Europe). The SACEUR in turn assigned to the Commander in Chief-Allied Forces South (CINCSOUTH) the responsibility of serving as the

Commander-in-Theatre, who then exercised control over the deployment and employment of all land, air and maritime forces assigned to the mission through his subordinate commanders.[6] The Allied Command Europe Rapid Reaction Corps (ARRC) was deployed to provide the command HQ for all forces in Bosnia. The overall line of command for all subsequent operations have followed a similar pattern, with CINCSOUTH being designated the theatre commander with control over NATO military forces. The ARRC was subsequently also deployed in several instances, such as Kosovo Force (KFOR), to provide the operational HQ for land forces on the ground, while for Operation Allied Harbor the Allied Mobile Force, Land (AMF[L]) was deployed to provide the land HQ, and in Operation Determined Guarantor, the force positioned in Macedonia to furnish an extraction capability for the Organization for Security and Cooperation in Europe (OSCE) monitors in Kosovo, the deployed force was made up of nationally contributed military units with the French providing the lead in the field.

There are several reasons to assume that this pattern of command arrangement, or some variation of it, will continue. First, the implementation of the new command structure means that theatre and sub-theatre command roles can be allocated to major and regional NATO commands. The "supported–supporting command relationship" of the new command structure has been created to facilitate the transfer of the weight of a military effort down to the regional HQ level if desirable; hence, command of a crisis response operation can be assigned without difficulty to the major or regional HQ closest to the emergency. Moreover, the new command structure accentuates the need for regionally based HQs "to be able both to receive forces and support inter/intra regional reinforcement."[7] In other words, NATO has sought to design a new command structure that facilitates the provision to any HQ, including regional HQs, of whatever military capabilities are deemed necessary to meet the political goals of an operational mission, from anywhere within the overall military command structure.[8]

Second, SHAPE has undertaken a number of innovations in the wake of the IFOR operation to enhance its ability to generate and sustain such operations. One initiative was to revitalize the ACE Reaction Force Planning Staff (ARFPS), which furnished the strategic planning for the IFOR operation.[9] In addition, SHAPE initiated the ACE Mobility Coordination Center (AMCC) in December 1995, the purpose of which is to provide for the coordination of "movements of national forces into theater [of operations] to meet the needs of the theater commander," and to work with "non-NATO nations . . . to ensure that their deployment plans fit into the overall flow of forces."[10] These and other innovations have contributed to SHAPE's ability to plan, generate and sustain the types of out-of-area military operations that were envisioned in 1993 when the CJTF HQ concept was first raised as a possible solution to some of the problems foreseen by NATO's military leaders.

Third, utilizing the force commander's current HQ staff provides a command staff that is unified and used to working together. Most commanders would prefer to work with the command personnel that make up their HQ rather than assume command with a new, unknown staff. An inherent problem perceived with the CJTF HQ concept is that the nucleus command staff will have to spend considerable time training together to develop a common understanding, a common mind-set and a fluency in a common working-language, in order to develop an efficient working relationship. There is no certainty that such training will create a unified command unit with these characteristics, particularly if the CJTF HQ nucleus is only trained every other year as is now contemplated.[11] A CJTF HQ nucleus staff also confronts, in the event of a crisis, the difficult task of integrating a wide range of individuals or units into the command structure on relatively short notice: staff officers with whom they have not worked with before, with whom there are likely to be misunderstandings or friction due to the lack of a common mind-set and even a lack of sufficient fluency in a common language.[12] Finally, it will take time to generate a CJTF HQ, for even with predesignated fill-in units and personnel, there will be a time lag in moving these personnel and integrating them into the HQ framework. This time lag means that a CJTF HQ is not capable of a rapid deployment in the same time frame that a standing formation such as ARRC is capable of managing.[13] These questions about the efficiency, and hence effectiveness, of the CJTF HQ concept suggests that NATO is likely to prefer turning to the range of alternative standing headquarter staffs available when designating command and control of a crisis operation.

Finally, the standing SACEUR is unlikely to be very willing to relinquish overall operational control of a NATO mission. The pervasiveness of the news media in the modern world, coupled with the speed at which news can be transmitted, increasingly means that a soldier standing on roadblock can create an international incident that will require the response of the SACEUR. As a consequence of this compacting of the command hierarchy, the SACEUR is likely to prefer a much more direct involvement in overseeing, if not actually managing, operations than was usual in the past.[14] Moreover, NATO commanders of the major HQs are likely to lobby the SACEUR to assign to them theater command of a real world operation, as military commanders are aware that with such a command comes a significant increase in resources.

These considerations generally suggest that NATO neither needs nor is likely to utilize the CJTF HQ to plan, generate and control an out-of-area military crisis response. SHAPE has demonstrated that it is capable of planning, generating and deploying a multinational military force, utilizing the principles of CJTFs to tailor the mission to meet the political aims of the Alliance in an out-of-area crisis, and of incorporating non-allied contingents.[15] The general pattern of command established through practice since 1995 has worked well. Moreover, NATO's military command has used this structure to generate CJTFs with the capabilities needed to pursue successfully the political aims of the Alliance, while at the same time being flexible enough to incorporate non-NATO military units. The ARRC and AMF(L) have proven that they can furnish a rapid reaction command framework for forces on the ground, and these are likely to continue to be the instruments that SHAPE will task initially with providing such command frameworks, particularly if the crisis is proximate to the Alliance's territorial boundaries, as have been those in the Balkans.[16]

The CJTF HQ concept may be perceived, however, as the best option should NATO undertake out-of-area military operations that are distant from Europe. In the wake of September 11, NATO is taking seriously the need to address the issue of terrorism. The widespread and diffuse nature of terrorism implies that NATO may need to be willing and able to operate much further afield than geographic areas immediately proximate to Alliance boundaries. NATO may, in taking on terrorism, thus be tasked at some future point to disrupt and destroy a terrorist organization well outside Europe, or to provide a follow-on peace support operation in a distant conflict. In the event of such a distant, "over-the-horizon" mission, political and military considerations may demand that the operational commander be based close to the operations.[17] NATO could for small, short-term operations turn to the ARRC, or even the AMF(L), to provide the command HQ in a rapid and efficient manner. Nevertheless, a sea-based or land-based CJTF HQ could be useful in mounting a non-time-sensitive, "over-the-horizon" operation, particularly if it is substantial in scale and scope.

The CJTF HQ concept still has some utility as a political symbol. NATO remains committed to permitting PfP states to contribute to military operations and to the principle that such contributing states should be allocated some posts in the operational HQ. The CJTF HQ concept furnishes evidence that this principle can be fulfilled.[18] Moreover, when NATO accepted the Czech Republic, Hungary and Poland as new members in 1999, it avoided agreeing to pre-position Alliance forces forward in these states. The Alliance increasingly looks set in 2002 to invite seven more states to accede to the Washington Treaty, and it seems unlikely that it will agree to pre-position forces in these new states or to establish a regional HQ in any of them. A CJTF HQ gives the Alliance the means to furnish an operational command to be based in these new member states if the need to do so should ever arise. The CJTF HQ concept in these instances thus serves as a material symbol of NATO's political commitment to protect its newest members as well as its commitment to work inclusively with PfP states.

In the final analysis, the existence of effective alternatives and the CJTF HQ concept's shortcomings means that NATO's military is unlikely to rely on such HQs in responding to future crises. Thus, just as NATO is moving toward the Initial Operational Capability of the CJTF HQ concept in 2004, the Alliance appears to have no critical military requirement for it; however, the concept does continue to serve as a symbol of NATO's new political commitments.

ESDP and CJTF HQ

The EU is moving forward to develop a rapid reaction force to support its ESDP. At the Helsinki European Council the European heads of state made a commitment both to a "headline goal" and a "capability goal." The fifteen member states plus some fifteen non-EU member states committed a range of national military capabilities to the ERRF at the Capability Commitment Conference in November 2000. The EU used these commitments to put together the "Force Catalogue" that comprises 100,000 troops, 4,000 combat aircraft, 100 ships and 100 buildings from which a force of up to 60,000 can be assembled and supplied.[19] More important then simple numbers, however, is the range of particular capabilities available to the ERRF, especially given the aspiration for this force to be able to engage in Petersberg Tasks. Of special concern was the clear need for the EU to have appropriate "command, control and intelligence" capabilities.

The Nice European Council in December 2000 set forth the main components of the political structure for the command and control of ERRF operations: the COPS, the Military Committee and the Military Staff. In spite of this progress, as the U.K. House of Lords Parliamentary Report on ESDP pointed out, EU "command and control mechanisms remain poorly thought out and must be considered as a matter of urgency."[20] A central issue that remains ambiguous is what the EU intends to use as its military command structure, including the important question of what is to serve as the operational HQs for a military operation.

The ERRF is not to be a standing army, but rather based on the concept that predesignated national forces will be brought together when necessary, that is, when a military crisis response is desired. Thus, by its very nature, the ERRF is based on the principles and practices of CJTF operations; indeed, reportedly the initial discussions at Saint-Malo between France and Britain about a European military capability were in terms of CJTFs.[21] EU member states recognize that, along with widely discussed deficiencies in strategic lift and an intelligence capability, what they critically need to have if they are to meet the HG is an operational HQ. The Military Capabilities Commitment Declaration indicated that the EU envisions two possible options for an operational HQ to command an ERRF operation: requesting that NATO release a CJTF HQ (among commonly held NATO assets are its two CJTF HQs) or requesting use of a member state's national operational HQ.[22]

For the EU to request the use of a CJTF HQ in the event of a crisis may be the most practical means to address the current shortcomings in the military command structure of the ESDP. Although officially the ERRF is solely European at the political level, militarily the conduct of operations in Europe is linked to, if not in fact embedded in, NATO. The EU's Military Staff, which are to conduct strategic planning, will "have working procedures and operational concepts based on, and in any case compatible with, those of NATO."[23] Such compatibility is coupled with the agreement that NATO's Deputy Supreme Allied Commander Europe (DSACEUR), alternately either a British or German officer, will serve as the designated operational commander of the ERRF. The Alliance heads of state confirmed the DSACEUR as the designated operational commander of the ERRF at the Washington Summit in April 1999, and further agreed that the DSACEUR would have NATO command and control assets at his disposal.[24] Moreover, the NAC has offered to grant the EU unrestricted access to and use of the planning capabilities of SHAPE for all aspects of ERRF operations, from peacetime training exercises to the conduct of crisis operations.

NATO has not, however, agreed to give the EU assured access to common Alliance-held assets such as the CJTF HQ. NATO's general position, rather, is that Alliance-held assets would only be released to the EU subject to the consensual agreement of the NAC, and that all requests by the EU would be considered on a case-by-case basis.[25] This formulation confronts the EU with the possibility that any Alliance member country that opposes a prospective operation by the EU could block requests for NATO assets in the NAC, including a CJTF HQ, which would render impossible the proposed EU operation. Simply put, this formulation potentially translates into a veto by a non-EU state over a EU military operation. Yet at the same time, there can be no expectation that NATO or any individual state such as the United States would be willing to release military assets to the EU by some form of "automatic" right.

If it decides to utilize a CJTF HQ, the EU would thus be dependent on NATO and the goodwill of the non-EU members of the Alliance should it want to mount a military operation. It can be argued that such a position of reliance need not necessarily be problematic, as the required cooperation would very likely be forthcoming from NATO and individual member countries in the event of a crisis sufficiently serious to warrant a military operation. However, the recent problem of Turkey blocking the NATO–EU agreement to furnish the EU with automatic access to Alliance planning assets does indicate that the Union cannot be certain that the assets would be released.[26] The implications of this particular dispute make clear that the EU capacity to act in the event of need could be held hostage to the political considerations of non-EU states (see chapter 7 in this volume). The very perception that this is the case does suggest a compromising of the EU's aspiration for "autonomy"; further, the material problem coupled with the political perception are not likely to be deemed acceptable to EU member states in the long run.

Another important issue is that reliance on a NATO CJTF HQ by the EU would mean that the United States would have a role in a European operation. The United States has said that it would support the detachment of a CJTF HQ for use by the ESDP on a case-by-case basis. However, U.S. military personnel make up about 30 percent of the NATO command structure, and the staffing of the CJTF HQs will certainly reflect this density. This raises two issues. First, if the United States believes that it does not have sufficient interests at stake to act, would it be willing to allow its military personal in a CJTF HQ staff to participate? Recent U.S. governments have demonstrated a political aversion to taking American military casualties, particularly if they believe they cannot convince the American public that there are important U.S. interests involved. There is a risk, albeit low, that a U.S. government might be willing to allow the EU to use a CJTF HQ, but at the same time withdraw its officers from the latter's staff. The EU would then be confronted with the need to find European replacements, the process of which would disturb even further the capacity to react quickly and upset the working effectiveness of the CJTF HQ.

Second, if the United States did allow its personnel to participate, there might be concern within the EU that the U.S. contribution of more than 30 percent of the command staff—and indeed the possible further contribution of American personnel involved in providing other particular capabilities—would give Washington an oversight role in a European operation. This contribution potentially could provide the United States with a substantial degree of influence on the operation. Excessive concern here would be unwarranted, for Washington is quite capable of taking a "hands off" approach. Nevertheless, to understand why EU governments may have such concerns, one only has to remember the dispute between General Jackson (the British Commander of the ARRC forces deployed in Macedonia) and U.S. General Wesley Clark (then SACEUR) over whether and how to respond to the Russian military dash to the Pristina airport in the summer of 1999, and that both reported back to their national political leaders for instructions.[27] Even if such latent concerns are misplaced, the question of the American content in a CJTF HQ could well be a significant issue for some EU states that are determined to make ESDP truly "autonomous."

The alternative means for the provision of an operational HQ is for the EU to rely on a member state to commit to furnishing one. The December 2001 Draft Presidency Report on European Security and Defense Policy notes: "Member States are offering a sufficient number of HQ at the levels of operations, force and component, as well as deployable communications units."[28] In particular, Britain and France have offered "the UK's Permanent Joint HQ and France's Centre Operational Interarmees and their planning capabilities as options to command EU-led operations,"[29] while Germany has also promised to make available an operational HQ.[30] The United Kingdom's Permanent Joint HQ is currently operational and available for the EU's use, France's Centre Operational Interarmées is near ready, and Germany is currently constructing the complex to house its designated HQ.[31] The British and French, when they first proposed their respective operational HQs for EU use in 1999, noted that "as part of this, we intend to develop standing arrangements for setting up multinationalised cells within these HQ, including officers from other EU partners."[32] In a similar fashion, the Capabilities Commitment Conference Declaration "welcomed" the decision by some member states "to open existing joint national HQ to officers coming from other Member States."[33] The indication that member states would be willing to incorporate officers from other national militaries into their national command HQs reflects, in a sense, the approach to constructing an operational HQ adopted by NATO in developing its CJTF HQ concept.

In the near to mid term, the deficiencies of the EU's shared command and control assets are such that, if the EU does not utilize NATO command and planning assets, the Union could only conduct an operation if one of the European great powers takes the lead. In principle, this would mean most probably that either Britain or France would take the lead and furnish the framework for the conduct of the operation through the provision of the designated operational command HQ.[34] There are several potential issues involved in choosing one state to provide the lead and framework concept for an operation. One such issue stems from the reality that states, rightly or wrongly, often perceive that there are gains to be made from providing the lead in an EU operation, in terms of increased political status in Europe or in terms of national prestige. If such a perception is present, as it may well be in instances when an operation is considered politically important, the EU could be confronted with two or more member states lobbying hard to be allocated the lead role, with the attendant possibility that such nationalistic competition could spill out into the public realm at the very time that the Union is attempting to generate a crisis response operation. At best, such an occurrence would be embarrassing, while at worst it could be politically disruptive at a time when the Union most needs harmony and consensus.

Another potentially problematic issue is the incorporation of officers from other member states into a national HQ. As the operational HQs are national assets, including other officers is most likely to occur only once a particular state has been asked, in effect, to take the lead and furnish the operational HQ. To replace standing officers with personnel from other states could impact effectiveness just as the HQ begins the concerted process of generating the concepts and forces for an operation. If the officers taken in are put into slots that are not critical or high profile, this impact may not be significant. However, if NATO's past experience is anything to go by, capitals tend to be keen to be allocated command slots in an operation that reflect directly the degree of military commitment they make; the greater the commitment, the greater the number of posts wanted, and the more serious interest there is in at least some command posts being important, high profile ones. National governments (and indeed, national military commands) can at times be quite insistent about such issues. The potential for significant political disagreement should not be overstated, for national capitals at a time of crisis are unlikely to be overly insistent on the matter of command slots. Nevertheless, it has the potential to be a problem, even if the problem is that festering political irritation or wounded political pride emerges post-operation.

A final issue that the EU needs to resolve is that of the training of the ERRF. As the U.K. parliamentary report pointedly stated, "training, field and command post exercises will be required to develop effective working practices, levels of professionalism and shared understanding. There is little evidence that sufficient attention has been paid to this and the EU must ensure that standards of training at all levels are laid down and monitored under the ESDP."[35] It should go without saying that the ERRF, if it is to be a serious and effective military capability, will need to engage in regular training exercises. Although the EU can exercise select elements and components of the ERRF, it also needs to conduct fairly large-scale training exercises that involve the entire command and control system along with select national forces. To conduct such large exercises the EU will need to establish an operational HQ. In principle, the EU could request the use of the three national operational HQs on a rotational basis, but this would mean that these are likely only to train in the context of the ESDP every eighteen to thirty-six months, depending on how frequently operational level exercises are conducted.

The problem with utilizing national operational HQs on a rotating basis is that no individual HQ is likely to develop the experience that is required to ensure effective working practices and common understandings. Moreover, the EU would be dependent, particularly in the case of Britain and France (which have extra-regional interests), on the operational HQ being available in the time frame needed to organize and conduct a training exercise. The same problem, it should be noted, is likely to be present should the EU decide to rely on NATO's CJTF HQ concept as its operational HQ. NATO already exercises its CJTF HQ in large training maneuvers biennially and the EU would need to negotiate and coordinate with the Alliance the release its CJTF HQ.

The question of utilizing national operational HQs for training exercises leads to a strongly related issue, that of standards of language, procedures, doctrine and concepts. Would each of the national HQs be required to operate in an EU-designated command language, such as NATO commands do? Would these HQs utilize EU-designated procedures and doctrine, either new or borrowed, or utilize their own national doctrines? To what degree are the command and control systems of national operational HQ systems compatible with the command and control systems of other EU member militaries? These questions are not necessarily easy to resolve, yet the EU must resolve them if it is to conduct training exercises as well as military operations, for it cannot proceed in a piecemeal fashion.

At present the EU does not have a permanent integrated, multinational command structure, and creating one in an ad hoc manner to generate a military response to an immediate crisis would be fraught with difficulties. The EU can request either NATO or an individual member state to provide an operational HQ for the ERRF. NATO's CJTF HQ concept has several advantages, including the fact that NATO's DSACEUR is the designated operational commander for the ERRF and that NATO commands have satisfactorily sorted out issues such as command language and doctrine. Nevertheless, there are potential downsides to relying on the Alliance's largesse that are mainly political in nature, including latent concerns about whether NATO would release a CJTF HQ for the EU to use, and the longer-term issue of the EU's stated desire for "autonomy." If, on the other hand, the EU determines to use national operational HQs, then it needs to address a range of practical issues such as how are other nationals to be integrated (and into which posts), training, language and doctrine. The resolution of these issues will not be insurmountable, but it also will not necessarily be easy. In the short term at least, these two alternatives will allow the EU to mount many if not most Petersberg Task missions. In the long run, however, the EU needs to consider whether it requires and indeed should have its own integrated military structure.

An EU Groupes de Forces Interarmées Multinationales?

The development by the EU of its own operational HQ in the mid to long term would serve to obviate most, if not all, of the deficiencies inherent in borrowing one either from NATO or a member state. Such a step would also furnish a significant political signal that the EU is indeed serious about its commitment to be able to generate a credible and effective military response to crises that affect its interests.

If the EU is to develop its own integrated military command structure, however, it needs to keep in mind a number of considerations. First, the recent transatlantic debate has made clear that the United States, and indeed other NATO members, would be seriously concerned if the EU were to develop an integrated command structure duplicating that of SHAPE.[36] If it seeks to develop a capacity to field its own command HQ, the EU would have proceed with care in order not to precipitate a political dispute over unnecessary duplication that could disrupt the transatlantic security link, as this would serve neither Europe's nor North America's interests. Second, the EU cannot be certain of the nature of future crises that may impact its interests, of whether it would respond militarily to such a crisis, or of what would be the political aims to be achieved if it did respond. Third, the military resources it can call on when seeking to generate a military force are constrained, with few member states being able to field the full panoply of military capabilities such as the U.S. military is able to do. Finally, the EU has to consider that any operation it launches is likely to include non-NATO militaries; fifteen non-EU states have committed forces to the Force Catalogue and hence the command structure developed must be capable of integrating a range of non-EU military capabilities.

The EU's strategic-political circumstances are strikingly similar to those NATO faced in the early 1990s. Now, as then, the principles of CJTF operations provide the flexibility that the EU is likely to need in developing a command capability and the flexibility it will need to generate rapidly an effective operational force to meet uncertain future contingencies. Further, NATO's experience with its CJTF HQ concept can furnish a template that the EU can draw on in developing a European command HQ capability. There are two plausible approaches that the EU can pursue in seeking to develop its own operational HQ. First, it may use a current European military structure as the nucleus from which to build an operational military HQ; the most obvious of such command structures is Eurocorps. And second, it may construct an operational HQ, both in terms of staff and physical resources, from the ground up, as something new.

There have been indications to suggest that Eurocorps may be a candidate to assume the role of the operational command. In late May 1999, France and Germany proposed that Eurocorps be transformed into an ERRF,[37] a move subsequently endorsed by both the WEU and Britain.[38] Moreover, NATO Secretary General Robertson, in discussing his decision to allow Eurocorps to take command of KFOR in April 2000, observed that he had "spent a lot of my time looking at the various non-NATO multinational forces in Europe and trying to make them serious"; his push to have Eurocorps take command of KFOR suggests that Robertson found it to be the most "serious" available alternative.[39]

Using Eurocorps as the foundation on which to construct a European operational command has several advantages. First, Eurocorps already exists as a multinational operational command and has been working on agreeing some of the central aspects of a unified command. Eurocorps has a multinational staff and has agreed that English will be the working language for operations. Moreover, Eurocorps' command of KFOR in 2000 has furnished it with real world experience that gives it a credibility it might previously have lacked. Eurocorps provided only 350 officers, about one quarter of the staff of the NATO HQs, to the KFOR command, with operational continuity depending largely on officers from the United States and Britain, neither of which belongs to Eurocorps. This "modular approach," as NATO Secretary General Robertson described it, was designed to allow the European officers of Eurocorps to gain command experience of a large operation while keeping a solid NATO system in place.[40] Even prior to its assumption of the command of KFOR, Eurocorps had worked to develop interoperability with NATO, through staff contributions to the Stabilization Force for Bosnia and Herzegovina (SFOR) and joint exercises with NATO. The ability of the Eurocorps command staff to integrate key personnel from NATO and non-NATO states when it assumed command of KFOR suggests that its structure could be adapted to permit the inclusion of command personnel from EU states. Further, though Eurocorps was originally designed to provide territorial defense, in recent years it has endeavored to adapt itself to peace support operations and Petersberg Tasks.

Second, the structure of Eurocorps is already geared to provide the operational command for a "pool" of capabilities. Currently, Eurocorps has only French and German units permanently attached to it, but Spain, Belgium and Luxembourg have worked out agreements whereby they will provide designated military elements. These agreements provide a framework that could be used by other EU members to provide forces for a European military crisis response. Moreover, the command structure, though it has never been utilized in this manner, is geared to construct a force comprising military elements and capabilities from different countries. Third, Eurocorps effectively is a stand-alone military formation, in that it has no official institutional affiliation. France and Germany, the primary agents of Eurocorps, have reached agreements with the WEU and NATO by which these two organizations can employ Eurocorps. The EU could utilize Eurocorps as the HQ for any European crises response, either by the simple expedient of reaching an agreement, as NATO and the WEU have done, or by negotiating with Eurocorps member states its inclusion within the institutional structure of the EU. Whichever approach is taken, the maintenance of the previous agreements, especially that with NATO, would contribute to the alleviation of the concerns of the United States and other NATO allies that the development of a European military capability contribute to NATO and that it not involve "unnecessary duplication."

This is not to suggest that the Eurocorps command structure could immediately serve as an EU-based CJTF HQ, or even necessarily as a nucleus for a European force. Britain, for example, is currently not a member of Eurocorps, yet it is a major EU state critical to the successful development and implementation of ESDP; the British military is one of the few European military organizations, along with the French military, whose command units have considerable experience in conducting large operations that combine ground, air and sea forces. Moreover, the original concept of Eurocorps being a fully integrated force has proved to be more difficult in practice than in theory.[41]

Eurocorps nevertheless provides the most suitable extant structure on which the EU can best begin to develop a command HQ capability. NATO's efforts to incorporate the principles of CJTF operations and to develop its CJTF HQ concept serve as a singular example that the EU can draw on in transforming Eurocorps into a European military command capability. The original concept of Eurocorps being a completely integrated military would have to be jettisoned in favor of an integrated multinational command structure that could draw on national military units in order to generate a military force tailored to the specific mission. A Eurocorps with an integrated command would have to comprise an officer corps drawn from all EU member states, even if this were confined to a core group of officers, as is the case in the CJTF HQ concept. This situation could be achieved even if the units being commanded on an ongoing basis remained only those France and Germany, for with a multinational integrated command it could, when needed, incorporate national military units from contributing EU states much as is envisioned in the case of NATO's CJTF HQ concept, and much as Eurocorps envisioned incorporating Spanish, Belgium and Luxembourg forces.

Transforming Eurocorps into a functional and effective operational command staff is easier in theory than in practice. There are a host of issues and problems both political and military that would need to be resolved, much as NATO had to resolve such issues in developing the CJTF concept, in adapting Eurocorps. On the political side, one such issue is whether France and Germany would be willing to give up the original idea of Eurocorps so that it can be reformed into a European command capability. Another political issue is the allocation of command positions within the integrated command structure. The experience within NATO suggests that nations can and will hotly contest the posts that their military nationals are allocated to fill, because of the prestige and influence that particular positions may have. On the military side, one of the most critical and potentially most difficult issues is the development of common procedures, doctrine and operability. In this vein, it is interesting to note that one of the things that the Eurocorps command learned in running the Kosovo operation is NATO procedures. Another issue is the working language. A common language must be used, and the level of language competence must be high. Eurocorps has decided on English as its working language, and any transformation of Eurocorps into an EU HQ could continue this practice; nevertheless, national political sensitivities may mean that the EU members would have to negotiate the question of language. These are but a few examples of some of the problems that the EU would confront in developing an integrated command HQ, even using Eurocorps as its nucleus; there are a range of other difficult issues that would need to be solved. It will thus take time and effort to transform the current Eurocorps command structure into a fully integrated and effective European operational HQ.

The second approach for the EU is to craft a new operational HQ capability. There has been no public indication to date that any EU member state favors the creation of a new command capacity. That such an approach does not appear to be particularly favored reflects the difficulty of creating a new organization when EU members already face difficult resource constraints in meeting the HG targets. Nonetheless, it would almost certainly be as easy, if not easier, to construct a standing EU operational HQ from scratch as it would be to transform Eurocorps to serve the same purpose. EU member states should have more than sufficient command staff available at present to man such an operational HQ without denuding their own command capability. Hence the primary financial cost would be in constructing the permanent infrastructure for the HQ (as Germany is currently doing for its national operational HQ that it has committed for EU use), with all this implies, and in providing the HQ with the requisite command and control capabilities. The EU could take the lead provided by NATO and fashion a nucleus command HQ that could be reinforced when needed. Clearly, such a nucleus EU HQ would be different from NATO's CJTF HQs: it would need to be a stand-alone HQ instead of being a core framework embedded in another HQ and hence it would need far more officers than NATO designates for its CJTF HQs to function independently on a daily basis. Should the EU decide to construct a permanent operational command structure over the long term, the same issues discussed earlier that would attend the transformation of Eurocorps would equally apply and would, therefore, involve considerable political negotiation. Should the EU ultimately decide to create an operational HQ from scratch, however, then NATO's CJTF HQ concept provides a structure and many specific practices that could be emulated and/or adapted to suit the needs of a standing European operational HQ.

Conclusion

When it was introduced, NATO's CJTF HQ concept was an innovative idea that provided a realistic response to a number of issues that the Alliance confronted in the early to mid-1990s. It offered the Alliance a command instrument that would enhance its capacity to respond quickly to uncertain out-of-area crises, while at the same time furnishing the material capability to implement an ESDI military operation. In spite of the concept's flexible utility, NATO today does not have an abiding military requirement for the CJTF HQ in order to organize and deploy an out-of-area operation. What NATO appears to need in the event of future crises is not so much the CJTF HQ concept, but rather more ARRC equivalent command HQs. NATO's military structure has proved to be sufficiently flexible to manage successfully the rapid generation of a range of operations in response to different types of crises. Its ability to do so has stemmed in part from a number of initiatives that SHAPE has undertaken, and in part from the fact that NATO's militaries have internalized the basic principles and practices of CJTF operations. Thus, while NATO may not have a clear military requirement for the CJTF HQ concept in order to mount a military crisis response, the introduction of the concept contributed significantly to the incorporation of the principles of CJTF operations into NATO thinking, to the extent that these are now guiding principles in the development of military operations.

The other potential requirement for NATO's CJTF HQ concept is to provide a command instrument for a European military operation. The CJTF HQ concept provided a material demonstration of NATO's stated support for the idea of a real and effective ESDI/ESDP. The fact that EU member states have committed operational HQs to the "Force Catalogue" does suggest that the EU, or at least some EU members, would prefer not to rely on NATO to provide the nexus point for its military command structure. Hence, in terms of ESDP, the CJTF HQ may be little more than a political symbol. Since NATO in and of itself does not absolutely require the CJTF HQ other than as a political symbol, continuing to invest in the development and implementation of the concept may seem wasteful in a time when the Alliance is hard-pressed to find adequate resources. Nevertheless, political symbols are often important in the world of diplomacy, and in light of the "Sturm und Drang" of some of the transatlantic rhetoric about the development of a European military response capability since the war for Kosovo in 1999, a decision to halt the implementation of the CJTF HQ concept could have adverse diplomatic repercussions.

Although the EU may not want or require a NATO CJTF HQ to mount a real world military operation, the concept does provide a practical example that the EU can draw on. The EU can refer to NATO's experience with the development of the CJTF HQ concept to help it identify the types of problems it would confront should it decide to develop its own command capability. Indeed, the EU could use NATO's CJTF HQ concept as a model that it can adopt or adapt to suit European goals. Whatever approach the EU decides to take should it move to create an operational command capability, it seems clear that the generation and conduct of future EU military crisis responses will embody the principles and practices of CJTF operations.

Notes

1. See General Klaus Naumann, "A New NATO for a New Century," Address to the Konrad Adenaur Siftung Group, Brussels, October 15, 1997, at www.nato.int/docu/speech/1997.
2. On the CJTF as a symbol, see Nora Bensahel, "Separable but not Separate Forces: NATO's Development of the Combined Joint Task Force," *European Security* 8 (Summer 1999), pp. 52–73.
3. For an early discussion of the NATO CJTF concept, and of CJTFs in general, see Charles Barry, "NATO's CJTFs in Theory and Practice," *Survival* 38 (Spring 1996), p. 82.
4. Lt. General Mario da Silva, "Implementing the Combined Joint Task Force Concept," *NATO Review* 46 (Winter 1998).
5. On the origins of the CJTF, see Terry Terriff, "U.S. Ideas and Military Change in NATO, 1989–1994," in Theo Farrell and Terry Terriff, eds., *The Sources of Military Change: Culture, Politics, Technology* (Boulder, CO: Lynne Rienner, 2002), pp. 91–116.
6. See *Information Booklet on NATO, SHAPE and Allied Command Europe* (Brussels: SHAPE Public Information Office, 2000), p. 13.
7. General Klaus Naumann, "NATO's New Military Command Structure," *NATO Review* 46 (Spring 1998).
8. For an overview of the new command structure, see ibid.

9. Ibid.

10. General George A. Joulwan, "SHAPE and IFOR: Adapting to the Needs of Tomorrow," *NATO Review* 44 (March 1996).

11. Interviews with officers in Allied Forces South (AFSouth).

12. Interviews with members of the International Military Staff and SHAPE.

13. Interviews with members of the International Military Staff. The ARRC is deployable within seven days, a time line that a CJTF HQ would not be able to meet.

14. Then SACEUR General Wesley Clark appears to have been directly connected to actual operational activities during the Kosovo campaign. See General Wesley K. Clark, *Waging Modern War* (Public Affairs: New York, 2001). This had the effect of circumventing, at times, the theater command based at AFSouth in Italy; indeed, this remains the case in regard to NATO's ongoing operations in Kosovo and Bosnia. Interviews with officers at SHAPE and AFSouth, and members of the International Military Staff.

15. Joulwan, "SHAPE and IFOR."

16. Indeed, NATO is seeking to have more ARRC-type formations available to it. See, for example, Nicholas Fiorenza, "ARRC Envy," *Armed Forces Journal International* (November 2001).

17. Interviews with officials at SHAPE and AFSouth.

18. Interview with official in AFSouth.

19. *Military Capabilities Commitment Declaration*, 4.a.

20. U.K., House of Lords, Session 2000–01, European Union Committee, *European Union—Eleventh Report* (London: European Union Committee Publications, January 29, 2002), paragraph 89.

21. Interview with former U.K. Ministry of Defense official.

22. *Military Capabilities Commitment Declaration*, Annex I to VI, 4.b, Nice European Council, December 7–9, 2000, at http://ue.eu.int.

23. Nice European Council, Presidency Report on European Security and Defence Policy, Annex VI, Sec. IV.

24. NAC, *The Alliance's Strategic Concept* (Washington, D.C.: NAC, April 1999), paragraph 18.

25. See "Building the European Security and Defence Identity within the Alliance."

26. For more on this issue, see Tofte, chapter 7, in this volume.

27. See, for example, Ivo H. Daalder and Michael E. O'Hanlon, *Winning Ugly: NATO's War to Save Kosovo* (Washington: Brookings Institution Press, 2000), p. 176.

28. "Statement on Improving European Military Capabilities: European Capability Action Plan, Annexe I," Council of the European Union, Draft Presidency Report on European Security and Defence Policy (Brussels: European Union, December 11, 2001), p. 17.

29. "Joint Declaration by the British and French Governments on European Defence."

30. Interviews with EU Council and Commission officials.

31. Interviews with EU and national military officials.
32. "Joint Declaration by the British and French Governments on European Defence."
33. *Military Capabilities Commitment Declaration*, 3.
34. See, for example, Marc Otte, *Preparing for Petersberg Tasks*, manuscript for intervention at the Royal Institute of International Affairs 2002 Defence Conference "Europe and American: A New Strategic Partnership," February 18–19, 2002, Chatham House, p. 3.
35. House of Lords, *European Union—Eleventh Report*, paragraph 89.
36. For a blunt statement of the U.S. view on this, see U.S. Deputy Secretary of State Strobe Talbott, "America's Stake in a Strong Europe," Remarks at a Conference on the Future of NATO, The Royal Institute of International Affairs, London, October 7, 1999, at http://www.state.gov.
37. See John Vinocur, "A Push to Redefine Eurocorps Role," *International Herald Tribune*, June 2, 1999.
38. See Western European Union, Ministerial Council, Luxembourg Declaration, Luxembourg, November 23, 1999, at http://www.defense-aerospace.com/data/verbatim/data/ve66/.
39. Joseph Fitchett, "Kosovo Task Bolsters EU Role in NATO," *International Herald Tribune*, April 20, 2000.
40. See Richard Norton-Taylor, "Eurocorps to run Kosovo peace force," *The Guardian*, April 18, 2000.
41. See Fitchett, "Kosovo Task Bolsters EU Role in NATO."

CHAPTER 4

The Effects of Kosovo and the Danger of Decoupling

Frédéric Bozo

After a period of certainty in the second half of the 1990s, the Atlantic Alliance is once again prey to self-questioning. Retrospectively, the shift occurred in the spring of 1999: upon approaching its fiftieth anniversary, the Alliance that had survived the Cold War and had established itself as the arbiter of European security, appeared to be stronger and more united than ever. Did not the "Allied Force" operation demonstrate just that? But this triumphalism was quickly transformed into skepticism as the "success" celebrated after the Kosovo Crisis gave way to a critical assessment that largely explains the subsequent revival of tension in transatlantic relations, accompanied by a forceful return of the European option.

The Crisis exposed the size of the gap threatening to open up between Europeans and Americans in the realm of capabilities, responsibilities, and especially strategic priorities, thereby highlighting structural flaws capable of leading eventually to a virtual decoupling of the two sides of the Atlantic. Separate dynamics at work since 1999 have fueled the questioning even more: does not the spectacular progress of ESDP in fact call into question the transatlantic "bargain"? Could the new "global" priorities of the United States, symbolized above all by the Missile Defense project, remain without consequences for Euro-American relations?

Is a divorce between Europe and America (as forecast by some) therefore inevitable? Or, on the contrary, is it possible to envisage a new transatlantic partnership (as desired by others)? In order to answer these questions, we must first go back to the Kosovo Crisis and its impact on U.S.–European relations, then study the nature and breadth of the political and strategic differences that it exposed, before considering the possibility of a more balanced relationship, a renewed partnership between America and Europe. The central question now is why such a partnership, so long improbable, today appears as the best hope of preserving a durable transatlantic relationship. Is this hope justified?

Back to Kosovo

Whether they confirm or reverse preexisting tendencies, crises have been inherently decisive in the history of the Alliance. Kosovo is no exception: since the NATO operation and its features were largely determined by the contemporary Atlantic context, it is indispensable to review what *ipso facto* has constituted a moment of truth for NATO, one whose ambivalent outcome places the Kosovo Crisis (unlike the one in Bosnia four years earlier) in the category of crisis that inverts preexisting tendencies—hence the current anxieties.

NATO Faced with the Kosovo Challenge

Of course, "Allied Force" was not launched, as some have maintained, with the aim of reconferring a "raison d'être" on NATO. On the other hand, the way in which the allies intervened did reflect the state of the Alliance ten years after the end of the Cold War: first, the dénouement of the Bosnia Crisis in 1995 had consecrated NATO as the true arbiter of European security; second, it had been enlarged by three new members in accordance with Washington's desiderata; last and most important, it was dominated by the United States alone. In short, it was an Alliance perhaps more "Atlantic" than at any time since its creation.[1]

The characteristics of the operation arose from this state of affairs. First, the very availability of NATO and the relative facility of the allied decision to resort to force in the spring of 1999—in contrast to Bosnia between 1992 and 1995—could scarcely be explained without the feeling of ultimate (albeit tardy) success engendered by the preceding crisis in Bosnia. Next, the choice of strategy—faith in the efficacy of air strikes—evidently resulted from an extrapolation derived from the precedent of the summer of 1995 when similar strikes had (at least apparently) made the Bosnian Serbs see reason. Last, the political and legal approach:[2] the decision to use coercion without legitimation by the UN Security Council, while justified by a probable Russian veto, must be related to the discrediting of the UN in the Bosnian Crisis and, especially, to the United States' search for a confirmation of the validity of this type of approach within the new strategic concept of NATO then under discussion. Did the Kosovo operation not furnish a useful precedent in demonstrating this?

Above all, this overall context accounts for the most striking trait of the Allied intervention. For the Europeans, a phase of political activism (the British and French, via Rambouillet, had involved the Americans in the process that would lead to the intervention) was succeeded by a phase of military conformism (the British and French relinquished significant influence over the definition of strategy and then its implementation as soon as the crisis was transformed into an open confrontation). It is obvious that such "sequenced" conduct on the part of the Europeans reflects the state of transatlantic relations in the spring of 1999, relations characterized by both the "lessons" of Bosnia (the dread of a new strategic divorce from the Americans pushing the Europeans to accept without balking their military leadership) and also by the desire to remedy the situation (the search for a new political balance within the Alliance was what first pushed the United States to take the lead in the crisis).

Victory or Non-Defeat?

Therefore the intervention could not help but become a moment of truth for the Alliance, but the examination of its strategic options, its conduct of the operation, and the results of the "NATO" intervention are all subject to criticism.[3]

First, the strategic options. The concept initially adopted failed: while the air strikes were supposed to lead Milosevic to yield in a few days (due to a shortsighted interpretation of the events of the summer of 1995 in which the same strikes had played only a symbolic role), it took seventy-eight days of constant "intensified" bombing to achieve this result. Nevertheless, the result cannot be credited exclusively to these air strikes; rather, a combination of several factors explains the decision of the Serbian dictator to yield: the risk of a possible land operation, the arrest warrant issued by the Court in The Hague (which such an operation could make into a credible threat to him), the feeling of no longer being able to count on Russian support, the political role of the EU, and the role finally granted to the UN in the solution of the crisis.

Second, the conduct of the operation demonstrated the limits of NATO's functioning in a major crisis and highlighted the relative unsuitability, politically and militarily, of the Alliance to perform its "new missions" outside Article V. On the one hand, this was because NATO had revealed serious gaps in the implementation of the initial strategy and particularly in the decision-making process,[4] and on the other hand, because it was not certain that the allies (assuming they had ultimately been convinced of the initial strategy's failure and of the need for a radically changed approach) would have been able to implement any strategy other than that of a mechanical pursuit of air strikes. Not only did there not exist from the start a "Plan B", but it is also doubtful that the land option discretely mentioned in the latter half of May in order to increase the pressure on Milosevic would actually have been authorized and then put into operation if needed. In short, the "chance" factor played an undeniable role.

In the end what was achieved left much to be desired. Yes, the allies were able to maintain their cohesion, and this demonstration of unity evidently weighed in the balance. And yes, the five goals announced at the start of the intervention were fulfilled.[5] But this should not allow us to forget that the initial effects of the operation had been the opposite of those sought (the air strikes had at first contributed to the ethnic cleansing and they had not been exempt from collateral damage), that the half-admitted aim of overthrowing Milosevic would not be achieved until well after Western intervention, which in fact played only a minor part in that event, and finally, that in fact the Alliance had nearly backed itself into a strategic impasse from which it escaped only thanks to a set of favorable circumstances and in line with a scenario unlike what had been initially anticipated (in terms of the roles of the UN, Russia, the EU, and so on). In short, the Alliance only succeeded to the extent that it did not fail.

Two Interpretations

This unsatisfactory outcome is undeniably the source of a reverse trend in transatlantic relations after Kosovo, a trend that is the opposite of that of the preceding crisis. Bosnia had given rise to a crisis in transatlantic relations before its dénouement following the summer of 1995; however, the largely positive assessment that people chose to give it had the opposite effect, that is, it permitted an unprecedented reaffirmation of Atlantic unanimity and the cohesion of the Alliance and of American leadership as a corollary. Yet in the case of Kosovo, it was the opposite dynamic that prevailed: while the management of the crisis had furnished a demonstration of real Atlantic cohesion, the outcome of the ordeal was perceived as mediocre and the lessons drawn from it caused profound differences to appear within the Alliance. This dialectic, inverted from one crisis to the other, basically explains how the first confirmed the transatlantic status quo while the second gave rise to a questioning of it—first and foremost (but not only) from a European standpoint.

With respect to official declarations, the Alliance certainly seemed to have emerged as strengthened by this trial as by the preceding one. But the reality is different: behind a façade of self-satisfaction, European leaders assessed the operation just as harshly as did the Americans. Yet each side differs radically from the other over the reasons for this semi-failure—attributing it, at least implicitly, to its partner. And so the consequences that the two sides draw for the future imply antithetical visions of the evolution of the Alliance. This explains the decisive meaning of the crisis for the Alliance, which justifies viewing the events of the spring of 1999 as a major turning point in its development since 1989.

It is not that the Americans are more satisfied with and the Europeans more critical of the Kosovo intervention: such a classic outcome would merely reproduce the customary situation within such an unequal relationship, that of the dominant power's self-satisfaction and the others' inevitable frustration. What gives the Kosovo Crisis decisive overtones is that both parties share the same critical judgment of the affair, but that the fundamental reasons for their dissatisfaction are divergent, if not opposite. For their part, the Americans deplore having borne an overly large share of the effort in an operation in which the European military contribution should have been greater, while complaining of having been prevented by the latter from conducting the strategy in a way that seemed best in their eyes. Meanwhile, for their part, the Europeans begrudge having had too small an influence upon the operation, with some of them (not always explicitly) believing that a more assertive Europe, and hence a more balanced Alliance, would have been in a position to promote a strategy that was better than the American one.

Hence the discordance between the consequences and lessons each draws from the Kosovo Crisis. While Europeans and Americans no doubt agree that Kosovo does not offer a model or a precedent (the opposite conclusion, hastily drawn from the Bosnian Crisis, largely explains the errors committed in 1999), there also exist radical differences over the prescriptions to apply in the future. While the Americans find an argument for requiring from their allies a larger military effort, the Europeans inversely deduce the need for better decision-sharing. While the former increasingly highlight the stakes of "global" security in their strategic priorities and proclaim their disdain for peace operations unworthy of American armed forces, the latter reassert the preeminence of the security challenges to their own periphery and adopt a "headline goal" for European forces that corresponds precisely to such operations. In short, while some basically want to Americanize the Alliance even more, others want to Europeanize it. At the risk of being overly schematic, this has been the state of transatlantic relations since Kosovo.

The Return of Decoupling?

If this crisis appears to be a turning point for the Alliance, it is because, beyond the event itself, it revealed the breadth of what separates Europeans and Americans in certain key aspects of their strategic relationship. Far from being accidental, the chasm that the operation exposed is related to a system of structural flaws whose interplay could lead, in the future, to alienating Europe and America in a dangerous way. The chasm is really three-fold, involving simultaneously problems of capabilities, responsibilities, and priorities.

A Three-Fold Chasm

First, the domain of capabilities.[6] The facts are well known: the "Allied Force" operation, by its very nature an intensive and prolonged aerial intervention, prioritizing precise and selective strikes and using sophisticated weapons, highlighted the distance today separating the United States and the European allies with regard to conventional military means, at least at the top end of the range. Although its exact measure is the object of debate, the scale of magnitude of this problem was unflinchingly stated by the former American Secretary of Defense William Cohen: "The European members of NATO spend about 60 percent of what the US spends, but they produce about 10 percent in terms of capabilities." The Europeans do not refute this comparison.[7] Hence we find a situation unprecedented since the era when the American rearmament precipitated by the Korean War left the Europeans (still badly armed, if not disarmed) way behind. And if subsequently the gap was narrowed by the necessities of the defense of Europe, the end of the Cold War has widened it anew. But current tendencies (budgetary in particular) on both sides of the Atlantic lead to the conclusion that the phenomenon could become still more accentuated in the foreseeable future.

Turning to the domain of responsibilities, here, too, the chasm separating Americans and Europeans within the Alliance has appeared in the spotlight, with Europe, through "Allied Force," simply tagging along behind U.S. strategy. But here too, the latest Balkan Crisis exposed a structural problem, a corollary of the preceding one: the Euro-American relationship, ten years after the Cold War, remained just as unequal as it had been at its origins. Of course, the end of bipolar confrontation could have removed the obstacle that for forty years had prevented European self-assertion, a development long considered to be incompatible with the maintenance of U.S. engagement in the defense of Western Europe. Nothing of the sort happened, and the decade 1989–1999 can be interpreted as a sequence of two successive failures in this domain: that of an autonomous European defense in relation to NATO (the project advanced by the French after 1990 in the framework of the relaunching of Europe at Maastricht), and that of a European defense integrated into the Atlantic organization (this was the objective of the "strategic revolution" attempted by Jacques Chirac between 1995 and 1997).[8] But without a "European pillar" within NATO or without—in other words with an Alliance that remained $1 + n$—there can be no real sharing of responsibilities.

There remains the question of priorities in the treatment of these twin problems: is it more urgent to upgrade European military capabilities or to grant the EU more responsibility within NATO? Kosovo and its after-effects also revealed the breadth of differences between Americans and Europeans in this respect, with the former promoting a DCI conceived before the crisis but actually launched in the spring of 1999, while the latter were undertaking an ESDP announced since Saint-Malo but really spurred by Kosovo. Here again, the conflict merely revealed fundamental tendencies at work since the end of the Cold War, if not well before: is the American desire to obtain from the Europeans a greater effort in the military domain not as old as the quest by the latter for increased strategic weight within the Alliance? This conflict over priorities has every chance of enduring as long as the givens of the problem remain unchanged or even deteriorate: Washington's growing exigency with regard to European capabilities will be answered by a European demand for a better reapportioning of responsibilities. A NATO aligned around the American military apparatus versus an Alliance re-equilibrated in favor of Europeans: such is the nature of the transatlantic debate today.

A Cycle of Mutual Recrimination

This debate can only feed a dangerous cycle of mutual recrimination, liable in time to bring about an actual strategic divorce. This is because the problem of military capabilities revives the old quarrel over burden sharing. Awareness of disequilibrium in the means deployed by the Europeans and Americans in Kosovo led William Cohen to denounce as "not acceptable" a "situation in which one country [of the Alliance] bears a disproportionate part of the burden."[9] Although this is not explicitly stated by officials in Washington (except in Congress), this really amounts to a warning to the Europeans: America will not maintain its engagement in Europe unless the latter agrees to contribute more to the common effort—a warning that one finds in coded statements made after the November 2000 election by members of George W. Bush's entourage with regard to an eventual American withdrawal from KFOR. But the recrimination is mutual: why should the Europeans "share the burden" of a strategy that is not theirs? Since "Allied Force" does not appear as a model for the future—notably due to the debatable choice of "air strikes only" intervention—the Europeans indeed can legitimately question the reasonableness of American demands regarding military capabilities; in fact, their response can be read between the lines of the *Headline Goal*, formulated more within a logic of land intervention than of coercive strikes.

The same cycle of reciprocal recrimination prevails in the debate over the sharing of responsibilities. Even if Madeleine Albright's three "D's" gradually gave way to Lord Robertson's suggested three "I's," the determination of the Europeans to obtain the means of autonomous decision-making with regard to defense within the framework of the Union has been, as we know, received by the Americans with reticence bordering on hostility. The same argument always reappears: why and how can one continue to justify U.S. involvement in the defense or security of Europe if the Europeans are in a position to take decisions without American participation that implicates them in crises and conflicts they would not have chosen? Or worse: isn't there a risk that Europeans might adopt such structures of decision making without having the military tools to face the possible consequences? Decision-making capabilities without operational means: the old American nightmare concerning Europe's defense is still very real.[10] Nor are the Europeans quiescent in the face of these recriminations. They inevitably interpret U.S. hostility to a European decision capability as a rejection of the demand for better sharing of transatlantic responsibilities and consequently as tangible proof of persistent unilateralism and even hegemonism.

But it is the controversy over priorities (Europeans upgrading their capabilities versus Americans accepting responsibility sharing) that today best crystallizes the mutual recriminations and reveals the most worrying defect: this is what separates an America that is strategically more and more "global" from a Europe that is steadily more "European." Each, naturally, interprets the priority of the other as reflecting strategic preoccupations detached from its own. For the Europeans, the American obsession with high tech (of which National Missile Defense (NMD), is the caricature), combined with their reticence about ESDP, is interpreted as follows: the United States sets up false threats or at least exaggerates their reality (the ex-rogue states, the ballistic risk combined with that of weapons of massive destruction); it wants to drag its allies into crisis scenarios or "global" strategies while disengaging itself from the Old Continent and the Balkans in particular—that is to say from where the "true" risks lie in the eyes of the members of the EU. In short, they see a bellicose United States and yet one that is steadily less interested in Europe.

For the Americans, conversely, the demand for autonomous decision-making about defense within the framework of the EU, along the lines of the HG, combined with a lack of European seriousness about military budgets, means only one thing: the Europeans are primarily interested in institutions, meaning in themselves, instead of dealing alongside America with the true threats confronting the West; at the most they want to confine their strategic assertions to a police role on the periphery of the EU, notably the Balkans, while nevertheless leaning on the United States to perform these tasks. In short, the EU presents itself as a provincial strategic partner, inward looking and ultimately "isolationist."

Toward Decoupling?

This situation, characterized by a growing divergence between the European and American strategic perspectives, suggests the famous "decoupling" that haunted Western strategists during a large part of the Cold War. Of course, adopting a historical perspective relativizes this danger. All in all, the Alliance has always been characterized by asymmetries that lie at the very heart of the creation of the Atlantic system: a United States that is militarily super-powerful, politically controlling, and strategically global guarantees the security of a Europe that is militarily weak, politically minor, and strategically regional. This was, *ab initio*, the raison d'être of the Atlantic system, as well as of its actual structure. Of course, these same asymmetries have simultaneously represented the fundamental problem of this essentially unequal Alliance, explaining the endless transatlantic crises. And yet each of these very crises has been overcome by the Alliance.

The Cold War system indeed had the advantage of allowing the allies to relativize the importance and to attenuate the consequences of military, political, and strategic disparities between Europe and the United States, thereby preventing any real decoupling at a structural level. First, this was because the disequilibrium in military means was acceptable to the Americans: the United States was prepared to defend Europe despite denouncing the "free ride" the Europeans were taking, because this was also in their vital interest. The second reason was because the deficit of strategic responsibilities was bearable for the Europeans: however dissatisfied they were (the French foremost) with the hegemony of the United States, the Europeans (including the French) recognized, in the final analysis, that this was the price to pay to be defended by America. Third, the divergences over strategic priorities were without real consequences, quite simply because the "European" threat and the "global" threat constituted, in reality, one and the same threat: that of the U.S.S.R.

But these factors do not operate today: the United States no longer sees a vital interest in the security of Europe; meanwhile the Europeans are less and less concerned about the necessity of an American guarantee, especially if bought at the cost of European identity; finally, the strategic stakes of the Old Continent are now less closely linked to those of the wider world. More than a decade after the end of bipolar confrontation, the prospect of decoupling ceases to be solely theoretical, and the Kosovo Crisis, in this respect, revealed and catalyzed a deep-seated tendency.

The Necessary Re-Balancing

Is the frequently heralded divorce thus inevitable? This question, so often formulated in critical moments in the Alliance's history, may seem hackneyed: has divorce not been avoided so often in the past? It may even seem incongruous if one considers that the Atlantic community is more closely knit together by values and cultures that are largely convergent.

Divorce is Less Impossible

However, the question is not unfounded in strategic terms: not only have the factors that made decoupling impossible during the Cold War—starting with the common threat—ceased to operate, but the respective situations of the United States and the EU (analyzed in terms of distribution of power and strategic options) could lead to a divorce. To deal with the United States first: American power (at least in relative terms) is today such that two questions must inevitably be raised. On the one hand, do the Americans still feel the need to have partner-allies in order to face their strategic challenges? On the other hand, do Europeans now see America as distant from them strategically—whether in terms of means or of preoccupations—to the point of judging it useless or illusory to maintain themselves "on a par" in order to perpetuate the partnership? More than the initial actions by the Bush administration, it was the fundamental tendencies of American policy over a number of years (Congress's increasing influence, a rejection of the multilateral rules of the game, a focus on powerful military means) that might legitimately fuel such lines of questioning.[11]

Turning to the EU: more than ten years after the end of the Cold War, have not the successive failures of Europeans to establish a strategic entity durably (if not irremediably) discredited in American eyes the aspirations of a *Europe puissance* to be capable of such a partnership? Are not the Europeans themselves convinced of the futility of their effort and have they not chosen, consciously or otherwise, a *Europe espace* that would *ipso facto* cease to be/constitute a strategic player for America? The questioning across the Atlantic in this vein is just as legitimate; the Americans must be struck by the growing weight of European institutions, by European reluctance to act in a decisive manner, and by their reluctance to take military means seriously.

This perhaps unprecedented situation in the transatlantic relationship, in which each of the partners questions the interest of the other in maintaining a real strategic partnership, may explain the kind of proposal being put forward these days, which, under cover of restoring harmony between the United States and Europe, would in reality merely instrumentalize their separation. For example, the idea of a deal whereby the United States would not oppose the setting up of the ESDP and the Europeans would not object to the launching of the NMD;[12] wouldn't such a bargain simply ratify the decoupling each was trying to avoid? How, except as a strategic divorce, can one describe a situation in which each of the partners accepts the deviations and infidelities of the other in order to follow its own? Harmony might be reestablished, but at the cost of the relationship itself.[13]

One could say that such a proposal is so unrealistic as to be of no consequence: apart from the fact that such a bargain appears highly improbable to the extent that it proceeds from a false symmetry (one of the projects already has substance while the other is just anticipated; one of the actors could block the other's project but the reverse is much less likely . . .), it is difficult to see how the United States and Europe could arrive at a sort of mutual agreement over what would amount in effect to ratifying their decoupling, if not divorce. Yet the risk with such a scenario is not that the actors might deliberately follow it but that it might be enacted without being actively or consciously envisaged. In other words, the current standing of the relationship, if nothing is done, might lead perhaps fatally to such a decoupling. The status quo, in this sense, is not a solution; it would only increase the asymmetry that today threatens the Alliance's cohesion. It is in this sense that a strategic divorce between Europe and the United States is today less impossible than ever before.

This is also why the rebalancing of the Alliance is more necessary than ever. Far from letting the transatlantic relationship take the path of least resistance that can only lead to exacerbating disparities and hence divergences, the Alliance's cohesion and its future depend quite evidently upon a new relationship between the United States and Europe, one that is more balanced. In fact, because it would reduce the military, political, and strategic chasm that the Kosovo Crisis revealed and that is currently widening, a more balanced relationship would allow the two parties to achieve the compromises necessary for a definitive transatlantic "bargain" that would endure.

This is evident with regard to capabilities and responsibilities; a deal presupposes a Europe in a position to demand the latter by arguing from the strengthening of the former. On the one hand, the United States cannot grant more influence to Europe in defining and implementing its strategy unless Europe is in a position to contribute more toward sharing the burden. On the other hand, Europe cannot consent to an increased defense effort unless it is guaranteed a significant strategic role. The same goes for priorities: it is only if the Europeans accept collaboration with the Americans in facing "global" challenges that the latter will make an enduring commitment to remain an active party in European security. And conversely, the willingness of the Europeans to broaden the scope of the Atlantic Alliance to encompass extra-European strategic issues depends upon the availability of the Americans to confront alongside them the problems (still prime in their eyes) of security on the periphery of the EU. More responsibilities granted by the Americans in exchange for increased capabilities to which the Europeans consent; better Euro-American cooperation outside Europe in exchange for a real American devolution of responsibilities inside Europe: these are the elements of a new grand "transatlantic bargain" that would perpetuate the strategic relationship between the United States and Europe, a bargain that by definition presupposes a minimum of balance between the protagonists.[14]

Less Improbable Partnership

Today it is the prospect of a more assertive EU that constitutes the true guarantee in such a strategic rebalancing, and hence its best hope of conserving a strong transatlantic relationship. This prognosis, previously unthinkable, is shared almost unanimously inside the Alliance, and, especially, inside the Union.[15] It has become a commonplace statement: in matters of European defense, more distance has been covered in two or three years than in fifty; the Europeans, after many false starts and pretences, are now "serious." The reasons for this are political, military, and strategic.[16]

We deal first with the political reasons: the decisive novelty is clearly the desire of the Fifteen to give the Union a defense capability. Of course, this conceptual leap could have been no more than an institutional "quick fix" similar to what had been attempted at the time of Maastricht ten years previously—in other words, a simple word game amounting yet again to instituting European defense by decree. It is nothing of the sort: the worst case scenario (of liquidating the old WEU once its failure was acknowledged without really giving the new EU the means to succeed where the former had failed) did not come to pass, largely because the British did not push for it or even perhaps plead for it (for which they are owed homage, as are the French who knew enough to take London's historic change on this matter at face value, which was not *a priori* obvious). On the contrary, the devolution of the defense role to the Union is part of a dual dynamic of legitimacy and efficacy. The legitimacy dynamic stems from the fact that if European defense has been revitalized by its wholehearted assignment to the EU, it benefits fully—without the damper of the WEU—from the political vitality intrinsic to the Union. (We have as proof the remarkable results of the EU in this domain, in contrast with almost all the rest, including the euro currency.) The efficacy dynamic stems from the fact that even if the European strategic revival cannot be reduced to a simple institutional expedient, it still relies on politico-military institutions that are able to function adequately (and essentially are copied from those of the Atlantic Alliance).

The military reasons include the fact that even if the impulse behind the European dynamic is supremely political and institutional, the process cannot be reduced to that. It has been said repeatedly that the novelty of the current renewal of European defense resides in the commitment made by the Fifteen to defense capabilities. The "Headline Goal" is both sufficiently ambitious to open the way, within a short time, to a significant military role for the Union in the scenarios envisaged under the Petersberg missions, but also realistic enough to avoid the pious wishes of the past. Political legitimacy and military credibility are thus the indispensable dialectic that reconciles the approach from above—dear to the French—and the approach from below—much prized by the British. From this dialectic results the current European defense dynamic and its inscription within the transatlantic relationship.

However, strategic factors figure most prominently in the current process. It is because the principal protagonists in European defense are converging that this goal has recently become realistic. We have seen a three-fold normalization: British normalization regarding the very idea of a European defense (indeed it is the changed policy of the U.K. under Tony Blair that permitted the current process); French normalization regarding NATO (despite stalled rapprochement with the integrated structure, the separate status of the French within the military organization no longer poses much of an obstacle to France's participation in NATO operations); and finally, German normalization regarding themselves, so to speak (i.e., with respect to power and the use of force).[17] The Kosovo Crisis confirmed and even accelerated this triple normalization—hence its decisive impact on the European strategic process. Indeed, frustration over the strategic inferiority of the Europeans was evident during the crisis, which led to the Copernican Revolution effected by London; moreover, the operation widely confirmed the banality of a pure and simple integration of French forces into the Allied operational apparatus; finally, the crisis demonstrated the maturity of German public opinion and politicians with respect to the issue of using force.

Moreover, beyond this convergence, one might ask if the Kosovo Crisis constituted for the Europeans a sort of revelation of what might in future be specific and legitimate about the EU's actions on issues of international security, notably in relation to U.S. perhaps less determined to be engaged in a conflict like that over Kosovo: their availability (perhaps due to the very raison d'être of European construction) to intervene in the name of defending human rights at least on the Old Continent.[18]

All the above—and most especially the Kosovo factor—may explain the current hope of a transatlantic rebalancing as well as the perception of its indispensability to the long-term survival of the relationship. Creating a Europe of defense would not turn the Alliance into a "relic of the past."[19] Not proceeding with ESDP would have this result. If the Europeans would only continue (in line with statements made at Cologne, Helsinki, and Nice) to establish and refine (and especially finance) a coherent defense project, if the Americans would only choose correctly between the devolutionist approach and the hegemonic temptation that are manifestly clashing inside the Bush Administration, and ultimately if both sides would only find a reasonable compromise over the decisive question of the articulation—political, military, and strategic—between the Union and the Alliance, in short, if only good judgment governs the actors' policies, such a rebalancing will be translated into actions and lead to a transatlantic relationship that is long lasting on its new foundations. A true transatlantic partnership, formerly unthinkable, is today much less so.

The Conjunctural and the Structural Factors

It is true that several conditions must be met: the undeniable progress of recent times is not guaranteed to bring about results, and there are limits to voluntarism and to simple policy making, limits that arise from conjunctural factors. The European project and the renovation of the transatlantic relationship are at the mercy of the next crisis, whether in the Balkans (alas, Macedonia is the probable candidate) or elsewhere; this time, will Europe be "ready" or will it once again invoke the unexpected nature of events in order to justify its possible failings? Inversely, will the United States finally be able to trust its allies? In this sense, the history of the Alliance will continue to be the history of its crises.

But in the final analysis, structural factors will be decisive. At this stage in the evolution of the transatlantic relationship and of European construction, these can be summed up in two sets of retrospective questions about why it was impossible until now for the Atlantic Alliance to be truly balanced. The first set is about Europe: why has it been incapable of asserting itself as a credible strategic actor for so long? Is the reason conjunctural in that the circumstances have never been propitious and so therefore European defense has been a series of missed opportunities? Or is it structural in that the necessary choices were never made, starting with that of a truly integrated Euro-defence that is alone capable, perhaps, of turning Europe into a coherent strategic actor? The second set of questions concerns the United States: why until now has it not been in a position to welcome with serenity a Europe that is strategically autonomous? Is this because Europe has never been in a position to demonstrate its seriousness of purpose? Or more fundamentally, is it because the United States is incapable of accepting involvement without being in control? "America," De Gaulle once remarked, "only envisages an Alliance on condition that it commands it."[20] This may have been a visionary statement.

Notes

Translated by Susan Emanuel.

1. For an interpretation of the post–Cold War evolution of the Alliance, see Frédéric Bozo, *Where does the Atlantic Alliance Stand? The Improbable Partnership*, Les Notes de l'IFRI, no. 6 bis, Paris, 1999.

2. On the legal aspects, see Serge Sur, *Le Recours à la force dans l'affaire du Kosovo et le droit international*, Note d'IFRI, no. 22, Paris, September 2000, and Catherine Guicherd, "International Law and the War in Kosovo," *Survival* 41: 2(Summer 1999), pp. 19–34.

3. For a critical analysis of the operation, see Ivo Daalder and Michael O'Hanlon, *Winning Ugly: NATO's War to Save Kosovo* (Washington: Brookings, 2000).

4. See Guillaume Parmentier, "Redressing NATO's Imbalances," *Survival* 42: 2 (Summer 2000), pp. 96–112; and Kori Schake, *Evaluating NATO's Efficiency in Crisis Management*, Note d'IFRI, no. 21, Paris, 2000.

5. These five objectives were: an end to the acts of violence perpetrated in Kosovo, the withdrawal of Serbian forces, the deployment of an international force, the return of refugees, and Belgrade's acceptance of substantial autonomy for the province.

6. On this subject see David Yost, chapter 5, in this volume.

7. Quoted by Yost, chapter 5, in this volume.

8. For an attempt to interpret the post–Cold War failure at transatlantic rebalancing, see Frédéric Bozo, "The Transatlantic Relationship: Change or Continuity? A European Critique," in S. Victor Papacosma, Sean Kay, and Mark Rubin, eds., *NATO after Fifty Years* (Wilmington: Scholarly Resources, 2001). On the changes in French policy during this period, see Frédéric Bozo, *La France et l'Alliance atlantique depuis la fin de la guerre froide. Le modèle gaullien en question?* (Paris: Cahiers du centre d'études d'histoire de la défense, 2001).

9. Remarks by William Cohen to the Wehrkunde, February 5, 2000, U.S. Department of Defense, *Defense Link*, www.defenselink.mil/speeches.

10. William Cohen, in the same speech to the Wehrkunde, was not coy: "My fear is that we will see a bureaucratic system [of European defense] set up. We will see declining budgets and we will not see the [military] capability to match the words that we have talked about so passionately . . ."; ibid.

11. These tendencies are well analyzed in Steven Everts, *Unilateral America, Lightweight Europe? Managing Divergence in Transatlantic Foreign Policy*, Working Paper, Center for European Reform, March 2001, www.cer.organization.uk.

12. See Joseph Fitchett, "U.S. and EU Ponder Defense Trade-Off," *International Herald Tribune*, February 8, 2001.

13. On this point see David C. Gompert, "America and Europe: Partnership, Division of Labor—or Worse?" Lecture to IFRI, March 8, 2001.

14. Such a scheme was outlined several years ago by David C. Gompert and F. Stephen Larrabee, in *America and Europe: A Partnership for a New Era*

(Cambridge: Cambridge University Press, 1997). At the time, the situation appeared unpropitious for its realization in that the Alliance, after the dénouement of the crisis in Bosnia, seemed seriously unbalanced; see Frédéric Bozo, *Où en est l'Alliance atlantique? Op. cit.*

15. See Jolyon Howorth's contributions to this volume as well as his book *L'Intégration européenne et la défense: l'ultime défi?*, Institut d'études de sécurité de l'UEO, Cahier de Chaillot, no. 43.

16. On this topic see the analysis by Gilles Andréani, Christoph Bertram, and Charles Grant, *Europe's Military Revolution* (London: Center for European Reform, 2001).

17. On this convergence, see Nicole Gnesotto, *L'Europe et la puisssance* (Paris: Presses de Sciences-Po, 1998).

18. See Martin Ortega, *L'Intervention militarie et l'"Union européenne*, Institu d'études de sécuritée de l'UEO, Cahier de Chaillot, no. 45.

19. In William Cohen's expression, *International Herald Tribune*, December 6, 2000.

20. Conversation between General de Gaulle and former Chancellor Adenauer, March 10, 1966, in *Lettres, notes et carnets (1964–1966)* (Paris: Plon, 1987), p. 267 ff.

PART TWO

The U.S.–European Capabilities Gap

CHAPTER 5

The U.S.–European Capabilities Gap and the Prospects for ESDP

David S. Yost

The defense-capabilities gap that divides the United States from its European allies is real, and it matters. The gap can most usefully be viewed as the aggregate of multiple gaps relating to the organization and conduct of large-scale expeditionary operations. Large transatlantic disparities in the ability to mount such operations became painfully obvious during NATO's Kosovo intervention in March–June 1999 and spurred commitments on both sides of the Atlantic to narrow the gap. However, a close examination of the EU's post-Kosovo efforts to develop an autonomous military capability reveals the serious obstacles to improving European forces.

Defining the Gap

It is difficult to make comparisons between U.S. and European military capabilities for at least three reasons. First, scenarios differ, and the employment of capabilities is scenario-dependent. Different capabilities can be used to achieve similar results; similar capabilities can be used in different ways to achieve distinct results and so on. Second, even in a simple comparison of similar capabilities (for instance, air-refueling aircraft) basic problems in counting rules arise, quite aside from the

quality of the aircraft and the readiness and proficiency of the personnel. The most fundamental "counting rule" question is, who is coming
to the party? What forces are likely to be made available in specific
contingencies? For example, with over 600 tanker aircraft (KC-135s
and KC-10As), the United States has about ten times as many aerial-
refueling tankers as the NATO European countries put together. It is
obviously preposterous, however, to suppose that all U.S. tanker aircraft
would be available to deal with a crisis in Europe: under all foreseeable
circumstances, the United States would retain some tanker aircraft in
East Asia, the Persian Gulf, and North America. For that matter, France,
the United Kingdom, and other European nations would also probably
retain some tanker aircraft at home for national defense purposes, unless
the contingency at hand threatened their own national survival.

As this judgment suggests, on the European side as well, the "who is
coming?" question also involves political and force-allocation issues.
Which European nations should be counted in a gap assessment? Should
all the EU nations be counted, or all the European members of NATO, or
both? Would it not be misleading to count all the capabilities of all these
nations when (1) participation in a "Petersberg Task" crisis-management
operation is voluntary and hence optional and (2) no nation is likely to
commit all of its military forces to such an operation?[1] Furthermore, the
15 members of the EU have approved the principle of ad hoc crisis-
management consultations with 15 other countries in so-called "15-plus-
15" meetings.[2] The other 15 countries consist of the six NATO European
countries not in the EU (the Czech Republic, Hungary, Iceland, Norway,
Poland, and Turkey) and nine countries that have applied for EU
membership (Bulgaria, Cyprus, Estonia, Latvia, Lithuania, Malta,
Slovakia, Slovenia, and Romania). Should the U.S. capabilities presumed
available for a specific operation be compared with those of all 30 countries that might hypothetically participate in an EU-led operation?

The third factor complicating a U.S.–European capabilities-gap
assessment also involves complex political judgments: the possibility of
EU access to common NATO assets and even, in some circumstances,
U.S. national assets under the auspices of Alliance-approved CJTFs.
What are the NATO assets of interest to the European allies in CJTF?
According to one definition, such assets are those funded by NATO
common infrastructure budgets: Airborne Warning and Control System
(AWACS) aircraft, HQ elements, pipelines, radars and other air-defense
and air command-and-control systems, communications equipment,
airfields, and storage depots. By another definition, NATO assets also
encompass the U.S. capabilities regularly put at the disposal of

NATO: air-refueling capabilities, heavy long-distance air transport for troops and equipment (such as C-141s, C-5s, and C-17s), satellite intelligence, communications, and navigation data. U.S. national assets clearly remain ultimately under U.S. control, however, and should not be attributed to Europeans in a gap assessment.

An Operational Definition of the Gap

The U.S.–European capabilities gap should be defined as an aggregate of many gaps. In some areas, there are technology gaps.[3] In most areas, there are investment and procurement gaps. These gaps add up to U.S. superiority, quantitative and sometimes qualitative, in many areas of military capability. These include strategic mobility assets (such as aerial refueling and air transport), surface ships and submarines, precision-strike munitions, electronic warfare, power projection (in the sense of long-range air and missile strikes), and what the U.S. military calls C4ISR (command, control, communications, computers, intelligence, surveillance, and reconnaissance). The United States is currently superior to any combination of its European allies in its ability to plan, conduct and sustain theater-wide expeditionary operations. Of all the NATO allies, only the United States can project power in the form of large-scale long-range non-nuclear air and missile strikes at great distances from its homeland. Only the United States can deploy hundreds of military aircraft far beyond its homeland and even transport the logistics to upgrade airfields with limited facilities. The synergistic effects of preeminence in these areas (and others) imply an even greater overall superiority. Broad-brush descriptions of the gap are abundant. According to former U.S. Secretary of Defense William Cohen, "NATO [European] countries spend roughly 60 percent of what the United States does and they get about 10 percent of the capability. That has to change."[4] As François Heisbourg has pointed out, "with defense spending close to 60 percent of America's, the Europeans could in theory be expected to achieve 60 percent of U.S. capabilities. They are probably below 10 percent in the realm of strategic reconnaissance and theater-level C4ISR, at substantially less than 20 percent in airlift capacity (by volume or tonnage), and possibly at less than 10 percent in terms of precision guided air-deliverable ordnance."[5]

Origins of the Gap

In contrast with most of its European allies, the United States has been preparing forces for transoceanic power projection for decades.

The Cold War scenario of a major NATO–Warsaw Pact war called for most NATO European military establishments to "fight in place" rather than to project troops or firepower at great distances. Partly because the United States was deploying forces from North America or even further afield, the U.S. defense establishment for decades built and improved fleets of large air-transport aircraft, air-to-air refueling tankers, carrier-battle groups, amphibious ships, and other mobility assets relevant to transoceanic power projection and expeditionary operations. The Americans also put more into logistic support than most of the other allies, who were generally even less prepared for prolonged operations than the United States. This pattern explains the situation alluded to by Robertson. Several European allies have found it difficult to organize forces to send to the Balkans for peacekeeping because their troops lack logistic support. During the Cold War, most NATO European troops were expected to leave their garrisons and defend their nations against a Warsaw Pact assault. The Soviet and other Warsaw Pact troops were expected to come to them. Several European allies have, however, adapted slowly to the new circumstances and requirements; they have continued with conscription and with Cold War force structures, training and procurement patterns, with comparatively little investment in mobility or logistic support.

Throughout the history of the Alliance, the United States has spent a higher percentage of its GNP on defense than most of the other allies and far more in absolute terms. Because the European defense ministries have generally spent significantly more than the Americans on personnel, they have spent proportionately less on procurement. Moreover, the Europeans have generally spent this smaller budget share less efficiently, partly because they have bought less and partly because they have paid more for comparable weapons.[6] Furthermore, the Europeans have invested much less than the Americans in military R&D, and the European efforts have for the most part been scattered and dispersed in national programs.

While the duplication of overhead costs in separate national procurement and training establishments accounts for part of the European capability shortfalls, the long-standing reliance on large conscript armies in most NATO European countries, with the exception of Britain, is even more significant. According to Heisbourg, "the single most important cause of the massive discrepancy between U.S. and European capabilities flows from European force structure policies...Indeed, the Europeans reign supreme in one area, that of unusable and ultimately unaffordable manpower. The forces of the European Union countries field 1.9 million under uniform versus 1.4 million in the U.S.... The net effect is that after spending for the corresponding force structures, there is little left for European R&D, acquisition or for O&M [operations and maintenance] spending."[7]

As Heisbourg suggests, some cases are more extreme than others. According to an Italian analysis: "After Luxembourg, Italy is the Alliance country which currently spends most from its defense budget on staff expenditure (72 percent, which mainly goes toward military pensions and the upkeep of the national service system). Thus, in 1998, only 12.7 percent of its budget was left for hardware ... as against, for example, Great Britain's 27 percent."[8] Political and organizational obstacles often hamper attempts to introduce new defense spending priorities or to change methods of force recruitment and procurement. France has, however, now completed its 1996–2001 transformation toward all-professional armed forces. Italy, Portugal, and Spain have also decided to end conscription. Germany is, however, unlikely to abandon conscription entirely in the foreseeable future. François Cailleteau has compared the U.S. military posture with the aggregate of the military postures of the five largest members of the EU (the U.K., France, Germany, Italy, and Spain), which together account for over 80 percent of its defense spending. Relying on data from the IISS *Military Balance*, Cailleteau has concluded that U.S. naval tonnage is three times greater than that of the "EU five" for nuclear-fueled ballistic-missile-bearing submarines (SSBNs) and surface combatants, and four times greater for operational transport and support ships; that the United States has 66 nuclear-fueled submarines (SSNs), and the "EU five" 18; that the U.S. Navy has 12 catapult-launch aircraft carriers and 29 cruisers, and that the "EU five" collectively have only one cruiser and one catapult-launch aircraft carrier. While the "EU five" have about 100 frigates against America's 40, the U.S. frigates are of a single type and displace 2,800 tons; and the European frigates are of "innumerable" types and a third displace 1,300 tons or less.[9]

Cailleteau's conclusions are similar for other military capabilities. For modern combat aircraft, the United States has a 2.5 : 1 edge over the "EU five." For airlift, the U.S. advantage is 3.5 : 1 in numbers of aircraft; and two-thirds of the "EU five" planes are C-160 Transalls, a third smaller than the C-130, the smallest U.S. transport aircraft. For tanker aircraft, the ratio is around 30 : 1. The United States has 7,600 main battle tanks, all variants of the M1 *Abrams*, while the "EU five" have 4,800 main battle tanks, of six highly different models (AMX 30-B2, *Leclerc*, *Leopard* 1 and 2, *Challenger* 1 and 2). The U.S. Army and

Marine Corps together have 1,664 attack helicopters, of which 753 are AH 64 *Apaches*, with "firepower very superior to that of the Gazelles and BO-105s in the European armies." Moreover, the U.S. Air Force has 366 A-10 ground-attack aircraft, for which the Europeans have no equivalent. The asymmetries are also acute in C⁴ISR capabilities such as submarines, intelligence and communications satellites,[10] aircraft for intelligence and reconnaissance,[11] and offensive electronic warfare.

Capabilities gaps have furnished the backdrop for burden-sharing debates, which have been virtually continuous since the founding of the Alliance. These debates have, for the most part, consisted of Americans asking Europeans to increase their level of defense spending. During the 1950s, as their postwar economic recovery proceeded, the Europeans could plead incapacity. Since the 1960s, Europeans have repeatedly stressed certain "output" measures instead of the input measures based on GNP percentages favored by American critics of European "free-riding." The outputs stressed in some European-authored comparisons have downplayed capabilities gaps or have portrayed them as favorable to NATO Europe. In 1990, Jane Sharp deplored "the myth that the U.S. bears a disproportionate share of the NATO burden, especially in terms of the contribution of conventional forces. Despite contin-ued complaints about 'free riders,' European NATO countries provide 90 percent of the manpower, 85 percent of the tanks, 95 percent of the artillery and 85 percent of the combat airpower in the Atlantic-to-the-Urals area covered by the CFE [Conventional Armed Forces in Europe] negotiation."[12] Sharp's statement is representative of the arguments advanced by Europeans in burden-sharing debates during the Cold War. Except for aircraft, it omits most of the advanced military capabilities relevant to power projection; and it obviously makes no allowance for the qualitative distinctions that matter more in combat than in arms-control negotiations.

Since the late 1970s, when the last great U.S. defense build-up began with President Jimmy Carter, the European allies have been unwilling to invest in military forces, notably in modernization and research and development, at levels approximating those in the United States. The Carter administration persuaded the allies to approve a Long-Term Defense Program (LTDP) and a goal of increasing defense spending by 3 percent a year in real terms, but the performance of the allies in meet-ing the goals was uneven. The LTDP objectives included capabilities that are currently identified as key elements of the gap, such as logistics, electronic warfare, and command, control, and communications (C^3).[13] Similarly, the Reagan administration pursued a Conventional Defense

Improvements (CDI) program that was formally endorsed by NATO's Defense Planning Committee in 1985. The CDI focused on several of the same capabilities as the LTDP, but was equally unsuccessful in preventing a widening of the U.S.–European gap in conventional military capabilities. The magnitude of the gap in logistics, C^{4}ISR, and long-range precision-strike capabilities became publicly manifest during Operations *Desert Shield* and *Desert Storm* in 1990–1991, but it was apparent to experts in the late 1970s and early 1980s.[14] Even in Bosnia, in close proximity to NATO European territory, the United States had to augment existing NATO capabilities with unique communications assets. According to General Klaus Naumann, the German officer then serving as chairman of NATO's Military Committee, the United States provided 46 of the 48 communications satellite channels used by IFOR in Bosnia in the period December 1995–1996. In Naumann's words, "It indicates quite clearly that without American support, an operation like [IFOR in Bosnia] could not be done...There is no security for Europe without the Americans."[15]

Many French analysts and officials argue that, despite the obvious capability gap, there is no technology gap. European science, technology, and industrial assets are up to U.S. levels, but the Europeans have spent less than the Americans and have pursued different research and development strategies and procured different types of equipment. According to an official French Ministry of Defense analysis, "this conflict illuminated the differences between the military means of the United States and Europe. The United States has developed extremely large military means that are justified by America's world ambitions since the end of World War II. These [European–American] gaps also result from the research efforts and armament programs underway [in the United States] since the beginning of the 1980s. ... Our technological backwardness in certain areas, such as information mastery in real time or stealth, is linked to the lower level of financial means allocated to research (Europe's defense research budget is a third of the U.S. one) rather than to the know-how of European companies. The Kosovo conflict has, moreover, revealed quantitative deficiencies that could affect our ability to sustain an operation of long duration as well as capabilities that were completely lacking (cruise missiles, radar satellite observation systems, offensive jammers, aircraft identification systems)."[16] Some French observers contend that the United States has spent more not only because it has security interests and commitments in several regions with correspondingly immense logistical requirements, but also because it has been engaged in over-insurance and excessive investment in the innovations associated with the so-called Revolution in Military Affairs.

The Gap in *Operation Allied Force*

Operation Allied Force consisted mainly of air operations, which involved 14 of NATO's 19 members. Four nations—the Czech Republic, Iceland, Luxembourg, and Poland—did not participate because they lacked relevant capabilities, while Greece chose not to for political reasons. While non-U.S. aircraft carried out over 15,000 sorties, about 39 percent of the total, U.S. aircraft delivered over 80 percent of the weapons. Certain capabilities were provided solely or almost entirely by the United States, including offensive electronic warfare, airborne command and control, all-weather precision munitions, air-to-air refueling, and mobile target acquisition. As a result, while non-U.S. allies conducted 47 percent of the strike sorties (principally during the later weeks, when weather conditions had improved), they accounted for only 29 percent of combat-support sorties for refueling, command and control, and suppression of enemy air defenses (SEAD). Indeed, an average of three American support aircraft was required for each European strike sortie.[17] For airborne command-and-control during *Operation Allied Force*, the allies relied on a U.S. Air Force EC-130 Airborne Battlefield Command, Control and Communication (ABCCC), a C-130 designed for airspace traffic control and battle management.[18] Within NATO, only the United States has a dedicated aircraft for this purpose. The NATO AWACS aircraft are optimized for early warning, not for airspace and battle management. The United States also provided most of the mobile target-acquisition capability via the two JSTARS (Joint Surveillance and Target Acquisition System) aircraft it deployed to the Balkans.

According to some U.S. accounts of the operations, only the United States employed air-launched all-weather precision munitions and the only all-weather precision munitions utilized by any of the Europeans were the U.S.-built *Tomahawks* launched from British submarines. However, the French Ministry of Defense's two official "lessons learned" analyses imply that *Mirage* 2000D aircraft delivered laser-guided bombs at night and unguided bombs in all-weather conditions. "France has very precise strike capabilities thanks to its laser-guided armaments, by day for all of the offensive aircraft of the air force and navy (*Mirage* 2000D, *Jaguar*, *Mirage* F1 CT, *Super Étendard*), and by day and night for the *Mirage* 2000D ... Moreover, the demonstrated capability of *Mirage* 2000D crews, in all weather conditions and with sufficient accuracy, to deliver unguided bombs made us the sole Europeans capable of participating in all the strike missions of the coalition. The arrival of the *Rafale* will make new progress possible in this capability."[19]

With regard to air-to-air refueling, over 90 percent of the sorties were accomplished by U.S. aircraft. The published sources are not entirely consistent on European aircraft contributions. According to the IISS, the United States had "some 150 deployed," while "France and the U.K. each had 12 tankers available for the operation, and Italy and Turkey had two each."[20] The French Ministry of Defense indicates, however, that France was able to deploy only ten tankers (KC-135s), while the British Ministry of Defense reports employing only nine tankers (four *Tristars* and five VC10s).[21] European contributions in *Operation Allied Force* were particularly strong in combat air patrol; air-to-ground strike operations in good weather; and in surveillance, reconnaissance, and battle-damage assessment with unmanned aerial vehicles (UAVs) and manned aircraft such as *Tornados*, *Étendard* IVPs, and *Mirage* IVPs. While the Europeans and the Americans both made successful use of UAVs, the capabilities of the U.S. *Predator* far outweighed those of the Franco-German *CL-289*. Thanks in large part to its satellites, superior UAVs and reconnaissance and surveillance aircraft, the United States met "approximately 95 percent of NATO"s intelligence requirements" in *Operation Allied Force*.[22]

Operation Allied Force also revealed that information systems pose great interoperability challenges. As in many areas, the problems derive from the rapid pace of U.S. innovation and modernization compared to that of the other allies. The U.S. military services have retained old-fashioned communications capabilities, euphemistically called "legacy" systems, to accommodate the "low-end" communications capabilities of U.S. allies and security partners. In national or coalition operations, it is essential for all participating forces to have a "common operational picture" (COP). The interoperability gap in information systems is worsened by the fact that most allied navies have only a limited ability to receive imagery; their encrypted communications capabilities rely mainly on voice and written messages. According to one expert, "the biggest complaint of the allies" is the reduced reliance of the U.S. armed forces on previous methods of communications-encrypted voice and teletype messages. The U.S. shift to electronic transmission of schedules, maps, images, and so on, via the SIPRNET (Secret Internet Protocol Router Network), a U.S.-only secure communications network, is seen as excluding the allies.[23] During *Operation Allied Force*, a significant proportion of allied air forces lacked even encrypted voice communications.

With time, some experts have argued, the retention of "legacy" systems for communications with allies and coalition partners will become costly, burdensome, and impractical, if new U.S. information systems cannot readily communicate with the old systems. As a matter of principle, the U.S. armed forces will not "dumb down" information systems or decline to develop them to their full potential for the sake of interoperability. Current U.S. policy is, however, to retain "legacy" systems for essential coalition communications. Interoperability problems highlighted in Kosovo include communications connectivity and divergences in computerized planning capabilities. But the most significant issues concern security. From a U.S. viewpoint, there are concerns about the security of U.S. technology, intelligence, communications, and plans. These concerns derive from the implications for the security of U.S. and allied forces and their ability to conduct operations successfully. The pace of modernization of U.S. information systems has been much more rapid than that of allied forces; and this has led to a widening gap in capabilities. The officially proposed remedies include simplifying the constraints on the release of information, reviewing and (when appropriate) eliminating or simplifying licensing requirements, and carrying forward Alliance efforts to establish interoperable communications architectures.[24] The fact that information systems are increasingly based on commercial off-the-shelf products could facilitate allied procurement of interoperable systems, if the allies chose to make the necessary investments.

Electronic attack capabilities constitute one of the most significant areas of continuing NATO European dependence on U.S. military forces. Such capabilities are essential to conduct air operations with minimal losses. Aircraft flying at a high altitude beyond the range of anti-aircraft artillery are still vulnerable to surface-to-air missiles (SAMs) unless the target-acquisition radars are neutralized by jamming or direct attack. Direct attack with a high-speed anti-radiation missile (HARM) is feasible only if the enemy radars are switched on. As in *Operation Allied Force*, however, the direct-attack capabilities may deter an enemy from switching on the radars. The operational significance of America's EA-6B *Prowlers* has been well summarized as follows: "The fundamental mission of the *Prowler* is to seize control of key segments of the electromagnetic spectrum in wartime, assuring that they can be exploited by friendly forces while denying their use to adversaries... Control of the electromagnetic spectrum has assumed a significance similar to command of the air, and that is precisely what the 19 squadrons of *Prowlers*... are designed to achieve... [T]he proliferation of advanced air-defense systems around the world has severely compromised the survivability of nonstealthy aircraft unless they receive continuous EW [electronic warfare] protection in combat."[25] Aircraft with capabilities like U.S. Navy and Marine Corps EA-6Bs are essential to NATO air operations, because NATO European air forces lack comparable capabilities. According to a French Ministry of Defense analysis, "The effectiveness of the American offensive jamming means is hard to quantify, but their absence constituted grounds for canceling the air raid."[26] The United States is unlikely to sell such capabilities to the allies because of the technology-transfer and intelligence-sharing issues (for instance, about the design of enemy radars). The allies must therefore develop such capabilities on their own or continue to depend on the United States to provide this protection, as in *Operation Allied Force*. The NATO European allies have at least two programs to develop jamming capability for tactical aircraft: the *Spectra* integrated countermeasures system for France's *Rafale*, and the EuroDASS (Defense Aids SubSystem) for the *Eurofighter*. Neither program concerns a dedicated tactical jamming aircraft, however. This implies a degree of continuing NATO European dependence on U.S. EA-6Bs in combat contingencies.

Scenario-Dependence and Capability Gaps

Electronic attack assets may help to illustrate another gap: that between America's capabilities and its official aspiration to be able to conduct two major theater wars almost simultaneously. Assessing America's capability to carry out its declared strategy of being ready to fight two major-theater wars obviously involves judgments about reasonable risks and many capabilities in addition to electronic warfare. It is nonetheless worth noting that the United States reportedly deployed more than 40 of its available fleet of approximately 95 EA-6B *Prowlers* in the Balkans during *Operation Allied Force*.[27] In view of the redeployments of EA-6B aircraft and crews in Turkey, Japan, and the United States to permit a concentration of these capabilities in the Balkans, Loren Thompson has concluded, "*Operation Allied Force* proved that, at least in the case of electronic-warfare aircraft, the United States did not have the capacity to prosecute two major theater wars simultaneously."[28]

Some experts maintain that U.S. authorities insisted on standards of performance (such as no U.S. or allied casualties) that called for force protection requirements more rigorous than were envisaged prior to *Operation Allied Force*. On some occasions, the ratio was one EA-6B to one strike aircraft, a higher level of electronic attack protection than had previously been planned for. Setting this high standard for force protection inevitably drove up requirements. This explains why it can indeed be argued that, at this level of electronic attack protection, the United States lacks "the capacity to prosecute two major theater wars simultaneously." As with *Operation Desert Storm* in 1991, *Operation Allied Force* has established new expectations and assumptions about acceptable risks, at least in some circles.

In October 1999, U.S. Secretary of Defense William Cohen and General Henry Shelton, Chairman of the Joint Chiefs of Staff, noted that U.S. participation in *Operation Allied Force* could not have been sustained at a high level if major conflicts had erupted elsewhere.[29] This implies that *Operation Allied Force* was conducted with exceptionally demanding force-protection criteria because they could be met, in view of quiet conditions elsewhere. If U.S. forces had been rapidly withdrawn for action in, say, Afghanistan, *Operation Allied Force* would have probably taken a different form. The NATO European allies might have carried out a much larger proportion of the operations; and they might have adopted different policies about force protection, targeting, and collateral damage. Thus, as British and French observers have pointed out, *Operation Allied Force* should not be seen as the last word on understanding U.S.–European capability gaps. Official French analyses have hinted at the limited value of the Kosovo experience as an indicator of these gaps.[30] In other words, the nature and scale of the capabilities gap should be evaluated across multiple cases, not a single scenario tailored according to U.S. specifications. The capabilities-gap concept too often reflects an unexamined American assumption that U.S. military forces and concepts of operations represent the sole standard of excellence. According to one British expert, the U.S.–European capability gap is "irrelevant if the Europeans can deal on a reasonable basis with the threats at hand and conduct any necessary interventions."[31]

Some French and British observers have argued that the American-defined way in which *Operation Allied Force* was conducted artificially inflated the apparent gap between U.S. and European military capabilities. It was the Americans, according to this argument, who insisted on fighting much of the war with standoff air-launched weapons at a height of 15,000 feet; and this approach played to American strengths in airpower and precision-strike munitions. These observers assert that it was the United States that insisted on a "zero death" strategy in

Operation Allied Force. In their view, the Europeans could have done this operation by themselves, even though it might have lasted longer and would have meant accepting greater risks and losses. Without U.S. electronic warfare assets and other capabilities for the suppression of enemy air defenses, it is argued, the Europeans might have engaged in air-to-air combat or resorted to other measures (perhaps the use of special forces or ground force operations to create a "safe haven" enclave for the Kosovar Albanian refugees). One French observer has estimated that the Europeans would have lost 20 to 30 aircraft, but that this loss would have been accepted by European publics.[32] In this event, the losses would have probably extended beyond aircraft to at least some crewmembers killed or taken hostage, without U.S. combat-search-and-rescue capability at hand to try to save them. France alone among the European allies had such capability ready for use in *Operation Allied Force*. The effectiveness of the U.S. capability (as during *Operation Deliberate Force* in 1995) and the comparative scarcity of European capability underscore how a European-only *Operation Allied Force* might have taken a different form.

Why the Gap Matters

Capability gaps have been a constant irritant throughout NATO's history, most acutely during crises and conflicts. During various Cold War crises, including those centered on Berlin and Cuba and on NATO nuclear force modernization, the most prominent capability gap resided in European dependence on U.S. nuclear forces and commitments. While the Alliance remains a collective defense organization, in post-Soviet, post–Cold War conditions its main operational tasks have included embargo and no-fly-zone enforcement, humanitarian relief, large-scale interventions (*Deliberate Force* in 1995 and *Allied Force* in 1999), and peacekeeping (in Bosnia since 1995 and in Kosovo since 1999). Americans resent European "dependents" telling the United States how to run Alliance operations, while Europeans resent dependence on U.S. capabilities. The U.S. resentment has never been great enough to place the Alliance's future in jeopardy, and the European resentment has never been great enough to motivate European governments to substantially improve their capabilities through increased spending and other measures. In its current and prospective form, however, the gap could lead to unhealthy divisions of labor, new resentments and burden-sharing debates, industrial "fortress" competitions, a weakening of Alliance cohesion, and/or marginalization of the Alliance.

As far as unhealthy divisions of labor are concerned, two hypothetical risks are often highlighted: that the Europeans might find themselves increasingly responsible for manpower-intensive operations with a high risk of casualties, while the Americans would carry out the high-technology lower-risk standoff precision attacks and intelligence functions; and that the EU would take on the low-end crisis management and peacekeeping tasks, while the Americans would conduct the more demanding interventions and thus bear the main responsibility for collective defense.[33]

In short, the gap has significant implications for the conduct of military operations and for transatlantic relations. There is no shortage of U.S. members of Congress willing to accuse the Europeans of being "free-riders" and to deplore NATO arrangements that seem to subsidize America's economic competitors. In *Operation Allied Force*, the irritations in some U.S. political-military circles regarding NATO's "consensus" decision-making system, which requires unanimity, were summed up in Lt. Gen. Short's declarations: "It's my evaluation that NATO cannot go to war in the air against a competent enemy without the United States. If that's the case, and we're going to provide 70 percent of the effort... then we need to have more than one of 19 votes." In General Short's view, the United States should have told its allies: "We will take the Alliance to war and we will win this thing for you, but the price to be paid is we call the tune."[34] Of course, from the perspective of some Europeans, the United States did call the tune. As a number of other chapters in this volume discuss, the post-Kosovo EU decisions to seek a defense dimension—including the December 1999 Helsinki "headline goal"—may be attributed in part to European frustrations during the Kosovo War with U.S. political dominance, which stemmed directly from U.S. preponderance in military capabilities.

Increased EU and NATO European military capabilities would be in U.S. interests. Under current U.S. national-security strategy, the United States has many commitments in several regions and its military capabilities are severely taxed in peacetime, to say nothing of crisis contingencies. Increased European capabilities would lessen the overall load placed on U.S. forces. Moreover, enhanced European capabilities could neutralize the "burden-sharing" argument for reducing or withdrawing the U.S. military presence in Europe. Improved military capabilities would also be in the interests of the EU and NATO European countries. America's European allies would be well advised to recognize the limits to U.S. military power and the multiplicity of U.S. security commitments in other regions of the world. U.S. military power is finite.

Once the U.S. Secretary of Defense, on the advice of the Chairman of the Joint Chiefs, declared that a particular regional commander in chief (CINC) was a "supported CINC," the military assets would start flowing in that direction. The finite character of U.S. capabilities and the risk of U.S. attention being focused elsewhere (considerably increased since September 11, 2001) have been recognized intermittently during NATO's history, for instance, during the Korean War and the Vietnam War. It was also recognized in the years immediately after the fall of the Shah in Iran and the Soviet invasion of Afghanistan in 1979, when the United States was so preoccupied with southwest Asia that the allies became aware that some U.S. forces were "dual-hatted"—that is, committed to serve as reinforcements in both Europe and the Persian Gulf. Furthermore, as the French have pointed out over the decades, despite the fact that the United States has remained faithful to NATO for over 50 years, the future course of U.S. politics is unpredictable.

According to some European observers, particularly in France, *de facto* U.S. constraints (via the NAC) on European access to commonly funded NATO assets could become a point of contention in European–U.S. relations. Simplifying access by abandoning NATO's consensus principle seems improbable, however. If this principle was abandoned, an "easy-access" arrangement for the EU could erode Alliance cohesion and lead to potentially risky situations—for instance, European-led operations utilizing NATO assets without the full endorsement of all the allies. If the contingency became an Article V case (i.e., if it threatened the security of one or more members of NATO and therefore constituted a basis for action under the mutual-defense pledge in the North Atlantic Treaty), the European allies would in all probability expect U.S. support. However, if the United States is expected to be present for the "crash landings," it will understandably want to be in for the "take-offs" as well.

Purposes of the EU's Defense Initiative

What do the EU countries want autonomous capabilities for, and what capabilities do they need for these purposes? The phrase "Petersberg Tasks" is used as shorthand for: "humanitarian and rescue tasks; peacekeeping tasks; [and] tasks of combat forces in crisis management, including peacemaking."[35] In NATO parlance, these are non-Article V tasks, including "crisis response" missions. However, there is no official definition (by NATO, the EU or the UN) of any of these terms. Moreover, "peacemaking" as carried out by NATO in *Operation Deliberate Force* in 1995 and *Operation Allied Force* in 1999 looks like warfighting. In February 2000, French Defense Minister Alain Richard identified three options for crisis-management interventions. The first would be a NATO action, as in Bosnia and Kosovo. In the second option, "the EU would take overall responsibility" and "would make use of NATO HQs such as CJPS and SHAPE for the planning of its operation, of the chain of command organized under Deputy SACEUR for the command of the operation, and of the operational HQ and troops earmarked for NATO for its implementation." In the third option, "there is a possibility that the EU might have to rely on strictly European capabilities to run an operation . . . In the short term this option will therefore be available only for more limited military operations."[36]

It is far from clear, however, that all EU nations share the objective of acquiring the capabilities necessary to conduct interventions similar to *Operation Allied Force*. Indeed, some expert observers, even in Paris, doubt whether the objective of pursuing such capabilities would be endorsed by EU nations such as Denmark, Finland, Ireland, and Sweden. The "illustrative scenarios" envisaged in the EU's force-planning process might throw light on this question. No geographical boundaries are indicated for the Petersberg Tasks. It remains to be seen whether the Europeans will select scenarios that are relatively modest, such as humanitarian and rescue tasks close to home, or whether they will pursue more ambitious aims. In September 2000, French Prime Minister Lionel Jospin suggested that the EU could intervene in Africa, under UN auspices and in close cooperation with the Organization of African Unity. For all the shortcomings of NATO's classified C^3 networks, they represent the principal multinational C^3 networks in NATO Europe. A key indicator of the EU's serious pursuit of autonomy from the Alliance would therefore be the development of classified C^3 networks and associated intelligence and information systems outside NATO. In view of the unwillingness of most EU countries to increase defense spending, it is hard to imagine them investing in expensive C^3 networks and information systems to avoid dependence on NATO.

In other words, financial as well as political and operational considerations stand behind the principle of minimizing gratuitous duplication with NATO in the pursuit of EU military capabilities. The duplication that could be most harmful to the Alliance's political cohesion (as well as being militarily unwise and financially wasteful) would be establishing a separate EU defense-planning process and command structure. In October 2000 U.S. Secretary of Defense William Cohen proposed that the 23 nations in NATO and/or the EU establish a consolidated NATO–EU defense planning mechanism, a "European Security and

Defense Planning System," with the European officer serving as Deputy SACEUR functioning as a "strategic coordinator" between NATO and the EU.[37] Major EU investments in classified C^3 networks and associated intelligence and information systems distinct from those of the Alliance are most improbable because of their cost. But it is worth noting that they also could be wasteful and divisive, at a time when it is imperative (as became evident in *Operation Allied Force*) to improve these capabilities within NATO.

The EU's "Headline Goal" for 2003

The EU's "Headline Goal" for 2003 is cast in such broad terms that the member states are almost certain to declare victory in meeting it. The HG suggests that the EU's current aspirations extend to being able to undertake operations like the SFOR and KFOR peacekeeping missions, not a combat action like *Operation Allied Force*. As François Heisbourg has pointed out, "since the Council decision indicates that the number mentioned includes both logistic units and combat support units, only 20,000 combat forces may be available. Such a fighting force could not be deployed for the *most demanding* Petersberg Tasks. For relatively large-scale sustained combat operations, the EU might need 50,000 to 60,000 combat forces. This would thus require a HG of 150,000–180,000."[38] The capabilities required for combat actions are expensive. The EU as a whole is likely to remain heavily dependent on U.S. forces for C^3, aerial refueling, electronic attack, precision strike, intelligence, and other functions.

Britain's official "lessons learned" analysis concluded in general terms that NATO as a whole should improve its capabilities "in such areas as precision attack weapons, secure communications and strategic movement assets" and that "we Europeans need to improve the readiness, deployability and sustainability of our armed forces and their ability to engage in both high intensity operations and those of an expeditionary nature."[39] In contrast, France's official analysis drew more precise and pointed inferences as to European military requirements, including: command and control of forces; all-weather intelligence acquisition; autonomous navigation systems; real-time data links; targeting and battle damage assessment; cruise missiles; all-weather strikes; offensive jamming and suppression of enemy defense systems; autonomous identification systems; support of operational means; and permanent presence of an aircraft carrier group.[40] France's aspirations for European autonomy in these areas are not mirrored with any precision in the EU's

HG. It appears that it was necessary to define the HG on a lowest common denominator basis that all the EU countries could endorse politically and contribute to militarily, hence the focus on ground forces for peacekeeping. Even for peacekeeping, the EU's dependence on U.S. military support is likely to continue. SFOR and KFOR required U.S. assistance for many functions in addition to the troops on the ground. Moreover, U.S. forces in Europe, including Marines afloat in the Mediterranean, are key elements for emergency reinforcements for SFOR and KFOR to call on if they find the situation getting beyond their capability. If a crisis led to a decision to extract SFOR and/or KFOR, augmented capabilities for C^4ISR, close air support, electronic warfare, large-scale logistical movement, and other purposes would be required; this circumstance also implies continuing EU dependence on NATO and the United States in particular.

Even with regard to the target of 50,000–60,000 troops, there are ambiguities. If the deployable force includes, as the document implies, "the necessary command, control and intelligence capabilities, logistics, other combat support services" and other support staff, the "tooth" put forward by this "tail" may be well below 30,000 troops. It is also unclear whether the goal of 50,000–60,000 troops deployable for "Petersberg Tasks" will count the forces of EU member states in Bosnia and Kosovo, on the assumption that NATO-led peacekeeping forces are still deployed in these territories in 2003.

From another perspective, the EU's declared force goals for "Petersberg Tasks" appear remarkably unambitious, since they are similar to the goals France announced for itself on a national basis in 1996. In February 1996, President Jacques Chirac said "it is imperative that France be capable of projecting abroad a significant number of men, 50,000 to 60,000, and not 10,000 as is the case today, in rapid and organized conditions."[41] President Chirac advanced this goal as one of his justifications for abolishing conscription and announcing that France would have all-professional armed forces by 2002, an objective that was achieved in May of that year. The HG was designed to be readily feasible, with minor budgetary consequences. The EU's aim seems to be to project a sense of progress and movement by establishing a vague goal that could, with minimal effort, be met. If necessary, the EU could even plausibly pretend that the goal had been met by assigning certain units special readiness categories: a "creative bookkeeping" means of meeting the target. The disadvantages of such solutions for EU governments could include a loss of credibility vis-à-vis other countries (including the United States) and their own publics if the EU's operational performance in the next crisis revealed little real improvement in capabilities.

For the foreseeable future, at least in major contingencies, European crisis-response decision-making and action will in all likelihood require close consultation with (and possibly participation by) the United States.

EU and NATO Efforts to Improve Capabilities

How is the EU tackling the challenge of improving the military capabilities of its member states? France has proposed that the EU examine scenarios of the Petersberg Tasks, from the simplest level to the level of an army corps; this would make it possible for EU military leaders to estimate requirements. In the presidency of the WEU and the EU during the latter half of 2000, France convened a meeting of the EU defense ministers in September 2000 to examine the requirements flowing from the EU's crisis-scenario analysis and to consider potential force contributions by the member states. This was followed by a capabilities-commitment conference in November 2000, with the commitments endorsed at the highest level at the EU summit in Nice in December 2000. Reflections in the EU about capability goals beyond the fulfillment of the HG in 2003 appear embryonic, where they exist at all. The June 2000 Venusberg Group report, authored by a group of defense and security experts from EU and NATO European countries, stands out as a noteworthy exception. The goals recommended in this report include an ability to "carry out a full Kosovo-type operation without recourse to U.S. assets" by 2015 and "a common defense by 2030."[42] The Venusberg Group report goals have not won support from EU governments, however.

NATO's DCI originated in U.S. proposals in 1998. The DCI's goals were initially articulated in terse conceptual terms. *Operation Allied Force* gave an impetus to the DCI and provided concrete indications of operational shortcomings. The DCI involves 58 areas for the improvement of NATO capabilities, to be pursued through the Force Goals established in NATO's collective-defense planning process, an arrangement that includes all the allies except France. In February 2000, Defense Secretary Cohen provided a list of allied shortfalls in meeting DCI-related commitments:

- Less than half of the nations who have agreed to do so have made their full contributions to an asset-tracking system for better logistical support.
- Less than half of the requested nations have contributed their full share to an advanced intelligence network.

- Less than half of the nations asked to provide deployable command-and-control modules—which will improve interoperability—have done so.
- Only two of the seven nations now providing air-to-air refueling assets for the Alliance have met their contribution targets for a Rapid Reaction Force.
- Only one out of 14 nations assigned to work on a deployable HQ that can withstand biological and chemical weapons attacks is on track to meet the goal by this year.[43]

This pattern is consistent with the continuing tendency of most NATO European allies, including major countries such as France and Germany, to cut their defense spending. The only exceptions to this tendency remain Greece, Turkey, and the United Kingdom. According to Frank Kramer, Assistant Secretary of Defense for International Security Affairs, "While allies acknowledge their capability shortfalls, few have made concrete efforts toward their amelioration by increasing their defense budgets and reallocating funds."[44]

What is the relationship between the HG and associated EU efforts and NATO's DCI? EU documents generally avoid referring to NATO's DCI, just as they refrain from employing the NATO expression "European Security and Defense Identity." There are nonetheless overlaps between the DCI and the HG, in that both argue that ground forces should have improved C^3I, sustainability and strategic mobility. The DCI differs from the HG in placing more emphasis on improvements in "effective engagement"—that is, power projection and precision strike. Another major difference is that the DCI highlights requirements that the EU documents generally do not even mention: the need for defenses against cruise and ballistic missiles and against chemical and biological weapons; and the need for improved electronic attack capabilities. As James Thomas has pointed out, more ambitious EU capability goals would entail greater overlaps with the DCI: "Meeting the requirements of the most difficult Petersberg Tasks would also furnish many of the capabilities needed to participate alongside U.S. forces in large-scale combat operations in, or beyond, Europe. This would help to reconcile the EU's Headline and Capability Goals with NATO's DCI objectives of improved deployability, logistics, strike assets, force protection and communications, command and control. On the other hand, if EU states choose more modest scenarios that emphasize threats closer to home and only at the lower end of the Petersberg spectrum, this is more likely to justify the continued slide in their defense budgets, making transatlantic imbalances more enduring."[45]

Conclusion: Narrowing the Gap may be Difficult

Efforts to build an ESDI in NATO—or an ESDP in the EU—have been pursued under various labels for the past half-century. Basic obstacles have proved difficult to surmount: a lack of political cohesion and unity in Europe, an absence of a shared vision of strategic requirements, and (on the part of several NATO European governments) an unwillingness to spend more than minimal levels on military capabilities.

The reversal of current trends toward reducing defense spending in most EU countries depends on at least three factors: economic growth, threat perceptions, and the prominence of social priorities other than national defense. Whether economic growth will lead to increased defense spending depends in large part on the other two factors. As far as threat perceptions are concerned, it is worth recalling that the EU's Petersberg Tasks—like non-Article V missions in NATO—are not vital matters of national or collective defense, but optional interventions. Such interventions do not provide compelling grounds for increased defense budgets in most NATO countries. Moreover, anecdotal evidence suggests that threat perceptions in the EU are not as acute as those in the United States, which helps to explain European non-comprehension of the U.S. interest in National Missile Defense (NMD). Thus, increases in Western European defense spending are unlikely. As far as social priorities other than national defense are concerned, the increased demand for pensions and health care is likely to constrain defense spending in all NATO countries. According to Paul Hazell, the Director from 1992 to 1998 of the SACLANT-sponsored study *The Implications of New Technology for Maritime Operations in 2015*: "In spite of the fact that NATO defense spending through 2005 is likely to be relatively stable, thereafter the prospects look grim. All NATO nations will come under increasing pressure to fund the retirement and social security/health costs of a growing number of post–World War II 'baby-boomers.' At best, defense budgets will remain level; at worst they could fall to 1 percent of Gross Domestic Product. From 2005 to 2020, when the pressures on defense budgets will peak, the need to replace major assets that were built at the height of the Cold War will become paramount. Because of the reduced budget levels, and the continuing growth in unit costs due to technical sophistication and falling production, the build rate for new ships and submarines may fall to 25 percent of Cold War levels. This will have a massive impact on fleet numbers, and could reduce the U.S. Navy to 150–200 ships." [46]

The French economist Claude Lachaux has argued that demographic and economic factors—these "stubborn facts"—are likely to constrain

West European defense spending more than that of the United States. The first fact Lachaux has emphasized is the changing demography of Western Europe: the decline in birth rates and the decline in the number of workers relative to the growing numbers of retired people receiving government pensions. According to his analysis, the growing pension and health care demands of ageing populations will make it difficult for European governments to increase spending on defense: "How will governments be able to obtain funds from their parliaments for high-tech armaments if the elected representatives of an aged population are only disposed to vote for funds for high-tech medicine?"[47] Other studies have reached similar conclusions about the implications of demographic change.[48] Lachaux's second stubborn fact is the cumulative U.S. advantage in spending a greater proportion of GNP on defense and in pursuing greater efficiencies, with less duplication and more attention to procurement, new operational requirements and military R&D. In view of the fact that the U.S. federal budget appears well enough balanced to permit Social Security reforms and real increases in defense spending in the coming years, while balanced budgets in Europe "appear, for a long time ahead, to be a dream," Lachaux has forecast that the United States will continue to make a greater defense effort than its European allies.

Finally, Lachaux has highlighted the enlargement of NATO and the EU, in conjunction with Balkan reconstruction efforts. Such endeavors also burden the economies of the EU countries and promise to limit the funds available for military capabilities improvements. Unless the Europeans can surmount such stubborn facts, Lachaux has concluded, "their speeches on European Security and Defense Identity will pass for pure rhetoric." In short, continued declines in defense spending in NATO Europe are in prospect, except perhaps for Greece, Turkey, and the United Kingdom. Since 1992, NATO European defense spending has dropped 22 percent in real terms.[49] While U.S. defense spending declined by 37 percent in real terms from 1985 to 2000, the United States nonetheless retained many of its capability advantages. An increase in U.S. defense spending in real terms began in fiscal year 2001 and was accelerated in 2002.[50] Representatives of EU organizations and like-minded European officials and experts frequently assert that the EU will be more effective than NATO in getting its member states to increase defense spending or, at least, to gain force improvements through more efficient spending. This remains to be seen; a number of European observers expect the pattern of U.S.–European capability asymmetries to remain essentially unchanged, although marginal improvements may be achieved via measures such as a projected pooling of air transport assets by some European countries.

Britain, France, and the United States are the three nations most determined to do something about the U.S.–European capabilities gap. London, Paris, and Washington all want to stimulate their European allies and partners to acquire improved military capabilities. Their motives are different, of course. Most Americans want more capable allies and coalition partners, though some have at times manifested reservations about diminished European dependence on the United States. The British and the French both seek more political and military options under national and/or EU control (and diminished dependence on the United States) and the greater influence in defining NATO strategy that would flow from increased capabilities. The British have played a leading role in this regard since late 1998, when Prime Minister Tony Blair announced, in a major change in British policy, an unprecedented readiness to bring security and defense matters into the EU. The British nonetheless remain more inclined than the French to think in terms of developing the EU's military potential within a broad NATO framework and in close cooperation with the United States. The French are more apt to think of an EU capability distinct from that of the Alliance and U.S. forces. As in the past, the concept of the EU as an autonomous great power—what the French call *l'Europe-puissance*—commands more interest and respect in France than in any other EU country. Long-standing patterns of capability dependence in transatlantic relations appear likely, however, to be prolonged and may well be deepened by factors affecting the willingness and ability of governments to spend on military forces, such as the low level of threat perceptions in NATO Europe and the imperatives of other social priorities in the EU. London, Paris, and Washington therefore face great challenges in their attempts to get significant improvements in capabilities. The way forward will demand shared determination, transatlantic cooperation and coordination, and increased European defense spending. This appears to be the only way to narrow the gap.

Notes

1. The unresolved issues in EU crisis-response decision-making (e.g., the possibility of a "mercenary scenario," in which some nations might offer financial support while others contribute forces to specific operations) are lucidly examined in Jolyon Howorth's *European Integration and Defense: The Ultimate Challenge?* (Paris: *WEU* Institute for Security Studies, 2000), Chaillot Paper 43.
2. European Council, Presidency Conclusions, Santa Maria da Feira, June 19–20, 2000, appendix 1.

3. See, among other sources, Richard R. Nelson, *The Technology Gap: Analysis and Appraisal*, P-3694-1 (Santa Monica, CA.: The Rand Corporation, December 1967).

4. William Cohen quoted in Elizabeth Becker, "European Allies to Spend More on Weapons," *New York Times*, September 22, 1999, p. A13.

5. François Heisbourg, "Emerging European Power Projection Capabilities," paper presented at the Joint RAND and GCSP Workshop, "NATO's New Strategic Concept and Peripheral Contingencies: The Middle East," Geneva, July 15–16, 1999, available at www.gcsp.ch.

6. For a fuller discussion of economic issues in the Alliance, see David S. Yost, *NATO Transformed: The Alliance's New Roles in International Security* (Washington: United States Institute of Peace Press, 1998), pp. 62–70.

7. Heisbourg, "NATO's New Strategic Concept," fn. 6.

8. Federico Fubini, "The Italian Paradox: We are Important but we Count for Little," *Limes*, October 20, 1999, in Foreign Broadcast Information Service, December 3, 1999.

9. François Cailleteau, "E pluribus unum," *La Revue Internationale et Stratégique* 34 (Summer 1999), p. 32.

10. France's two *Hélios* optical reconnaissance satellites, with Italian and Spanish shares, are the only European intelligence satellites. No EU or NATO European country has satellites for radar, infrared, or signals intelligence. Britain has a dedicated military communications satellite, Skynet, while France relies on its Syracuse system, part of the Telecom family of telecommunications satellites.

11. Britain and France alone among the "EU five" have invested in national AWACS aircraft. Three European allies have electronic-intelligence aircraft—the British *Nimrod* R-1s, the French *Sarigue* DC-8 and *Gabriel*-160s, and the German *Atlantic*-1s.

12. Jane M. O. Sharp, "Summary and Conclusions," in Jane M.O. Sharp, ed., *Europe After an American Withdrawal: Economic and Military Issues* (New York: Oxford University Press, 1990), p. 49.

13. Robert Komer, "Ten Suggestions for Rationalizing NATO," *Survival* 11 (March–April 1977), pp. 67–72; and "The Origins and the Objectives," *NATO Review* (June 1978).

14. The United Kingdom was better prepared for the operational demands of the conflict than any other European ally. Despite their expeditionary warfare traditions, the French found the magnitude of the Gulf War's requirements (and the military–technical gap with the United States in strategic intelligence and other areas) a sobering revelation. See David Yost, "France and the Gulf War of 1990–1991: Political-Military Lessons Learned," *Journal of Strategic Studies* 16 (September 1993).

15. Rick Atkinson and Bradley Graham, "As Europe Seeks Wider NATO Role, Its Armies Shrink," *Washington Post*, July 29, 1996, pp. A1, A15.

16. Ministère de la Défense, *Premiers Enseignements des Opérations au Kosovo* (Paris: Délégation à l'Information et à la Communication de la Défense, June 1999), pp. 8–9.

17. Carla Anne Robbins, "No Parades: To All but Americans, Kosovo War Appears a Major U.S. Victory—Display of Military Might Makes Allies, Adversaries Doubt Their Relevance," *Wall Street Journal*, July 6, 1999, p. A1.

18. See Robert Wall, "Airspace Control Challenges Allies," *Aviation Week and Space Technology*, April 26, 1999.

19. Ministère de la Défense, *Premiers Enseignements des Opérations au Kosovo* (Paris: Délégation à l'Information et à la Communication de la Défense, June 1999), p. 6.

20. "Lessons From Kosovo: Military Operational Capabilities," in *The Military Balance 1999–2000* (London: The International Institute for Strategic Studies, 1999), p. 290.

21. Ministère de la Défense, *Premiers Enseignements des Opérations au Kosovo*, p. 7.

22. James P. Thomas, *The Military Challenges of Transatlantic Coalitions*, Adelphi Paper 333 (London: Oxford University Press for The International Institute for Strategic Studies, 2000), p. 52.

23. Author's interview in London, April 13, 2000. The SIPRNET (Secret Internet Protocol Router Network) is an encrypted global communications network employed by the U.S. Department of Defense (DoD) and some other agencies.

24. Greg Schneider, "U.S. Will Relax Arms-Sale Curbs: Allies to Gain Greater Access," *Washington Post*, May 24, 2000, p. E1.

25. Loren B. Thompson, "The Future of Airborne Electronic Warfare," *Sea Power*, March 2000.

26. Ministère de la Défense, *Les Enseignements du Kosovo* (Paris: Délégation à l'Information et à la Communication de la Défense, November 1999), p. 19.

27. Greg Seigle, "Radar-Jamming Prowlers Played Big Role in the Balkans," *Jane's Defense Weekly*, July 7, 1999.

28. Loren B. Thompson, "The Future of Airborne Electronic Warfare," *Sea Power*, March 2000.

29. Secretary of Defense William S. Cohen and General Henry H. Shelton, Chairman of the Joint Chiefs of Staff, Joint Statement on the Kosovo After Action Review before the Senate Armed Services Committee, October 14, 1999, pp. 7–8.

30. Ministère de la Défense, *Les Enseignements du Kosovo*, p. 21.

31. Author's interview in London, June 28, 2000.

32. Author's interview in Paris, April 21, 2000.

33. David C. Gompert, Richard L. Kugler, and Martin C. Libicki, *Mind the Gap: Promoting a Transatlantic Revolution in Military Affairs* (Washington: National Defense University Press, 1999).

34. Michael Evans, "General Wanted U.S. to Call the Shots in Kosovo," *The Times* (London), January 27, 2000.

35. Western EU, Council of Ministers, Bonn, June 19, 1992, "Petersberg Declaration," paragraph 4 of Part II, "On Strengthening WEU's Operational Role."

36. Alain Richard, "European Defense and the Transatlantic Link," speech at Georgetown University, Washington D.C., February 23, 2000, pp. 5–6 of text furnished by the French Ministry of Defense.

37. Cohen quoted in Jim Garamone, "U.S. Proposes 'More Positive' Vision of NATO–EU Partnership," American Forces Press Service, October 10, 2000.

38. Heisbourg, *European Defense: Making it Work* (Paris: Institute for Security Studies, Western EU, September 2000), Chaillot Paper no. 42, p. 80; emphasis in the original.

39. Lord Robertson of Port Ellen, Secretary of State for Defense, *Kosovo: An Account of the Crisis* (London: Ministry of Defense, October 1999), p. 23.

40. Ministère de la Défense, *Les Enseignements du Kosovo*, p. 21.

41. Jacques Chirac, television interview on February 22, 1996, text furnished by the French Foreign Ministry, p. 2.

42. *Enhancing the EU as an International Security Actor: A Strategy for Action by the Venusberg Group* (Gütersloh, Germany: Bertelsmann Foundation Publishers, June 2000), p. 5.

43. William S. Cohen, "European Security and Defense Identity," Munich, Germany, February 5, 2000, remarks as prepared, available at http://www. defenselink.mil/.

44. Quoted in "DoD Reports on Progress of NATO's 'Defense Capabilities Initiative,'" *Inside the Pentagon*, March 16, 2000.

45. James P. Thomas, *The Military Challenges of Transatlantic Coalitions*, Adelphi Paper 333 (London: Oxford University Press for the International Institute for Strategic Studies, 2000), p. 69.

46. Paul Hazell, "Beyond 2015: The NATO Way Forward," *Jane's Navy International* 104 (December 1999), p. 13.

47. Claude Lachaux, "Alliance atlantique et Europe de la défense: les faits sont têtus," *Défense Nationale* (August–September 1999), p. 82.

48. Anne Swardson, "A Pension Crisis Looms in Europe," *Washington Post National Weekly Edition*, May 1, 2000, p. 17.

49. "The NATO Capability Gap," in *Strategic Survey 1999/2000* (London: The International Institute for Strategic Studies, May 2000), p. 19.

50. For an analysis of the implications of post-9/11 U.S. defense spending, see Michael O'Hanlon, "Rumsfeld's Defense Vision," *Survival* 44 (Summer 2002).

CHAPTER 6

The United States, ESDP and Constructive Duplication

Kori Schake

Introduction

The terrorist attacks on September 11, 2001 triggered an outpouring of public sympathy and government solidarity toward the United States among its European allies. But the stirrings of a new transatlantic relationship were clear several months earlier, as the rancor that had accompanied the debate over a common European defense policy ebbed away. The Bush administration has taken a more positive approach than its predecessors to the EU's attempts to develop its own military capacity. And the EU has worked to reassure that ESDP will not undercut NATO.

These changes have created a more balanced and constructive relationship between the United States and the EU. But they fail to address two serious problems that are threatening the ability and willingness of U.S. and EU forces to work together: the divergence of European and U.S. armed forces, and the question of "assured access" to NATO and U.S. military assets by the EU. Divergence means that U.S. forces are developing in a fundamentally different way than their European counterparts, due to different budgets and policy priorities. This growing dissimilarity is already making joint military operations more difficult, and the gap is increasing steadily. Assured access means that a European defense force, operating on its own initiative, could be certain of getting

NATO and U.S. military support; however, that expectation may prove unrealistic, which could leave the EU with serious problems in a crisis.

The status quo is unsustainable. Substantial as the divergence between U.S. and European forces is already, it will grow decisively as a result of September 11. American defense spending will increase dramatically, the changes occurring in U.S. forces will accelerate, and U.S. interest in and support for crisis-management missions will decline further. Moreover, while the attacks have reinforced European solidarity with the United States, the military operations in retaliation may yet prove divisive. Few NATO allies have the ability to participate, and the United States does not want to share intelligence with, or have its operational choices constrained by, states that are not directly involved in the operations.

The most productive way to redress these political and military problems is to encourage not only the emergence of a viable European military force, but also the duplication of capabilities already existing in NATO and U.S. forces. Some duplication already exists; much more will be necessary if European defense policy is to be more than mere rhetoric. At present, duplication is regarded with suspicion, particularly in the United States, which is worried that it might damage NATO. But a constructive approach to duplication could ameliorate the problems of both divergence and of European reliance on U.S. assets. This approach would allow the EU to conduct military operations without relying on U.S. assistance. It would also increase European influence over U.S. decisions about the use of force. For if EU states are able to participate in the more demanding sorts of combat, their views on how to conduct the military campaign will carry more weight in U.S. decision-making.

A New Approach to U.S. National Security

As previous chapters have discussed, the Clinton administration's policy toward ESDP was marked by major concerns that Secretary of State Madeleine Albright described as "the three Ds." This approach mellowed toward the end of the administration, but it continued to shape U.S. thinking toward European defense policy.

Many in the EU hoped for a more positive approach from the incoming Bush administration. The first comments on EU defense aspirations, from Secretary of Defense Donald Rumsfeld, expressed serious concerns about the potentially damaging impact of ESDP on NATO. Addressing the Wehrkunde security conference on February 3, 2001, just a week after taking office, Rumsfeld said:

> I favor efforts that strengthen NATO. What happens within our Alliance and what happens to it must comport with its continued strength, resilience, and effectiveness. Actions that could reduce NATO's effectiveness by confusing duplication or by perturbing the transatlantic link would not be positive. Indeed they run the risk of injecting instability into an enormously important Alliance. And if I may add one more point: whatever shape the effort may finally take, I personally believe it should be inclusive/open to all NATO members who wish to take part.

ESDP supporters interpreted Rumsfeld's remarks as a disappointing regression to the strident days of the Clinton administration's three D's policy. Many carped that the new team did not understand the post–Cold War evolution of the EU that had occurred in the eight years since Republicans were last in power. But Rumsfeld's comments accurately represent the continuing concerns many Americans have about the European defense initiative. Most U.S. policy-makers and defense experts continue to be skeptical of the value of ESDP and wary of the problems associated with it; that is the baseline American reaction.

Nevertheless, the Bush administration very quickly adopted a more encouraging approach. At the first meeting between President Bush and U.K. Prime Minister Tony Blair, the two leaders expressed their support for ESDP, while affirming that "NATO will remain the essential foundation of transatlantic security."[1]

In the press conference following the meeting, Bush and Blair outlined a transatlantic bargain on European defense. The United States would support ESDP, on condition that it be limited to peacekeeping missions where NATO chose not to be involved.[2] Blair made the terms reassuringly explicit:

> ...the important thing to remember is that, as the President has just outlined to you, this is in circumstances where NATO as a whole chooses not to be engaged; it is limited to the peacekeeping and humanitarian tasks that are set out. It is not a standing army, it is a capability that Europe should have, but the sovereign decision of each nation is necessary for each operation. And speaking together as the founders of NATO, we would never do anything to undermine NATO. But where NATO as a whole chooses not to be engaged, it is important that we have the capability, where it's right and within these limited tasks that I've set out, to be able to act, should we choose to do so ourselves.[3]

In return, President Bush unequivocally endorsed ESDP, saying "I support what the Prime Minister has laid out. I think it makes a lot of sense for our country." What he endorsed is a very limited vision of ESDP—a back-up peacekeeping force for cases where the United States does not want NATO involved. Whether all the other EU states, and notably France, will continue to accept that approach, remains to be seen. Still, this limited version of European defense policy allowed the Bush administration to be much more positive about a European military capability than its predecessor had been.

The architect of America's more affirmative approach, Secretary of State Colin Powell, has continued to assuage Europeans' concerns about U.S. opposition to its defense plans. The sigh of relief was audible across the Atlantic after Powell's first trip to Brussels in February 2001, where he not only reaffirmed the new policy, but also assured Europeans that the United States would not force an early test of EU capabilities by unilaterally withdrawing its troops from the Balkans (as had been suggested by both National Security Advisor Condoleezza Rice and Rumsfeld). Powell also left Brussels believing that all EU states had accepted Blair's version of ESDP.

European defense policy is now effectively off the transatlantic agenda. It is no longer a source of friction between the EU and United States. The Bush administration has welcomed a leading role for EU High Representative Javier Solana in the Balkans, encouraged efforts to achieve the Helsinki Headline Goal and backed away from internal EU deliberations about decision-making structures. The only time ESDP has been an issue was when the Bush administration endorsed the suggestion by the EU Balkans Representative François Léotard that the EU should take responsibility for the Macedonian mission. The EU declined.

It is striking, however, that despite the more sympathetic tone, the substance of U.S. concerns about European defense policy remains largely unchanged. Even Secretary of State Powell has worries: after his first meetings in Brussels, he said the other NATO foreign ministers had agreed that the EU would "push this program in a way that will be fully integrated within the planning activities of NATO. So, I leave comforted by that thought."[4] At the NATO summit in June, President Bush further elaborated on U.S. policy, saying:

> It is in NATO's interest for the EU to develop a rapid reaction capability. A strong, capable European force integrated with NATO would give us more options for handling crises when NATO, as a whole, chooses not to engage. NATO must be generous in the help it gives the EU.

And similarly, the EU must welcome participation by NATO allies who are not members of the EU. And we must not waste scarce resources, duplicating effort or working at cross purposes. Our work together in the Balkans shows how much the 23 nations of NATO and the EU can achieve when we combine our efforts.[5]

It is more graceful than the Clinton administration's "three Ds," but President Bush hit all three concerns about a European force that needed to be integrated with NATO (decoupling), should welcome participation by NATO allies (discrimination), and should not duplicate NATO's efforts. Moreover, by asserting NATO's "right of first refusal" over which missions to undertake, Bush gave a particular interpretation to the formula agreed at the Franco-British summit at Saint-Malo in 1998, that a European force would act only "when NATO as a whole is not engaged." In Bush's thinking, the EU would act only if NATO had decided against a leadership role. Less has changed in the U.S. position than the upbeat tone of transatlantic discourse might suggest.

While the substance of policy has changed relatively little, the greatly improved tone is important because of what it demonstrates about the Bush administration's priorities. Despite misgivings about ESDP, it has chosen not to fight about it. That decision marks five significant developments in security policy. First, the Bush administration has greater confidence in the United States' ability to lead when it chooses to; consequently, it is less defensive about ensuring a U.S. role and less inclined to intervene in internal EU developments. Second, the Bush administration is less interested in dealing with the kinds of crisis-management missions that ESDP is designed to address, because of concerns with the efficacy of intervening militarily in failing states, as well as burdens on the U.S. military. Third, President Bush has changed the terms of the U.S. debate on ESDP by emphasizing that a more capable European military force is in America's interests. If the United States does not want to take a lead in dealing with many sorts of crises, it must foster means for others to manage them. Fourth, the Bush administration is shifting greater responsibility for sustaining transatlantic relations on to Europe. If the Europeans want to work with the United States on security issues, they will need to sustain that cooperation through NATO. If the Europeans do not keep NATO at the center of the European security agenda, the United States will simply not be involved. Fifth, the Bush administration has a less ambitious agenda for NATO than its predecessors. Clinton tried unsuccessfully to build a consensus for NATO action anywhere in the world that NATO allies had common interests and a willingness to use military force. The Bush administration places less emphasis on U.S.–European partnership outside Europe, instead tending toward a less constraining "*à la carte* multilateralism" of temporary regional coalitions.

Since September 11, NATO states have made very important contributions to the fight against terror, but principally by using nonmilitary means. Politically, the invocation of Article V bolstered U.S. morale and made the construction of a broad international coalition easier, while diplomatic efforts by European statesmen have been particularly useful in the Middle East. Economically, European states were essential in stabilizing the international financial system, injecting liquidity and reducing interest rates in conjunction with the United States to reduce capital flow from the latter. The swift and effective work of European law enforcement and intelligence agencies in collecting evidence, apprehending suspected conspirators, and sharing expertise has been crucial in bringing terrorists to justice.

These contributions contrast starkly with the limited military contributions of European states. Britain was the only European country that openly participated in the opening campaign in Afghanistan. Few European militaries have the capability to contribute substantially to high-intensity combat operations of the kind the United States is carrying out; they lack the equipment and as a result operate very differently from U.S. forces.

The September 11 attacks on the United States, and Europe's response, have reinforced the forementioned tendencies in U.S. policy. The United States will be more likely to give the EU a leading role in crisis management in Europe, and less likely to put pressure on European allies to play a greater military role elsewhere. Perhaps the only remaining transatlantic obstacle to the development of Europe's defense policy is the dispute over links between NATO and the EU.

The Turkish Veto

Turkey, a member of NATO but not the EU, has for the past year held up an agreement between NATO and the EU during 2001 that would allow the EU assured access to NATO planning facilities, and presumed access to other NATO capabilities. The other 18 members of NATO signed up to this agreement in December 2000. After extensive mediation by the United Kingdom and United States, and bilateral assurances from other EU states, Turkey accepted the NATO–EU agreement at the December 2001 NATO meeting. However, Greece quickly rejected the deal as too great a concession to Turkey, preventing the agreement from going into force. Even when the general issue of NATO assistance to the EU is settled, the problematic relationship between the EU and Turkey (see chapter 7 for more detail on this issue) is likely to continue bedeviling the ESDP, since numerous agreements on the implementation of that assistance still need to be settled.

Many in the EU explain Turkish objections to its use of NATO assets solely as a tactic to promote the case of Turkish accession to the EU. They fail to appreciate that Ankara has legitimate concerns about the deployment of EU forces in the Aegean, especially if Cyprus becomes an EU member, and about EU intervention in the Caspian region or in support of Palestinians or Kurds. The EU is willing to give Turkey extensive consultative rights over its military operations, but unwilling to allow any state outside the Union a decision-making role in EU councils. Turkey—as a NATO member—would be able to veto any EU mission that depended upon NATO but unable to prevent EU operations that did not directly employ NATO assets.[6]

Turkey's ability to prevent the EU's use of NATO planning staffs and other assets can potentially force three damaging effects on the EU: (1) an expensive duplication of NATO headquarters (which together currently have about 13,000 staff); (2) estrangement between the United States and EU, as the Bush administration continues to oppose duplication of NATO planning; and (3) uncertainty on the part of potential adversaries that NATO would be willing to come to the aid of an EU operation.

It is unlikely that the United States will want to do anything more to twist Turkey's arm on ESDP. Ankara and Washington have common interests in managing Turkey's neighbors (Iraq, Iran and Syria), and both are strong supporters of Israel. Moreover, Turkey's strategic significance has increased since September 11—it can offer practical support for military operations in Afghanistan and moral support as a Muslim country within the anti-terror coalition. Also, Americans are more sympathetic than EU states to Turkish concerns about ESDP; they believe that rights that had been granted to Turkey as an associate member of the WEU should be carried over to ESDP, and they are skeptical about the soundness of bringing Cyprus into the EU.

In reality, however, Turkey's potential veto is not the major block to the development of a viable European defense force. Even if Turkey were to allow NATO assets to be used in support of EU military operations, two problems remain that could lead to serious transatlantic conflicts in the longer term: the divergence of U.S. and European military forces, and the assumption of assured access by the EU to U.S. assets. More generally, Turkey's potential veto forces the EU and the United States to address the issue of the duplication of capabilities. So, the veto may eventually turn out to be beneficial to the success of ESDP.

Diverging European and U.S. Military Forces

As David Yost discussed in chapter 5, European military forces are losing the ability to work in coalitions with U.S. forces. This is largely a result of efforts by the United States to transform its military capabilities, and the speed of that transformation, but it has important consequences for Europe. If European forces are no longer able to form viable coalitions with U.S. forces, European allies will become less valuable to the United States. At the same time, they will grow more dependent on U.S. support to fight wars.

America's armed forces have always been different than those of its European allies. Global responsibilities give U.S. defense policy a strategic perspective shared only by Europe's former colonial powers. The public acceptability of high defense spending in America is a point of envy in most NATO defense ministries. Even as American voters express concern about the quality of medical care and the viability of social security pensions, there is almost no pressure to reduce defense spending.

The United States now spends 3 percent of GDP on defense, roughly what NATO's European states spent during the Cold War (when U.S. spending hit 6.7 percent). Following the attacks of September 11, Congress approved a $40 billion supplemental spending bill, $18 billion of which is allocated directly to the defense department, with at least $10 billion a year more expected for a program of improved national defense and military restructuring. In addition to this enormous budget, likely to be about $340 billion in 2002, the economies of scale, the earlier adaptation to all-volunteer forces (in the 1970s) and the more rapid consolidation of the defense industry (during the 1990s), give the United States dramatic advantages over the military forces of all European states.

The innovations in American military forces are beginning to affect how the United States organizes and trains for warfare, and even how it thinks about it—and the pace of change is accelerating. The accuracy and destructive power of conventional forces, for example, have made a nuclear response unnecessary in virtually every planning scenario. Even before September 11, there were concerns that this military strength could prompt a skilled adversary to avoid engaging U.S. military forces directly and instead use "asymmetric" threats—such as terrorism, missile proliferation, computer warfare or other means of disrupting the army's ability to operate. Needless to say, the terrorist attacks have highlighted the need to improve capabilities for operating in areas where there are neither stationed troops nor support bases.

The impetus for innovation comes from the wars the United States expects to fight. The most likely conflict scenarios are no longer European in nature, which is certainly a development to be celebrated both in Europe and the United States. Contingencies like defending Taiwan against Chinese amphibious assault or attack by ballistic missiles, or ensuring passage through the Straits of Hormuz when Iran becomes a nuclear power, pose very demanding challenges for the most advanced U.S. forces.

The need to prepare for and conduct asymmetric warfare will also transform U.S. forces. Initially, only a small part of the U.S. forces will undergo a radical transformation, but it is this part that will be used for the most demanding missions and be the engine of change. In the longer term, the new approach will be incorporated into doctrine and organization, further reshaping U.S. forces.

The Bush administration has placed innovation high up on its defense agenda, since even before the election. The Quadrennial Defense Review, the blueprint of U.S. defense strategy and spending that Secretary Rumsfeld presented to Congress on September 30, 2001, reiterated the need for innovation. Although the defense program outlined in the review was completed before September 11, Rumsfeld emphasized that the war against terrorism "requires the transformation of U.S. forces, capabilities, and institutions to extend America's asymmetric advantages well into the future." The terrorist attacks, he said, "will require us to move forward more rapidly in these directions."

America's European allies are not keeping pace with military innovation. The latest U.S. Congressional Budget Office report on burden sharing concludes that "a failure by many of NATO's European members to keep up with technological advances could render them incapable of operating alongside U.S. forces in future military conflicts."[7] Different ways of operating will mean that U.S. forces face less risk than their European counterparts.

The problem is not that European forces are failing to innovate: much creative planning has gone into the Helsinki rapid reaction force, and especially into improving the ability to deploy forces. The United States is also not claiming that its European allies are failing to do their fair share in areas of common interest—Europeans have committed more than 80 percent of the ground forces that have been deployed in Kosovo and are also bearing more than 80 percent of the reconstruction and assistance costs. The point is that the United States and its European allies have different priorities for their military forces.

Most European governments do not perceive the same magnitude of new threats or imagine themselves fighting the kinds of wars that are driving U.S. innovation. Therefore adapting their military forces to ensure they could win those wars is not a priority. Even if expectations were more closely aligned, Europeans would be constrained by the size and allocation of funds in their defense budgets.

The ESDP is not responsible for the divergence between the American and European forces, but it could aggravate the problem. The United States is concentrating on high-technology improvements—such as striking targets precisely from great distances, and integrating air and ground operations—and eschewing peacekeeping. The EU, on the other hand, is focusing on crisis management—getting forces into a region in a timely way and establishing basic communications for passing information within a multinational force. While EU defense planners concentrate on constructing multinational forces that can operate together at the lower end of the conflict spectrum, the U.S. armed forces are accelerating their efforts to exploit the information and communications technologies that are transforming U.S. forces at the higher end.

The Fallacy of Assured Access

At their 1994 summit, the NATO countries' heads of government gave their approval to European attempts to develop "separable but not separate" defense capabilities through the WEU. Behind that approval lay the U.S. proposal for CJTFs that would allow NATO allies to work in smaller, variable coalitions that drew on NATO assets.[8] The United States thought that by agreeing to second NATO assets to other organizations (like the WEU, OSCE and UN) for specific missions, it would prevent competition and duplication between NATO and the Europeans. In particular, the CJTF concept was intended to remove any rationale for the WEU developing headquarters and military staffs that would duplicate those in NATO. The concept also aimed to involve NATO headquarters in the planning and management of non-Article V missions, such as peacekeeping. The project had the beneficial effect of facilitating participation by France, which is not integrated into the commands, as well as non-NATO allies edging closer to Alliance structures through the PfP.

Initially, the concept of CJTFs seemed promising (see Terry Terriff's discussion in chapter 3), but the elegant political solution quickly ran into difficulties over practical questions regarding the assurance of access to NATO assets. Both the United States and the EU were willing to declare most of these problems resolved in 1996, with the signing of the Berlin agreements. However, these accords did not—and probably could not—resolve the fundamental problem of assured access: how to guarantee the availability for European crisis management of scarce assets that the United States needs for fighting wars and managing crises globally. The Berlin agreements offered the WEU assured access to NATO assets, but in order to use them effectively, it would also need access to U.S. assets.

A real assurance of availability would mean that the EU's crisis-management priorities would take precedence over the other global responsibilities and interests of the United States. But if U.S. commanders worry about committing assets during a NATO operation, it is even more likely that the United States would withhold or withdraw them from an EU operation. Assured access is a faulty premise even for some NATO operations, much less for those in which the United States is not directly involved. Moreover, in the wake of September 11, America's willingness to commit assets to solving problems in areas of peripheral concern to Washington is likely to be highly limited.

An EU Approach to Warfare?

The defense budgets on which European states operate are too small to permit them the luxury of replicating the same patterns of military organization and operation that exist in NATO. Likewise, the dependence of European military forces on U.S. assets like airlift, secure communications, precision strike forces, theater reconnaissance and strategic intelligence is simply too great for the EU to overcome without major budget increases. In order to operate without depending on U.S. capabilities, the EU will need to develop an identifiably different approach to warfare from that practiced by the United States.

Given budget constraints, if the EU is serious about building a force that is capable of operating without U.S. support, it will need to experiment with new ways of carrying out the military tasks it cannot afford to replicate. EU members may have to relinquish some national autonomy. They will certainly need to pool resources to buy the necessary equipment and systems. And they will need to integrate their forces multinationally, to a far greater degree than is already done in NATO.

The EU will need to learn to prepare for military operations in ways different from NATO or the United States.

The U.S. approach to war emphasizes advances in technology that reduce the risk to military personnel, and consequently the political cost to leaders of engaging in war. The technologies range from mundane innovations like night-vision goggles, to exotic developments such as miniature robotics for intelligence collection. The EU will be operating without many of these risk-reducing technologies. As a result, EU political leaders will have two options: either greater tolerance for risk when choosing to use military force in crises, or an extraordinary amount of creativity to keep risks manageable when intervening with force. In either case, the internal dynamic of autonomous EU military action will encourage the development of a unique EU approach to warfare.

Rather than worrying about the rapid changes in U.S. forces and the shaky premise of "assured access," the EU should welcome the opportunity to develop a different strategic perspective. This challenge presents Europe with the chance to build affordable capabilities that do not require a major increase in European defense spending. NATO is going to have to develop new ways of working in coalitions whatever happens—not due to the EU's military development but because of the changes occurring in U.S. forces. If the EU were to emphasize *constructive duplication*—innovative ways to replicate by cost-effective means the high-end capabilities on which U.S. forces depend—it would be able to deploy force in a genuinely autonomous way. It would also make the EU states more valuable allies for the United States. Instead of relying on scarce U.S. military assets, they would complement U.S. forces, even if in some respects they might find it harder to operate together with U.S. forces.

Constructive Duplication

At the Capabilities Pledging Conference in November 2000, the EU identified a substantial catalog of forces available to meet the Helsinki Headline Goal.[9] However, all the assets pledged already existed in the military forces of EU states and nearly all were committed to NATO or UN forces. All the shortfalls identified by the WEU audit in 1999 remain; European military commanders, moreover, are concerned about the quality and availability of some of the assets pledged.

The EU now faces the dilemma of how to set priorities for improvement. The EU states in NATO have already committed to the 1998 DCI list of force capabilities that need to be developed, and these would improve Europe's military forces. However, the capability targets that the EU has set for the fulfillment of its HG are not fully consistent with the priorities of the DCI. The EU must decide whether to build its own planning process around NATO plans, or create a different set of priorities, more suited to fulfilling the HG.

For the EU to simply take over NATO plans would be politically difficult. France is not part of NATO's force planning process and does not want it carried over into the EU. More importantly, the requirements of the kinds of force promised in the HG are appreciably different to those of a DCI force. For example, an EU force would not be able to wage the kind of air campaign that NATO fought in Kosovo. But if EU members agreed to a different set of spending priorities from those already committed to in NATO, it would raise concerns in non-EU states about the EU's commitment to NATO and the seriousness of the Helsinki process. NATO and the EU, it seems, are on a collision course. The conflict could be reduced, however, if both sides accepted that duplication of assets and planning will occur, and the EU focused spending on the kind of military asset it had planned to borrow from U.S. forces.

From a military perspective, most duplication of U.S. and NATO assets would be constructive. The assets of greatest interest to the EU are also in short supply in U.S. forces. Furthermore, the high tempo of operations in the past ten years is wearing out some sorts of equipment at a much faster pace than expected—the United States had not foreseen routine use in long-term engagements in northern Iraq and the Balkans. This accelerated pace of use for U.S. forces requires the faster replacement of equipment and creates more concern about their use in marginal operations.

If the EU wants to avoid unnecessary duplication, improve its capacity to act autonomously, and engender support in the United States, it needs to choose areas of duplication that would reduce the burden on over-extended U.S. assets. In particular, it should focus on "strategic lift," intelligence, reconnaissance, strike capabilities, mid-air refueling and, finally, research, development and procurement.

Strategic Lift

The key constraint on the ability of Europeans to deploy force is their inability to shift troops by air, sea, rail and road. EU states already have procurement plans to improve the airlift capability of their forces. The United Kingdom has bought 25 C-130J transport aircraft and leased four C-17s from the United States; Italy has bought 20 C-130Js and is also buying 12 C-27J tactical transport aircraft; and Spain is buying nine C-295 light transport aircraft. Eight European states have plans to buy 196 of the new Airbus A400M strategic lift aircraft, to be available by 2007. Although these purchases mark a substantial improvement, they will not make the EU autonomous, even at the relatively modest level of the Helsinki Headline Goal force. Further purchases will be necessary to meet Helsinki requirements, and the United States would not object to such spending—it would relieve America of responsibilities that could slow down its ability to deploy force.

While airlift is generally the best way to move forces quickly, and EU states deserve praise for focusing on the high end of the spectrum, other less expensive alternatives also deserve consideration. Buying or leasing existing airlift from Russia or Ukraine could provide a cheaper means of quickly acquiring the necessary lift, although availability and safety might be counterbalancing concerns.[10] Another cheap and speedy fix would be to create a civilian reserve air fleet program (CRAF), allowing EU governments to requisition civilian aircraft, ships, trains and lorries in crises at previously agreed rates.

The Dutch and the Germans have embarked on a creative funding scheme, in which the Dutch invest in improving the German airlift fleet, in return for the right to use the fleet for Dutch operations. This important effort is the first attempt to use national spending to create a common pool of EU assets,[11] and has considerable merit as a model for more effective European defense spending. But the Dutch–German approach has potential drawbacks. By combining cross-funding (paying for another state to own an airplane) and pooling of assets (building multinational units out of nationally owned aircraft), it raises the potential drawbacks of access and buck-passing.

On access, countries would need a high degree of confidence that they had guaranteed usage, even when the country holding the common asset was not contributing forces to the mission concerned. The level of confidence is probably far higher among Europeans than across the Atlantic. First, there would be fewer concerns about the assets being engaged in other areas of the world or committed to higher-priority potential conflicts. And secondly, disagreements over the use of force are likely to be less trenchant among the 15 EU states than between NATO and the EU as a whole. Consequently, it is less likely that one member state would deny access to another.

The second potential problem with the Dutch–German model is buck-passing—states commit too little money because they are not themselves responsible for producing the necessary aircraft, ships, trains and lorries. As a result, the EU may end up lacking the necessary assets. NATO members routinely fail to spend all they have promised, and while the EU may prove better at enforcing commitments, that is certainly not a given.

Several EU states have looked at ways of improving European lift. Germany and France have proposed the creation of a joint air transport command, while France and the Netherlands have mooted an EU maritime lift force and coordination cell (with a substantial commitment of 70 ships). These are useful initiatives, but in order to provide the best cross-pollination, the EU should consider creating an overall EU transport command, as suggested by General Klaus Naumann, the former chairman of NATO's military committee.[12] An EU command would give the Helsinki process a concrete and visible result: aircraft, ships, trains and lorry transports flying the EU flag and committed in the first instance to EU operations. As long as these EU resources were available to NATO, neither the United States nor other states should have any reason to block an EU transport command.

Strategic Intelligence Collection and Assessment

Whether strategic intelligence collection is a genuine EU requirement is questionable. Satellites are not optimal for the kind of crisis-management operations outlined in the Petersberg Tasks. Europeans are divided on whether an autonomous EU force needs independent satellite intelligence. While many members regard government-owned reconnaissance satellites as a low priority in EU defense spending, France considers them critical. It has legitimate concerns about U.S. intelligence sharing and the availability of commercial data in crises.

In principle, the United States can have no objection to the EU acquiring strategic intelligence assets. The dominance of the United States in intelligence issues is neither conducive to cooperative policies, nor beneficial to the United States or Europe. Better intelligence would allow Washington's NATO allies to replicate and validate the factual basis of U.S. assessments. Disagreements over interpretation would certainly occur; they are common within and among U.S. intelligence agencies. But, overall, better European intelligence is likely to produce more transatlantic agreement, if only because the act of collecting and assessing intelligence would encourage European governments to think rather more—and more commonly—about long-term foreign policy issues than some of them do at present.

A more important priority than collection of intelligence, however, would be to improve intelligence sharing and assessment capabilities. The critical shortfall for Europe is not lack of information—the United States relies on intelligence provided by European allies in many parts of the world. The EU's problem is that since most states do not share their intelligence, they cannot arrive at a common assessment. The EU's Policy Planning and Early Warning Unit has some modest multilateral assessment capability, but most European intelligence remains jealously guarded in national channels.[13] The varying histories and commercial interests of the EU states give them different competitive advantages; these could be profitably combined without the sacrifice of vital national interests.

The United States will, however, be wary of intelligence sharing across the Atlantic until the EU establishes standards for security that bring its governments, and its institutions, up to the level at which member and allies can be confident about sharing intelligence. The war on terrorism will exacerbate U.S. fears. Catching terrorists requires tactical surprise, which places a premium on secrecy. The United States will not allow the kind of difficulties it experienced in Bosnia—on one occasion there were allegations that a French officer passed tactical intelligence to suspected Serb war criminals—to endanger the success of operations against the likes of Osama bin Laden and his associates. The need for secrecy and surprise will starkly restrict the sharing of intelligence, even with America's closest allies.

Those countries with privileged access to U.S. intelligence, such as Britain, will be loathe to encourage more intra-European sharing if it risked access to U.S. intelligence. Consequently, better EU intelligence capabilities depend crucially on raising the standard of information security in all EU states to the level of those countries with privileged access, and making the United States comfortable that the highest common denominator is reliably met.[14]

Intelligence hardware is high-tech and glamorous, but is ultimately less important than the ability of trained analysts to interpret what they are seeing intelligently. The U.S. experience on September 11, as on many other occasions, has been that intelligence failures are usually a product of insufficient analysis, not inadequate information. The training of analysts would improve Europe's intelligence capability faster, and less expensively, than investment in new equipment.

The EU's existing Situation Centre (linked to both the EU Military Staff and the Policy Planning and Early Warning Unit, in the bureaucracy that reports to Javier Solana, the High Representative for EU foreign and security policy) is insufficient. It does not receive enough intelligence from EU states, it is not large enough to provide analysis on demand, and its staff lack the links into national intelligence staff that would allow them to share ideas and receive feedback. The EU should consider creating a new and larger specialist unit, under the control of Solana, with responsibility for collating and analyzing information from national intelligence channels.

Theater Reconnaissance

There can be no doubt that better reconnaissance of the region in which EU forces operate is essential for improving its capacity for crisis management. Both the former and current chairmen of the NATO Military Committee have highlighted theater reconnaissance as a critical shortfall in European forces during the Kosovo campaign.[15]

The United States conducted over 90 percent of advanced intelligence and reconnaissance missions during the Kosovo campaign. Given the other demands on U.S. intelligence capabilities, the EU would be wise to reduce this dependence, focusing its spending on tactical assets, such as unmanned aerial vehicles and AWACs aircraft. EU countries could save money by pooling the cost of developing and buying these systems, and then run them as EU squadrons, just as NATO has its AWACs aircraft. Provided that these EU units were also available to NATO, they should pose no political problem.

Strike Forces

If the EU wants to improve the political visibility of its contributions to NATO, and the power to "shock and awe" potential adversaries independently of NATO, it needs to build a precision strike force that can attack from beyond the battlefield. This would be a welcome duplication, given Europe's heavy reliance on U.S. assets in Kosovo. Building a strike force will require upgrading both the platform for operations—predominantly fighter aircraft—and the precision munitions they use. Some improvements are already planned: France is buying 61 Rafale fighters that will enter into service in 2005; the United Kingdom, Germany, Italy and Spain are buying 620 Eurofighters; while Belgium, Denmark, Norway and the Netherlands are upgrading their F-16 fighters to provide an all-weather operating capability. With respect to precision weapons, France, the U.K., Italy and Greece are purchasing the Storm

Shadow air-launched cruise missile; Germany has a similar program under development but has not yet targeted funds.[16]

The potential impact of these improvements would be maximized if Europe pooled them into an EU strike force. The Benelux Deployable Air Task Force might provide a good model for pooling forces, especially among countries with smaller military organizations. This Task Force combines fighter aircraft from three countries that train together and can be deployed as a single squadron. EU states with similar aircraft and munitions, which are used to training together, could create multinational fighter squadrons for strike missions. This kind of multinational integration comes at a price, in terms of national sovereignty and military efficiency. But the advantages are substantial: a better sharing of the defense burden among EU states, and the opening up of a meaningful role for the smaller European countries on the leading edge of combat.

For the longer term, General Naumann's idea of a force of unmanned aerial vehicles with supersonic cruise missiles has considerable merit.[17] This option would reduce concerns about national sovereignty, since unmanned vehicles are a strictly mechanical weapon that could easily be reshuffled into different formations. Whether manned or unmanned, either approach would enable Europe to be at the forefront of a high-intensity combat mission, ensuring its involvement in the early stages of operations.

Air-to-Air Refueling

Another area for duplication that would garner U.S. support is in-flight refueling of transport, reconnaissance and fighter aircraft. In Kosovo, the most critical constraint on operations was the limited number of RC-135 refueling aircraft. Denmark and the Netherlands are pioneering the development of compatible systems in Europe through a bilateral agreement for Dutch tankers to refuel Danish F-16s. An EU refueling unit could be planned, organized, trained and commanded multinationally, as a separate force under EU auspices. This would give the EU a visible presence in operations and an essential niche that could be the basis for mission specialization within NATO or in non-NATO international coalitions.

EU Research, Development and Procurement

European R&D funding is insufficient for existing needs and is unlikely to increase substantially in the foreseeable future. One way of addressing the problem would be to secure national commitments in the EU for an agreed percentage of GDP to be spent on defense, and for R&D funds to be specially fenced within defense budgets.[18] This approach would take up the kind of quantitative criteria and careful scrutiny that fostered discipline for Europe's monetary union. But it is not clear that national governments are willing to be held to account for those kinds of targets in the area of defense, or that Europeans are willing to spend for Europe, given that they have not wanted to increase defense spending to meet NATO goals. The same idea has guided NATO defense planning for decades, but with little effect, for NATO has not found a way of holding governments accountable for failing to meet targets. The EU will need to convince governments to develop a stronger system in order to bring about progress.

EU governments need to think more about collective research, development and procurement. While R&D tends to be treated separately from procurement, the EU governments should think about combining the three processes. Potential improvements in weaponry could be evaluated in tandem with the restructuring of forces. One feasible solution would be to create an EU body under High Representative Solana to pool some of the national contributions to research, development and procurement. Members would certainly want to retain some of their funds for national programs, but an EU body collecting the contributions of member states could have five great benefits. It would: take advantage of potential economies of scale; help reduce the detrimental duplication of effort that exists in member states' budgets; work with the EU Military Committee to establish common priorities for equipment purchases that would advance the Helsinki Headline Goal and future objectives; establish the basis for an EU-wide defense market; and help to build a common strategic and operational vision of the future of EU forces.

Despite the exemption of defense industries from the competence of the EU under Article 296 of the EU treaties, a high-level coordinating body could build on the existing agency for managing joint weapons programs, the Organization for Joint Armaments Cooperation (OCCAR). The original participants in OCCAR—Britain, France, Germany and Italy—account for 80 percent of EU spending on research, development and procurement. Spain, Belgium and the Netherlands are in the process of joining, and Sweden is considering doing so—which would bring most of the EU's defense industry within the ambit of OCCAR.

A genuine transatlantic defense market would be preferable, but the political and economic impediments to transatlantic cooperation are prohibitive. Both European governments and the United States want the employment and technological benefits of domestic defense industries, and none of them wants to depend solely on foreign suppliers for critical war materials. However, consolidation among European industries could create some competition for America's defense industrial behemoths, thereby alleviating Pentagon concerns about monopoly suppliers in the U.S. market.

An EU research, development and procurement agency would duplicate the work currently undertaken by the Conference of National Armaments Directors, which tries to push governments to choose the systems that best serve NATO's military needs. That would be no bad thing. NATO armaments directors have failed for the past ten years to agree on whether to buy a U.S. ground surveillance system, identified by NATO military commanders as the top priority need, or to wait for a European system to be developed. If the EU could bring greater political impetus to decision making and thus break the gridlock in NATO committees, this would be an area of NATO planning where the risks of competition between NATO and the EU are worth taking.

Does the EU Need Its Own Planning Capability?

The duplication of expensive logistical and war-fighting assets is unlikely to raise objections in the United States or NATO—the benefits to all concerned are obvious. The difficulties will start when EU initiatives duplicate NATO's planning role.

Skeptics on both sides of the Atlantic question why the EU cannot manage its military operations through NATO, with or without U.S. participation. Employing the NATO machinery to organize, plan and conduct military operations has three enormous advantages. First, it ensures constructive U.S. involvement. Whether or not U.S. forces are involved, a NATO operation would commit the United States to a common approach. That would avoid the kind of divisiveness that occurred during the Bosnian War, when U.S. advocacy of a "lift and strike" strategy made life difficult for European states that had forces committed in the United Nations Protection Force (UNPROFOR). If Europeans were to work through NATO, the Americans would have a vested interest in the success of its operations.

The second advantage of using NATO's planning apparatus is the ability to call on extra support if necessary. The United States would not allow a NATO operation to fail and would act as a strategic reserve if the mission proved more demanding than expected. NATO's experienced planning staffs would ensure a smooth transition between operations of varying levels of intensity. Joint and combined military operations are taxing under the best of circumstances—and these exist only when a standing multinational HQ practices regularly and thoroughly for specific missions, and forces are trained to work together.

Third, for the EU to manage operations via NATO maximizes the likelihood of it being able to draw upon NATO assets. Military operations can be planned on an ad hoc basis if necessary, but doing so increases the risk of failure and casualties, and also increases the influence of the strongest contributors since little time will be available to share responsibilities. NATO headquarters are the backbone of the Alliance's military effectiveness. They allow NATO states to develop an intimate understanding of each other's military forces and practices. Such routine interaction, prior to a crisis, is the most reliable way to ensure that forces can work together smoothly when pulled into a multinational coalition.

But it would be simplistic to suggest, even in the short term, that the EU can develop an autonomous force without some independent strategic planning capability. Moreover, once the EU is capable of operating autonomously, its military staffs will need to go beyond strategic planning, to more detailed force and operational planning.

The EU needs a strategic planning capability so that ministers can receive advice on questions such as, for what purposes does the EU want to use force, in which parts of the world might it wish to intervene, which non-EU states might be asked to participate in an EU mission and are the operational plans supplied to ministers good ones? In short, strategic planning should help the EU and its governments to develop a common approach to the use of force and the mechanisms for taking military decisions.

The EU has already done a substantial amount of strategic planning. It has established the post of High Representative for its CFSP, charged him with overseeing the embryonic defense policy, and given him a military staff that can prepare issues for decision. It has set up a Brussels-based committee of senior national officials, to coordinate work on the CFSP, as well as an EU military committee to advise decision makers and coordinate progress on defense goals. All of these people and committees are engaged in strategic planning, without causing much conflict within NATO.

Force planning and operational planning, both essential to organizing and conducting military operations, cause more concern. Force planning is the long-term coordination of the size and capabilities of military forces. It deals with the number of troops, the kinds of units they are organized into, how they are trained and what types of weapons they have. NATO does an enormous amount of force planning to maximize the ability of its members' armed forces to work together, and to ensure that it has the capabilities it needs to carry out missions.

The EU does not yet engage in significant force planning. It is still debating whether to use NATO plans or to develop a unique system unrelated to NATO reporting requirements. And preparations for the Helsinki Headline Goal are now approaching the stage when force planning will be required; so far they have focused on drawing upon the present rather than shaping the future capabilities of forces. But if the EU intends to fight as an autonomous multinational force, it needs to train as an autonomous multinational force. This means that in the long run the EU will have to build staffs that duplicate NATO force planning: when the EU runs autonomous missions, it will sometimes need different types of forces, trained and equipped differently from NATO forces.

The EU will also need to conduct its own operational planning—that is, orchestrating the use of existing forces and weapons for specific military missions. NATO's military staffs carry out this planning for multinational operations; national military staffs then check the plans before NATO's nations commit to an operation.

The size of operations envisaged by the Petersberg Tasks suggests that a regional HQs would be the appropriate level for operational planning. To meet this need, the EU has four options: standing joint HQs designated by the EU, such as the Eurocorps, the five-nation HQs that is led by France and Germany; rely on national HQs (such as the British Permanent Joint Headquarters that so ably planned and executed operations in Sierra Leone in 2000); create ad hoc multinational headquarters; or revive the concept of NATO CJTFs (i.e., a modified version of a NATO HQ, adjusted to fit with the nationality of the countries taking part in the mission).

Defense leaders in both the United States and Europe are concerned about creating EU force or operational planning staffs. They want to sustain the advantages of U.S. involvement, such as a greater prospect of access to NATO assets, and—if an operation encountered problems—of U.S. assistance.

In the longer term, however, the EU may have to build full planning capabilities. Once the EU is able to take independent military action, it will naturally start developing an approach to the use of force that is different from, and competes with, NATO's. For example, NATO still has to plan for collective defense and high-intensity conflict, while the EU's more limited planning scenarios focus on crisis management.

If both the EU and NATO military staffs are planning to use the same forces for managing crises in different ways, political leaders will be faced with conflicting options. Even if the two staffs retain a common approach—which is unlikely—the process of presenting advice to decision makers is likely to be confusing and delay decisions. Over time, the two staffs are very unlikely to retain a similar approach, if only because the EU military staffs will be planning without reliance on U.S. military assets.

The problem of separate planning is a serious one, both politically and militarily. But it is not insurmountable. The United States has military staffs independent of NATO for planning, organizing, training, equipping and employing its military forces. There is no reason why the Europeans should not also create that capability within the EU. In any case they may be forced to do just that, if the EU and Turkey cannot reach a full agreement over the EU's assured access to the use of NATO planning staffs. And NATO planning staffs are already fully employed; given how different operations will be in NATO and the EU, both planning staffs will be kept busy. If the EU has a choice, however, it would be better to postpone the building of force or operational planning staffs until it has moved further down the road toward autonomous military operations.

The Benefits of European Military Autonomy

Constructive duplication will not come cheaply, but adding the capabilities outlined here would not be prohibitively expensive either. ESDP advocates may well be overestimating both the willingness of Europeans to spend more "for Europe" and the scale of potential savings that can be squeezed out of existing budgets. But if governments are serious about ending their dependency on the United States, raising defense spending by 10 percent per annum should be possible. This would yield an additional *Euro* 16 billion per year, which would go a long way toward providing the kind of improvements suggested. If EU members were to match the next phase of Helsinki Headline Goal planning with a commitment to contribute that extra 10 percent to a common EU fund to finance priority improvements, the United States would find it much harder to question Europe's seriousness on defense.

The EU could also earn America's respect by focusing on improvements at the war-fighting end of the Petersberg Tasks—lift, intelligence, strike forces, air-to-air refueling and research, development and procurement. This would reduce U.S. concerns that the EU is creating "the worst of all worlds. ... a new institution that complicates NATO's cohesion but without providing new capabilities."[19] It would make European forces more useful to the United States in the wars it fights, both in Europe and beyond. That, in turn, would expand the political influence of European states in U.S. decision-making. It would also give the EU a more strategic perspective on foreign and security problems, since it would have a fuller range of choices available in protecting and advancing its interests.

It is a major disadvantage for the EU not to have the option of conducting operations outside NATO. Without having genuinely autonomous military forces, Europe's needs are subordinated to U.S. priorities. The EU is left hostage to the concerns and potential veto of the United States and Turkey, both of which may well evaluate their interests as opposed to an EU operation. More generally, the lack of an EU military capability forces Europe into continuing dependence on the United States, which is politically unhealthy in states as powerful and independent-minded as those of the EU. Finally, as the war against terrorism is beginning to show, dependence leaves the EU unacceptably few options when higher-priority demands engage the United States.

The EU was right to set itself the goal of being able to run autonomous EU military operations, and it should remain committed. Europe needs, perhaps, to be more sensitive to U.S. concerns about EU rhetoric outstripping its capabilities. And Americans must understand that reducing Europe's dependence does not reduce its desire to work with the United States. There are substantial enough challenges to U.S. interests in the world that it needs allies out of strength, not allies out of weakness. The experience of September 11 has reinforced transatlantic political cohesion in ways that should allow for more EU activism on defense issues. And NATO will benefit from the new-found U.S. appreciation of the value of allies and from the pride Europeans feel in having honored the Article V pledge when America was unexpectedly in need.

An EU that is able and willing to take more responsibility for managing crises, with less reliance on the United States, need not damage NATO. If the EU allocates scarce defense euros to duplicating capabilities that both enhance its autonomy and reduce the burden on heavily taxed U.S. military assets, duplication can be constructive rather than wasteful. The practical problems of adapting NATO are manageable. For the EU to develop real competence in security and defense matters will require changes in the comfortable patterns of transatlantic relations, and these could make cooperation difficult. But the benefits of the status quo should not be overstated—it is not satisfactory to either the United States or Europe. The NATO Alliance is important enough on both sides of the Atlantic to be of continuing value for the management of common security problems and coalition military operations. And it is strong enough to manage the transition from a U.S.-dominated Alliance to a collaboration among more equal partners.

Notes

1. Joint statement, February 23, 2001.
2. Ibid.
3. Joint press conference at Camp David, February 23, 2001.
4. "Powell, Patten Discuss ESDI and Iraq," February 27, 2001 (uspolicy. usembassy.be).
5. President Bush, press conference with NATO Secretary General Lord Robertson, Brussels, June 13, 2001.
6. For a European perspective on Turkey and the ESDP, see Gilles Andreani, Christoph Bertram and Charles Grant, "Europe's Military Revolution" (Centre for European Reform, March 2000).
7. Congressional Budget Office, "NATO Burdensharing After Enlargement," August 2001.
8. Aside from headquarters, "NATO assets" generally refers to U.S. military capabilities such as strategic intelligence collection and assessment, theater reconnaissance capabilities, communications equipment, airlift and logistics to sustain deployed forces.
9. Assembly of the WEU, "Implementation of the Nice Summit Declarations in the Operational Area of the European Security and Defense Policy," Document A/1734, appendix 1.
10. Stephan de Spigliere and Dmitri Danilov, *From Decoupling to Recoupling: A New Security Relationship between Russia and Western Europe* (Paris: WEU Institute for Security Studies, 1998), Chaillot Paper 31.
11. "Keynote Address by Dutch Defense Minister de Grave to the Defense Planning Symposium," Oberammergau, January 15, 2001.
12. Klaus Naumann, "Europe's Military Ambitions," *Centre for European Reform Bulletin* (June/July 2000).
13. Alessandro Politi, *Toward a European Intelligence Policy* (Paris: WEU Institute for Security Studies, 1998), Chaillot Paper 34.
14. See Charles Grant, "Intimate Relations: Can Britain Play a Leading Role in European Defense—and Keep Its Special Links with U.S. Intelligence?" *Centre for European Reform Bulletin* (April 2000).
15. See Admiral Venturoni, NATO press conference, June 30, 1999, and General Naumann, NATO press conference, May 4, 1999.
16. See Robert Grant, "The RMA—Europe Can Keep in Step," Occasional Paper 15 (Paris: WEU Institute for Security Studies, June 2000).
17. Naumann, *Centre for European Reform Bulletin*, June/July 2000.

18. See Francois Heisbourg, *Centre for European Reform Bulletin* (June/July 1999) and Charles Grant, "European Defense Post-Kosovo," Centre for European Reform Working Paper, June 1999.

19. Peter Rodman, "U.S. Leadership and the Reform of Western Security Institutions: NATO Enlargement and ESDP," speech given at a German Foreign Policy Association conference, December 11, 2000.

PART THREE

NATO Enlargement, ESDP and the Discrimination Issue

CHAPTER 7

Non-EU NATO Members and the Issue of Discrimination

Sunniva Tofte

Introduction

The issue of discrimination with regard to the six non-EU European members of NATO (the Czech Republic, Hungary, Iceland, Norway, Poland and Turkey) is proving to be one of the most difficult circles to square as the EU develops its ESDP. The EU is seeking guaranteed access to NATO assets for its operations, including those "where NATO as a whole is not engaged," but the modalities for this assured access depend to some extent on the unresolved issue of what role the Six should be allowed in the ESDP in return. The extent of participation offered to these countries will be a significant indicator of the actual meaning behind the EU's stated aim of becoming an *autonomous* actor in security and defense, and will substantially affect the relationship between the EU and NATO.

The Six do not form a very cohesive group. Norway and Turkey have been the most eager to take part in the evolving project. The Czech Republic, Hungary and Poland are at the front of the queue for accession into the EU and all have a realistic prospect of full EU membership in the not too distant future, which will entail full participation in the ESDP project. Iceland does not have its own forces, and it therefore seems likely that this country's involvement in ESDP would necessarily be limited, regardless of the issue of membership.

Turkey and Norway have both seen exclusion from ESDP as highly problematic. There has been a greater concern in these two countries of isolation and marginalization outside the new European security structures, since for Norway and Turkey nonmembership is likely to be a more permanent characteristic than for the Czech Republic, Hungary and Poland. They will not be allowed full integration into the EU's security structures and fear at the same time that as these develop, they might also undermine NATO's cohesion and commitment to their security. Another concern is that a U.S.–EU bilateral relationship will emerge, from which these countries will be excluded.

In other words, there is a concern about falling between two stools: an EU that increasingly takes over responsibilities in the area where the two countries are situated geographically but which is less committed to their concerns, and a NATO/United States that increasingly delegates these responsibilities to the EU, and where the United States increasingly deals with the EU directly. Turkey and Norway have thus become strange bedfellows, sharing the same goal of obtaining the closest possible involvement in the EU's evolving security structures. However, the unlikely team members have had their cooperation impeded by their very different relationships with the EU and their vastly different strategies for achieving their aims.

The Non-EU Allies in the Post–Cold War European Security Conundrum

There are strong reasons in both Ankara and Oslo why the exclusion from ESDP is seen as problematic. Some of these are shared concerns, while others diverge considerably. For both Norway and Turkey it is vital that NATO remains the linchpin of an integrated security policy covering the whole of Europe. It seems unlikely that a Norwegian government will call for a new membership referendum, risking a third rejection, unless it is virtually certain that the electorate will return a yes majority. There are few indications that such a change is likely to take place in the near future. For Turkey, the EU's 1999 Helsinki summit reversed its own decision from the Luxembourg summit in 1997 and offered Turkey EU candidature. However, the prospect of Turkey actually becoming a member in this generation is as unlikely as the emergence of a yes majority in Norway.

At present, the EU does not have the capacity to deal with a crisis of any considerable dimension. Although the EU aims to handle smaller crises independently of the Americans, such a situation would not have to escalate very far before the EU would have to draw on NATO assets, at which point Norway and Turkey would come into the decision-making process on the supplier side. Some have therefore argued that the importance of finding an extensive role for the Six in ESDP is exaggerated. It is not, however, given that NATO will be asked to get involved in such a situation. The EU might decide to ask the United States directly for necessary technical assistance, especially since most NATO assets are American anyway. It seems unlikely that Icelandic or Norwegian considerations will weigh very heavily in such a situation or that the EU will bend over backwards to involve Turkey. For the EU, such a bilateral relationship might even prove less complicated than having to deal with NATO as a whole. Although countries like Norway and Turkey might feel jilted, the military action would not necessarily be adversely affected.

Norway

Norwegian concerns about the strengthening of ESDP flow mainly from the assumption that this will entail a weakening of NATO and a continuation of a reorientation of security priorities away from the northern region. Norway has been largely negative toward the integration of the WEU into the EU, but since such a development is taking place anyway, it is seen to be of utmost importance that ESDP should be as closely linked to NATO as possible. Norway looked with skepticism on the EU's stated objectives in the Saint-Malo Declaration and the Cologne summit to develop the means for "autonomous action backed by credible military forces, the means to decide to use them, and a readiness to do so."[1] Unless this capacity is *firmly* based within the NATO framework, and with at least an implicit, but preferably an explicit supremacy for the commitments of the Alliance, Norway might find itself in a weakened NATO and outside a strong and exclusive EU–U.S. bilateral relationship.

This is in part a reflection of the special position Norway held in the "old" NATO. As the only NATO member sharing a land border with the Soviet Union and with the high strategic importance given to the High North, Norway developed strong ties with the United States; indeed, this relationship was termed "an alliance within the alliance."[2] Norway had a large share of its military expenditure shouldered by NATO, and above all by the United States. Much of Norwegian infrastructure was funded through the NATO shared investment budget, which had considerable positive effects on the Norwegian civilian economy. These investments declined abruptly with the end of the Cold War. Moreover, whereas the security of most countries was vastly increased with the end of bipolarity, the Russian troops were still where they always had been in the North: right on Norway's border. There were also concerns about the stability and political control over these and the safety of their equipment. Such concerns were not lessened by the Kursk catastrophe, which took place close to the Norwegian coast. The end of the Cold War thus did *not* have exclusively positive effects on Norway, and this has contributed to Norway's slow adaptation to the new security reality.

As a nonmember of the EU and as a NATO member, Norway has on several occasions been seen by Russia as an "extended arm" of the United States in the North.[3] This becomes problematic due to the multiple areas in which there is potential for conflict in Norwegian–Russian relations, above all that of unresolved jurisdictions. Russia and Norway have unsettled border disputes on the Barents Sea continental shelf, and a long-standing disagreement over what jurisdiction applies around the archipelago of Svalbard. The disputed areas between the two countries equal 150,000 sq.km.—half the size of mainland Norway.[4]

Torunn Laugen contends that bilateral Norwegian–Russian relations are a function of the combined effects of Russia's relations to the West in general, internal Russian developments, and Norwegian policies in the north. Developments in all three of these arenas caused bilateral relations to take a negative direction in the latter half of the 1990s.[5] The temperature in Norwegian–Russian relations in the 1990s was not so much a result of developments between the two countries, but more often directly proportional to relations between Russia and the West, and in particular relations with the United States and NATO. Because Norway is not an EU member, it views itself as more vulnerable to instability in Russia. When it comes to condemning internal Russian affairs, Norway has thus maintained a lower profile than EU members Sweden and Finland. A bilateral relationship between a former superstate and a small country that has placed itself outside the main arena for political cooperation in Europe is not an easy one. Norway has therefore chosen a "Russia-first" policy in the Baltics, opting not to comment on developments between Russia and Ukraine or the former central-Asian republics and striving to have such potential conflict handled within multilateral frameworks.[6]

The Norwegian fear is that a situation might occur, such as increased tension in the dispute over jurisdictions in the Barents Sea, in which the spark might originate from outside the bilateral relationship. In such a scenario, support from Norway's Western allies would be vital.

If, however, NATO's Article V commitment is weakened and responsibility for European security is increasingly delegated to the EU, a conflict might emerge that is too great for Norway to handle on its own but not compelling enough for either NATO or the EU to get involved.[7] "If Norway should find itself in such a situation, a worst case scenario could be that it will be left on its own with Russia in the north, without being able to count on support from any of the other two corners [i.e., EU or NATO]."[8]

Until Saint-Malo, Norway took little notice of the EU's CFSP. The Norwegian acronym for CFSP, FUSP, was—until the implications of Saint-Malo had sunk in—often referred to as "FUSK" (fake). The rejection of the very idea of the EU as a political actor until the very late 1990s and the strong belief in NATO contributed to the continuous denial of any foreign and security role for the EU.

To the extent that the 1990s saw new directions in Norwegian security and defense policies, these were largely due to external pressures rather than internal developments, and *not* a result of the end of the Cold War as such.[9] Experiences deriving from the Gulf War had a larger impact in instigating change within the army than the complete rewriting of the political map of Europe between 1989 and 1992.[10] The pressures on the Norwegian defense concept can thus be said to be mainly organizational/institutional rather than military/strategic. In addition to NATO, the pressures for change have increasingly originated from an organization in which Norway is not a member—the EU.

Turkey

Since 1981, when Greece became a member of the EC, tensions in EU–Turkish relations have been further strained by Turkey's fractious relationship with EU member Greece. The most serious cause of tension is the long-standing dispute over the control of the island of Cyprus, dating back long before the Turkish invasion of the northern parts of Cyprus in 1974. Cyprus fell under Turkish rule in 1571, but was annexed by Britain in World War I and made a Crown colony in 1925. Cyprus became an independent nation on August 16, 1960, with Britain, Greece and Turkey as guarantor powers; however, the Greek inhabitants, who make up some 80 percent of the total population, have for centuries sought self-determination and reunion with Greece.[11]

In July 1974, Turkish forces were deployed to the island to protect the Turkish minority after Greek-Cypriot extremists threatened to make Cyprus part of Greece.[12] Since then, Greek-Cyprus has claimed that the

Turkish troops are an invasion force, while Turkey has claimed that it had to move in and remain to protect the 200,000 Turkish residents in the north of the island. The Turkish minority has since 1974 lived separately from the Greek majority in what in 1983 was proclaimed the "Turkish Republic of North Cyprus" (KKTC). This declaration has not been recognized by any country other than Turkey, and the UN Security Council declared the action legally invalid and called for its withdrawal.[13]

One of the most problematic issues for Turkey regarding ESDP is that, unlike the WEU, it did not have any promise that EU forces would not be used against a NATO member. One of Turkey's main concerns about being outside ESDP is that Greece might attempt to get the EU involved in Turkish–Greek bilateral disputes, and that when Cyprus becomes a member, Greece will effectively have two votes in the EU institutions to involve the EU in a conflict against Turkey. The main point of disagreement is Cyprus. Turkish-Cypriot leader Rauf Denktas has warned that the Greek-Cypriot EU bid is a continuation of the campaign starting in the early 1960s to achieve union with Greece (enosis) and that it is now hoped this can be achieved through the EU door.[14]

Turkey argues that out of sixteen potential threats to NATO's security, thirteen lie in close vicinity to Turkey, which should automatically entitle Turkey to a seat at the ESDP table. Turkey has also stressed how the events following the September 11 attacks highlighted its importance in the region and the pivotal strategic role Turkey plays as a bridge between the East and the West, the Christian and the Muslim world, and as a juncture between the Balkans, the Caucasus and the Middle East. Turkey insists that this strategic importance warrants a right to participate fully at all stages, including the decisions on whether to launch an EU-led operation that does not require recourse to NATO assets, but which takes place in Turkey's neighbourhood or affects its vital interests.[15] In other words, Turkey wants a guarantee from the EU of veto power if such a situation should arise. This point alludes not only to Turkish fears that an EU force might interfere in Turkish–Greek disputes but also to issues such as Iraq, where Turkey has special interests.

Turkey's bid for ESDP involvement cannot be, however, separated completely from the Turkish bid for EU membership. Developments in the aftermath of September 11 initially led many Turks to the conviction that now EU membership would be automatic despite continued EU concerns regarding Turkey's democratic and human rights credentials. By the Helsinki summit, there was growing recognition that "Europe's own economic and security interests would not be adequately served if Turkey was allowed to drift toward isolation and authoritarianism."[16] A serious roadblock nevertheless remained: the fact that Turkey is a Muslim country, which might make it difficult to reconcile Turkish membership with the self-image and identity of the EU.

European Identity: Not Welcomed by Norway and Turkey Not Welcomed

Although both Turkey and Norway have been unhappy with the roles they have been assigned in ESDP, their reactions to the EU have been almost diametrically opposite. This is clearly due to the fact that their means to obtain maximum influence, as well as their motivations, vary considerably. Norway realizes that its nonmember status is a self-inflicted problem. This is evidently going to reduce its leverage with the EU compared to that of Turkey. Turkey is *very* keen to become a member of the EU and there is a certain feeling of guilt within the EU about the way Turkey has been treated. To fully understand both Norway–EU and Turkey–EU relations, one must explore the very different identities of these two countries vis-à-vis Europe.

Turkey

The success of Turkey's enthusiastic bid for EU membership would be a crowning of the efforts over eight decades to westernize Turkey. Since the days of Mustafa Kemal Atatürk, Turkey has wanted to confirm its identity as a European country. Atatürk, after proclaiming the Republic of Turkey in 1923, imposed a mix of nationalism and secularism and "wanted Turks to turn their backs on the Ottoman past and become modern by imitating Europe."[17] This "Westernization project" is often referred to as "Kemalism" and rests on six pillars: Secularism, republicanism, populism, nationalism, statism and reformism.[18] These principles are still upheld by the westernizing elites, though while the statist, nationalist and authoritarian elements have been strong, the commitment to democracy and pluralism has been weaker.[19]

Despite the importance of Kemalism, Turkey (and before that the Ottoman Empire) has represented one of the most important elements of "otherness" in the European identity.[20] Not all EU members can picture an EU that includes Turkey, which is seen by many as where Europe ends and Asia begins. In a speech on behalf of the Dutch presidency of the EU to the European Parliament in January 1997, van Mierlo spoke of how he understood Turkey's frustration over progress toward its integration with the EU. However, he noted it was "time to be honest" in this matter and acknowledge that the problem was largely that of admitting a large Muslim state into the EU.[21] Not surprisingly, such rejection by the EU has contributed to Turkey's tough stance on ESDP.

Norway

In certain ways, this dilemma is reversed when it comes to Norwegian identity vis-à-vis Europe. In the Scandinavian states there is a sense of being part of "an exceptional family of nations."[22] As Wæver notes, "Nordic identity is about being better than Europe."[23] The Norwegian national identity is vital in understanding why Norway is not a member of the EU—and consequently of ESDP.

Norway is a young state, which only gained independence in 1905. The nation-building project is older, however, and gained (rather than lost) momentum through the almost six centuries of involuntary unions with Denmark (1319–1814) and Sweden (1814–1905). As a result, national sovereignty has subsequently been very highly rated, as has skepticism of power politics, which was largely seen as a (continental) European phenomenon. The first foreign minister, Jørgen Løvland, proclaimed: "We will not have a foreign policy." By this was meant that Norway should not concern itself with diplomacy or get involved and entangled in power politics with what were referred to as the "European war-nations." Relations with Europe should be along the dimension of trade only.

Until April 9, 1940 there was a widespread view that Norway's geographical and political distance to the "European war-nations" would make it an unlikely target for a military invasion.[24] This Norwegian perception of being remote from Europe in geographical, security, as well as political terms had to be readjusted following the German World War II occupation. Its geographical and political distance no longer provided it with the necessary protection, and it was clear that Norway would have to rely on foreign assistance for its security in the future. Before the war a tacit guarantee from Great Britain was one of the most important security principles for Norway. After a short period of attempting to play the role of nonaligned "bridge-builders," it seemed more self-evident in Norway than in the other Nordic countries to side with the Atlantic powers, above all Britain and the United States, when the policy of neutrality had proven not to work. Norway thus became a founding member of NATO in 1949.

The Norwegian view of the European continent did not change significantly, however. A 1990 survey indicated "Norwegians have about the most weakly developed identifications with Europe."[25] Traditional concerns about EC membership were reinforced not only by the deepening of European integration from the mid-1980s onward, but also by the EC's shift in identity to the European *Union*. In Norwegian national discourse, the word "Union" has very negative connotations derived from the experience of six centuries of forced unions with Denmark and Sweden.[26] Such identity issues have not been overwhelmed by economic arguments for EU entry in Norway, as in some other states, mainly because of the effects of North Sea oil.[27]

From an Inclusive WEU Family to an Exclusive ESDP

As NATO members, Norway and Turkey have held associate membership in WEU since 1992.[28] The many WEU declarations and treaties during the 1990s stressed the organization's holistic approach and allowed for further and further involvement of the associate members in WEU activities, which meant that the associate members in practice were treated as full members. This was particularly due to NATO's decision in Berlin in 1996 to allow the WEU to "borrow" NATO assets for military operations. The decision ignited a dispute over the role that non-EU allies should have in WEU-led operations, mainly due to the conflict between Greece and Turkey. The result was the "All European Allies" decision in spring 1997, which led to all decisions in the WEU being taken in the group of 18.[29]

Although neither Norway nor Turkey maximized the potential for activity and influence in the WEU due to their continued stress on NATO as the sole "real" actor in European security, the developments in WEU meant that the lack of EU membership did not as yet entail exclusion from the revitalized organization, which was seen to have the potential to develop into the European pillar of the Alliance. This role of the WEU was used as a counterargument to the pro-membership argument in the 1994 Norwegian referendum campaign, which held that Norway needed to become a member of the EU so as not to be excluded from the security structures developing in Europe.

Associate membership of the WEU could therefore be seen as a "security political EEA agreement."[30] The Amsterdam Treaty, in Article 17.1, opened up the possibility of integration of the WEU into the Union. Article 17.3 stated "[t]he Union will avail itself of the WEU to elaborate and implement decisions and actions of the Union which have defense implications." The Amsterdam Treaty did not explicitly address the issue of WEU associate members' involvement in WEU-led operations under the EU, but such participation was regarded as *acquis* by the associate members deriving from the Petersberg Declaration, "with associate members participating on the same basis as full members in WEU military operations to which they committed forces, irrespective of whether they were EU-led operations carried out through WEU using European assets or operations with recourse to NATO assets and capabilities."[31]

This picture was to change quite rapidly, however, starting with Tony Blair withdrawing Britain's long-standing veto over merging the WEU with the EU. At the Cologne European summit in 1999 it was decided that the WEU would *not* merge with the EU, but that the EU would create its own functions similar to those of the WEU, rendering the WEU redundant and not transferring the rights of the WEU associate members to the EU. It had long been clear that with its combination of members' statuses, rights and obligations, the WEU held very little potential for becoming an effective organization in the field of security and defense. By relegating the organization to the historical graveyard altogether, the EU could get round this problem by taking over the functions that were seen as useful, while not being obliged to take over the ones that would cause problems such as obligations in connection with associate memberships. As if to add insult to injury for the associate members, the Americans also lent their support to the developments.

The first EU declarations on ESDP and nonmember involvement were conveniently vague about the future role of the non-EU NATO members. At the European Council in Cologne, the Presidency Conclusions stated that a successful ESDP would require "satisfactory arrangements for European NATO members who are not EU Member States to ensure their fullest possible involvement in EU-led operations, building on existing consultation arrangements within the WEU."[32]

The Cologne Conclusions differ from previous EU declarations in that they extend nonmember involvement to give a more prominent role to non-NATO EU applicants. At Santa Maria de Feira (June 2000), the "appropriate arrangements" to "ensure the necessary dialogue, consultation and cooperation" with nonmembers were further clarified.[33] It was also decided that the issue of nonmember involvement was to be dealt with "in a single, inclusive structure" called the EU + 15 format.[34] This includes the 15 EU countries, 13 candidate countries, Norway and Iceland. After insistence on the part of the non-EU NATO members, and against French objections, the EU agreed to an additional EU + 6 format, which allows for closer contact between the EU and the Six within the EU + 15 framework.

The Nice Conclusions (December 2000) mapped out further the modalities for nonmember involvement, and further extended this framework to include cooperation and consultations with countries such as Russia, Ukraine and Canada, amongst others.[35] This extension of cooperation to more countries has annoyed the Six because this reduces the "exclusive" role to which they feel NATO membership should entitle them. While stressing the importance of pragmatism and efficiency, it was decided at Nice that during noncrisis periods there would be a minimum of two meetings in the EU + 15 format during each presidency "on ESDP matters and their possible implications for the countries concerned."[36] In addition, there should be two meetings in the EU + 6 framework. Dialogue and consultation would be intensified at all levels in the event of a crisis.

From Washington to Nice: Tables Turned or a New Tableau?

The modalities elaborated in the Nice Declaration fell *far* short of original Norwegian and Turkish expectations. The Norwegian expectations are set out in a *Pro Memoria* from the Norwegian Foreign Minister, Knut Vollebæk to all NATO and EU countries in October 1999. The document requests the inclusion of the non-EU allies in all aspects of ESDP.[37] Turkey has argued that they have not been offered "the influence they deserved" in the EU's structures, but it has been difficult to get a clear definition of what such influence should include. Charles Grant has claimed the Turkish public relations strategy to be "little short of disastrous," as the Turks for a long time made little effort to explain the merits of their case.[38]

The June 4, 2001 Information Note from the Turkish Armed Forces, which followed the rejection of the Istanbul Letters, is the closest to a clarification of what Turkey (or at least the Turkish military) demands. The six-point, "non-paper" Istanbul Letters document was brokered with Turkey by the Americans and British and worked out by the then Foreign and Commonwealth Office (FCO) Political Director, Emyr Jones Parry in May 2001. The Turkish Foreign Minister Ismael Cem, had agreed to the compromise. Upon return to Turkey, however, it seems that the foreign minister was overruled by the Turkish general staff. The Information Note clarifying Turkey's "rightful expectations" sets out four criteria to be met for Turkey to be able to accept an agreement to ensure EU access to NATO assets: a more important role for the Committee of Contributors, automatic access for non-EU allies to decision-making process when NATO assets are used, automatic invitation to operations in Turkey's geographic proximity and no use of EU-led forces in bilateral disputes between allies.[39]

The main issue of disappointment for the non-EU allies was the discrepancy between NATO's 1999 Washington Communiqué on the one hand, and the Nice Conclusions on the other. The Washington Communiqué states that "NATO and the EU should ensure the development of effective mutual consultation, co-operation and transparency, building on the mechanisms existing between NATO and the WEU ... We attach the utmost importance to ensuring the fullest possible involvement of non-EU European allies in EU-led crisis response operations, building on existing consultation arrangements within the WEU."[40]

Because of the long-standing distrust between Greece and Turkey, Turkey has argued that the bilateral guarantees from other EU members that Turkey will be invited to an EU operation in its proximity are not enough. Turkey fears that although the fourteen other members might want to invite Turkey to such an operation, this could be vetoed by Greece, and in the near future also by Cyprus, and has therefore insisted that there can be no permanently assured access for the EU to NATO planning without permanently assured participation for the Six in ESDP.[41]

The non-EU allies have therefore been disappointed that the EU is not willing to go as far as the WEU in including them in decision making. Turkey has argued particularly strongly that the eleven EU members who are also members of NATO did not keep the promises they had made in the Washington Communiqué when they later signed the Nice Conclusions.

The Turkish position must be seen in the light of the major discrepancy between Turkey's position in the WEU and the decisions taken at NATO's Washington summit in 1999 on the one hand, and the EU's offer to Turkey on the other.[42] Turkey has argued that the guiding principles for EU access to NATO assets should be those given by NATO at the Washington summit, which states that EU's access to NATO resources would be subject to "a case-by-case decision by the North Atlantic Council." Turkey's Foreign Minister Ismail Cem summed up the main causes for Turkish bitterness over the issue as follows: "In most transactions between a donor party and a receiving party, it is the donor that sets the terms. In the case of ESDP, however, we find the reverse: the EU, despite being the recipient, wants to define the rules for assured access to NATO assets ... the EU's proposals oblige NATO to accept a set-up that, for the first time in its history, would discriminate between NATO members, categorizing them as EU and non-EU allies."[43]

The crux of the disagreement between the Six and the EU is thus the question of how the WEU should relate to the EU and NATO. The Six interpreted the statements of "fullest involvement" based on WEU arrangements in a maximalist way.[44] Associate membership in WEU, when offered to European NATO members who were not members of the EU in the Maastricht Treaty, was based on the assumption of the WEU as an interface *between* NATO and the EU. Before Maastricht, WEU was linked to NATO rather than to the EC/EU. In the former WEU, the non-EU NATO allies had enjoyed a stronger position than the non-NATO EU "neutrals." Under ESDP the reverse became the case. The Six have not been happy about seeing the tables turning. To the EU, on the other hand, it is a totally new table, for which only members can expect an automatic invitation.

The modalities for non-EU involvement in ESDP will also have to be judged according to how they work in practice rather than in principle. Norway and Turkey were said to be irritated by the fact that at an EU–Russia meeting following September 11, Russia was offered monthly consultations with COPS, while the Six are only granted three meetings with the EU per presidency to discuss ESDP matters.[45] Moreover, these meetings are held between the EU and the Six as a group, rather than with each separate country.[46] The Six were upset that the EU created a privileged status for a country that, although crucial to Europe's security and beyond, is not a member of NATO, when the principle of independence of decision making has been the basis for refusing the non-EU allies' requests for increased influence.[47] However, the focus of all parties should be on the content of cooperation and not its frequency, and "procedural arithmetic," with which Norway and Turkey indeed have been overly preoccupied, should be avoided.

It is nonetheless hard to imagine that the arrangements offered to the Six will amount to real influence for nonmembers such as Norway and Turkey in the EU institutions. The EU does not have a history of being generous about letting nonmembers take part in its decision-making processes. This implies that, in a crisis situation in Europe similar to that of Kosovo, countries like Norway and Turkey might find themselves outside when the EU, on the basis of the interests of its members, makes a decision on what military action should be taken, but afterwards they will be asked to provide troops and pay their share of the bill for the operation. At the same time, there is no similar way in which Norway or Turkey can ensure that the EU will listen to their particular security concerns. Moreover, if the EU decided to get involved in a situation, and this escalated and activated NATO's Article V, the non-EU allies would be drawn into the situation while the EU neutrals could retreat, as they have no commitments of solidarity. This has been one of the main arguments of the Six in their case for ESDP involvement.

On Offer: Decision Shaping

What is on offer to the Six from the EU is that they cannot be parties to the decision *making* of the EU, but may be involved in all aspects of the decision-*shaping* process. In theory, this means that although Norway and Turkey will have to leave the room when the final votes on an issue are cast, they will be fully involved in the process leading up to and following a decision. The way this works in practice is, however, less straightforward.

One example of this is that the Six are not part of the particular institutional culture developing in the corridors of the buildings where the ESDP is taking shape. The lack of participation in the day-to-day running and shaping of ESDP means it will be more difficult for them to follow the dynamics and methodologies of this process, as well as to appreciate how best to influence it. A distinct discourse is taking shape from which the nonmembers are excluded. As a consequence, by the time the non-EU allies enter the process of decision shaping, the parameters for future decisions are likely to have been set down already through informal conversations in the corridors as well as more formal working groups.

The nonmembers will not have seen the briefs and intelligence reports the EU members will have shared. The Amsterdam Treaty obligates the member states to provide "to the fullest extent possible, relevant information, *including confidential information*."[48] Access to the same information is essential to reach the same conclusions and agree on the same policy. Such reports are often of a sensitive nature. Member states have been skeptical about sharing intelligence with other members due to numerous leaks in both the Council and the Commission. It is therefore reasonable that the nonmembers cannot have access to this classified information. For nonmembers, this means that they step into "consultations" on a very different footing from the EU members. The members are likely increasingly to speak with one voice—decided on before the non-EU countries are called in. The consultation process might therefore increasingly take the shape of the EU *informing* their non-EU partners.

Whereas Turkey–EU relations have always been impeded by a plethora of obstructing factors, Norway's lack of membership has traditionally not prevented it from taking part in the areas of cooperation within the EU framework that have been of interest to Norway. Examples of this are the EEA Agreement, which makes Norway a member of the economic side of the EU, and the Schengen Agreement, which means Norway is part of the passport free area. Such special arrangements have served as Norway's substitute for membership, and have been seen by some as an *à la carte* member status, allowing Norway to participate in areas of cooperation that are important to it while sovereignty is retained *de jure* if not *de facto*. Jörg Monar offers a less positive evaluation, describing nonmember inclusion in Schengen as "inclusion without participation."[49] He argues that the agreement is supposed to allow countries such as Norway and Iceland to take part in "decision-shaping," but that in reality there is little room for such influence. The reason why these countries still agree to such arrangements is that "they find themselves caught between the political inability to join the EU on the one hand and potentially rapidly escalating costs of exclusion on the other."[50]

It seems that Norway assumed something akin to the EEA or Schengen Agreement would be worked out for the area of ESDP, as Norway's requests for participation without membership have "always" been accommodated in the past. ESDP is, however, an area where there is not only less to gain for the EU by nonmember involvement, but also one in which such involvement can jeopardize the success of the project as a whole. The Six have much weaker hands than the EU in the negotiations, and it is also the EU that is dealing the cards. Some formula of cohabitation is necessary, but it is unlikely that this will be as close or as equal a relationship as Turkey and Norway had hoped.

The issue of autonomy will potentially be one of the greatest litmus tests for the success of ESDP. With the EU's stated aim of becoming an *autonomous* actor in the European security arena, the involvement of nonmembers is necessarily a difficult balancing act. With the various functions of the WEU progressively having been transferred to the EU, rights are created for the fifteen, and for them alone. The EU is a highly regulated organization, and there are no "grey-zones" for who has the right to vote or not.[51] France in particular has been said to be skeptical about allowing non-EU allies too much influence, as this might indirectly open up opportunities for American influence via NATO. More members mean that it will be even harder than at present to reach consensus quickly, which will be one of the measures for the EU's success in this field. Also, a successful ESDP must include the coordination of military instruments with instruments from the other pillars. Because these are of an internal nature, nonmembers cannot be party to the decision.[52] Such means will include nonmilitary instruments, for example, economic ones, which Norway has often advocated and used in its security policy in the past. But as these also become increasingly important to the EU, this will further limit nonmembers' scope for influence. Norway has not been happy about these developments.

If the EU cut a "special deal" with Norway, Turkey or both on ESDP involvement, the same offer would probably be extended to *all* present and possibly also future non-EU NATO countries. The decision as to which countries would qualify for preferential treatment would thus be in the hands of another organization: NATO. Letting some countries into the EU's decision-making process in this area would also make it hard to deny similar arrangements to those candidate countries that are likely to become members in the near future. Bringing a large group of countries into the club could jeopardize the chances of ever achieving a successful ESDP through being too vast and complex a task. With the upcoming eastern enlargement, as chapters 8 and 9 discuss, the challenge of integrating the new members into the ESDP will be formidable enough for the EU even without a host of "special arrangements" for various nonmembers. This was one reason why WEU failed as an effective actor in the European security arena. Moreover, the EU wants to keep the pace on the entry of the different applicants under control, and this might be undercut if all get the same "back door" to ESDP.[53]

Norwegian and Turkish influence in ESDP is likely to become even more marginalized when the EU enlarges to the East. When there are more countries that want to be heard, it seems likely that the EU will be more willing to listen to the voices of states that want to and are likely to become members than to a country that has turned down membership twice and one that might never qualify. Also, once the EU has been enlarged, it is unavoidable that the security interests of its new members will be more central than the concerns of nonmembers.

There is also a difficult issue of timing. Especially at such an early phase of the ESDP project, the EU will want to deepen and cement cooperation amongst its members before extending it to nonmembers. As seen from Ankara and Oslo, however, inclusion in the project from an early stage would make their role an interwoven component of ESDP, which would develop as an integral part of the ESDP project's evolution. It will be more difficult to obtain satisfactory arrangements at a later date, when the ESDP structures have been established without an extensive role for these countries in mind. When nonmember involvement is added as an auxiliary feature at a later date, it is likely that their involvement will remain just that—auxiliary rather than integrated.

Moreover, by the time the EU might be ready to extend ESDP to nonmembers in a real sense of the word, it will in all likelihood have more members and their concerns to cater for. There is therefore a vicious circle of timing to this; the EU is unlikely to offer permanent structures and solutions at an early stage or isolated from other structural decisions, while the Six want an early decision both to decide what attitudes they should adopt on key issues,[54] and also because involvement at an early stage is likely to mean more extensive involvement at a later stage.

Norwegian and Turkish Responses: Same Goals, Different Means

Turkey and Norway share the same goal concerning ESDP, namely to maximize their influence within these structures. Before NATO's Washington summit in 1999, there were reports that the two countries worked closely to coordinate their positions. As the above outlines of the two countries' approaches to the EU suggest, this sudden common predicament was indeed only superficial, and the cooperation, although a pragmatic one at the time, hardly amounted to a basis for a lasting partnership. Although there are some similarities in the situations of the two countries, they have adopted very different strategies to achieve maximum influence and have at times been annoyed with the strategy adopted by the other.

Turkey has repeatedly insisted that it will block any EU access to NATO capabilities through exercising its veto in the NAC, unless Turkey is given "appropriate" influence in the ESDP structures. The Turkish demands have been a major stumbling block for the infant ESDP project, and the two-year long acrimonious negotiations between the EU and Turkey can in large part be seen as a stalemate. At several points in time there have been reports that the impasse has been broken, but these have so far not led to a concrete agreement. The failure of the aforementioned six-point, "non-paper" Istanbul Letters, illustrates the role of the military in Turkish political life and how this adds another layer of complications to the efforts to solve the conundrum.

Greece has repeatedly argued that it will not accept an agreement on ESDP that undermines the EU's autonomy. In early December 2001 there were reports that an agreement had been reached between Turkey and the EU, but this was later rejected by Greece.[55] One might speculate whether the likelihood that an agreement would be blocked by Greece might have been part of the calculations during the negotiations in the first place. This in any case forced the Greeks out of Turkey's shadow on this issue, as now it is the Greeks standing in the way of a solution and in whose corner the ball currently is. Greek Foreign Minister George Papandreou has stated that Greece might if necessary use its veto to stop moves to include nonmembers in ESDP decision-making and that "there is no compromise on the ESDP between EU and non-EU NATO members."[56] However, it seems unlikely that Greece wants Turkish exclusion enough to be willing to pay the political price this would entail in NATO and the EU. There is a lot to suggest that the Turkish approach on ESDP has harmed rather than helped the Turkish bid for EU membership.

The Norwegian response to ESDP has in several respects been almost diametrically opposite to Turkey's hard-line approach. Norway has lent its support to the project from the beginning, at least in public statements. In the year following the Saint-Malo Declaration, this support was conditioned by the priority of NATO and the necessity of a holistic approach including nonmembers in the structures. This must in part be seen as a reflex reaction due to Norway's strong transatlantic orientation and lack of faith in the EU, and in part as a reflection of the fact that the Bondevik government was in a difficult position, as the three parties in the coalition had argued against membership in 1994 and had dismissed the argument of security as irrelevant to the issue of membership. It would therefore have been political poison to admit that this was not the case after all.

The Stoltenberg government, which took office in March 2000, adopted a different approach and a clearer strategy. This included a change of focus from insisting on priority being given to NATO to suggesting how Norway could contribute to the ESDP. Norway has shown a keen interest in participating in EU-led operations, both because this creates visibility and because it has been signaled that the more a nonmember is willing to take part, the greater the influence it will be given. Norway offered more troops per capita (3,500) than any other state at the EU's Capabilities Commitment Conference in November 2000. If the EU were to establish a similar sized corps compared to population size, it would be a force of 300,000 troops.[57] So far there is little evidence to suggest that the second Bondevik coalition government, which took office after the general election in September 2001, will depart significantly from the line pursued by Stoltenberg.

Before Turkey threatened to use its veto, officials traveled between Oslo and Ankara to discuss their positions in NATO on ESDP. Norwegian politicians have looked at the Turkish approach with concern and even annoyance, as it was feared that the Turks were playing into the hands of those in the EU system (in particular the French) who argue that the EU needs to be independent of NATO and needs to set up its own structures. Oslo felt Ankara was lending these groups another argument in the case for "necessary duplication," and that this was a dangerous game to play.

Conclusion

For Norway and Turkey, exclusion from ESDP is problematic for reasons of both security and politics. The EU might not be aiming at a role *separate* from NATO, but the fact that security in Europe seems increasingly to be in the hands of an organization with the stated aim of a role *separable* from NATO holds serious implications for these countries. They are also concerned that the evolving EU security structures might weaken the transatlantic security relationship or develop toward a bilateral relationship between the United States and the EU from which Norway and Turkey will be excluded. To play on Kissinger's metaphor, the two countries are worried that when the United States finally gets its phone number to Europe, there will be no extension codes to Oslo and Ankara, nor will the conversation be put on a "speaker phone." It is therefore considered as important to become as integrated as possible in the EU's security structures so as not to become isolated.

Although the conundrum of nonmember involvement in ESDP has held the ESDP project hostage for over two years and the solution to the EU–NATO disagreement over assets has still not been found, this should not be interpreted as a dead-end. After all, a similar agreement between the WEU and NATO took three years to negotiate.[58] While considerable hurdles remain to be cleared before a formula for non-EU allied involvement in ESDP may be found, it seems more than likely that this will happen in the not too distant future. All parties involved have too much political capital vested in the project for this not to happen.

Notes

1. European Council, "European Council Declaration on Strengthening the Common European Policy on Security and Defence," Annex III.1 in Presidency Conclusions, Cologne, June 3 and 4, 1999.
2. Rolf Tamnes, *Oljealder 1965–1995*, Vol. 6 of *Norsk Utenrikspolitikks Historie* (Oslo: Universitetsforlaget, 1997), p. 61.
3. Iver B. Neuman, "Norges handlingsrom og behovet for en overgripende sikkerhetspolitisk strategi," *Kort-Info fra DNAK 1-2001*, The Norwegian Atlantic Committee, 2001.

4. See Olav Orheim, "What are the Strategic Challenges Norway is Facing in the High North?" *Security Policy Library*, No. 7-2001, The Norwegian Atlantic Committee, 2001.

5. Torunn Laugen, "Mot et kaldere klima? Utviklingen av det bilaterale forholdet mellom Norge og Russland på 1990-tallet," *Internasjonal Politikk* 59 (2001), pp. 91–109.

6. See, for example, Iver B. Neumann, "Russlands utenrikspolitikk—fra supermakt til regional stormakt," in Iver B. Neumann and Ståle Ulriksen, eds., *Sikkerhetspolitikk. Norge i makttriangelet mellom EU, Russland og USA* (Oslo: Tano Aschehoug, 1996), pp. 103–133; Clive Archer, "Nordic Swans and Baltic Cygnets," *Cooperation and Conflict* 34 (1999), pp. 47–71.

7. Neumann, *Kort-Info fra DNAK*.

8. Neumann, ibid.

9. Helene Sjursen, "Med ryggen mot Europa? Endring og kontinuitet i norsk sikkerhetspolitikk," in Dag Harald Claes and Bent Sofus Tranøy, eds., *Utenfor, annerledes og suveren? Norge under EØS-avtalen* (Oslo: ARENA Fagbokforlaget, 1999), pp. 39–58.

10. Iver B. Neumann and Ståle Ulriksen, "Norsk forsvars—og sikkerhetspolitikk," Torbjørn Knutsen, Gunnar Sørbø, and Svein Gjerdåker, eds., *Norges utenrikspolitikk* (Oslo: Cappelen, 1997).

11. www.infoplease.com (November 2001).

12. "Divided Cyprus. The Danger of Over-Doggedness," *Economist*, July 19, 2001.

13. United Nations, "Resolution 541: Cyprus," November 18, 1983, at http://www.un.org/Docs/scres/1983/scres83.htm.

14. "Denktas Warns of Post-EU Accession Scenarios of Greek Cypriots," *Turkish Daily News*, November 13, 2001.

15. "Turkey Delays EU Defence Plans," *Jane's Intelligence Review*, August 1, 2001.

16. Ziya Önis, "Luxembourg, Helsinki and Beyond, Toward an Interpretation of Recent Turkey–EU Relations," *Government and Opposition* 35 (October 2000), pp. 463–483, 470.

17. "Ataturk's Children," *Economist*, October 27–November 2, 2001.

18. Andrea Smutek-Riemer, "Die Türkei: Wandel und Kontinutität," *Österreichische Militärische Zeitschrift*, cited in Barry Buzan and Thomas Diez, "The European Union and Turkey," *Survival* 41 (Spring 1999), pp. 41–57, 44.

19. Ibid., p. 45.

20. See Iver B. Neumann, *Uses of the Other: "The East" in European Identity Formation* (Minneapolis: University of Minnesota Press, 1999) and Ziya Önis, "Turkey, Europe and Paradoxes of Identity: Perspectives on the International Context of Democratization," *Mediterranean Quarterly*, Vol. 10, No. 3, Summer 1999, pp. 109–136.

21. Neumann, *Uses of the Other*, p. 62.

22. Peter Lawler, "Scandinavian Exceptionalism and European Union," *Journal of Common Market Studies*, Vol. 35, No. 4, December 1997, pp. 565–594.

23. Ole Wæver, "Nordic Nostalgia: Northern Europe After the Cold War," *International Affairs*, Vol. 68, No. 1, 1992, pp. 77–102.

24. Roald Berg, *Norge på egenhånd* (Oslo: Universitetsforlaget, 1997).

25. Beate Huseby and Ola Listhaug, "Identifications of Norwegians with Europe: The Impact of Values and Centre-Periphery Factors," in Ruud de Moor, ed., *Values in Western Societies* (Tilburg: Tilburg University Press, 1995), p. 158.

26. See Inge Lønning, "1905 and 1994—et perspektiv på unionsdebatten," in *Fellesskap og frihet: Tid for idépolitikk* (Oslo: Genesis, 1997), as translated by and quoted in Neumann 2002, p. 123.

27. On the oil issue, see Christine Ingebritsen, "When Do Culture and History Matter? A Response to Neumann and Tiilikainen," in *Cooperation and Conflict*, Vol. 36, 1, 2001, pp. 99–103.

28. The then three non-EU European NATO members, Iceland, Norway and Turkey, were invited to become associate members through Declaration No. 30 attached to the Maastricht Treaty.

29. Sjursen, "Med ryggen mot Europa?"

30. Tamnes, *Norsk Utenrikspolitikks Historie.*

31. WEU Assembly, "The WEU associate members and the new European security architecture," Report submitted on behalf of the Political Committee by Mr. Martínez Casañ, Rapporteur, and Mr Adamczyk, co-Rapporteur, WEU Document A/1690, June 5, 2000.

32. European Council, Cologne, June 1999, Annex III.5.

33. European Council, *Presidency Report on Strengthening the Common European Security and Defense Policy*, Annex I to the Presidency Conclusions, Santa Maria de Feira, June 19 and 20, 2000.

34. European Council, Feira, 2000. Annex I, appendix 1.7-22.

35. European Council, Presidency Conclusion, Nice Summit, December 2000, Annex VI to Annex VI.

36. European Council, Nice Conclusions, 2000.

37. The document is available at www.atlanterhavskomiteen.

38. Charles Grant, "A European view of ESDP," Presentation at CEPS-IISS meeting, Brussels, September 10, 2001, available at www.cer.org.uk.

39. See "TSK reveal that EU's proposal to Turkey on ESDP issue far from satisfies Turkey's rightful expectations," *Turkish Daily News*, June 5, 2001; Michael R. Gordon, "In Accord, Turkey Tentatively Agrees European Union Force may Use NATO Bases," *The New York Times*, June 5, 2001; "Turkish military presents note on European security stand," *Turkish Daily News*, June 4, 2001; *Jane's Intelligence Review.*

40. North Atlantic Council, "Washington Summit Communiqué," Washington D.C., April 24, 1999.

41. Jiří Šedivý, "The Ins and Outs of ESDP: The Question of Participation," *World Defense Systems, RUSI Journal* Vol. 3, Issue 2, July 2001.

42. Nathalie Tocci and Marc Houben, "Accommodating Turkey in ESDP," *CEPS Policy Brief* No. 5, Centre for European Policy Studies, Brussels, May 2001, p. 3.

43. Ismail Cem, "A Necessary Role in Defense," *Financial Times*, May 29, 2001.
44. Šedivý, "The Ins and Outs of ESDP."
45. Antonio Missiroli, "EU–NATO Cooperation in Crisis Management: No Turkish Delight for ESDP," *Security Dialogue* Vol. 33, No.1, 2002, pp. 9–26.
46. Ulf Petter Hellstrøm, "EU omfavner Russland," *Aftenposten*, March 6, 2002.
47. Zecchini Laurent, "Notre ami Vladimir Poutine...," *Le Monde*, October 11, 2001.
48. European Council, Amsterdam Treaty, June 1997. Emphasis added.
49. Jörg Monar, "Justice and Home Affairs in a Wider Europe: The Dynamics of Inclusion and Exclusion," in Proceedings from the ARENA Workshop "Redefining Security? The Role of The European Union in European Security Structures," *ARENA Report* No. 7/2000, Oslo, March 9–10, 2000, pp. 129–147.
50. Monar, "Justice and Home Affairs," p. 136.
51. Alyson Bailes, "Europe and the United States II: Organizing the Cooperation between NATO and WEU/EU," DGAP Summer School, August 20, 1999.
52. Ibid.
53. Alyson J.K. Bailes, "NATO's European Pillar: The European Security and Defense Identity," *Defense Analysis*, Vol. 15, No. 3, 1999, pp. 305–322.
54. Ibid.
55. See Judy Dempsey, "Greece Blocks EU Accord with NATO," *Financial Times*, December 11, 2001.
56. *Turkish Daily News*, June 13, 2001.
57. NRK, April 13, 2000.
58. Luke Hill, "Turkey slows build-up of EU defence," *Jane's Defense Weekly*, May 30, 2001.

CHAPTER 8

NATO Enlargement and European Defense Autonomy

Mark Webber

Introduction

The enlargement of NATO and the development of a European-based military and defense capability have been hailed as among the most significant developments in European security affairs since the early 1990s. Not surprisingly, a great deal has been said and written about these twin processes. The relationship between them, however, has not given rise to anything close to the same degree of interest. This situation notwithstanding, NATO enlargement does have certain consequences for the two organizational forms in which European military and defense autonomy has developed. A link with the ESDI—the "European Pillar" of NATO—has been implicit since at least the mid-1990s. Somewhat more obvious is the link between NATO enlargement and the ESDP developed within the EU. Insofar as the ESDP requires the development of an effective institutional and operational interface between the EU and NATO, the entry of the Czech Republic, Hungary and Poland into the Alliance in March 1999 complicated this already difficult task. The issuing of invitations to other NATO candidates at the Alliance's summit in Prague in November 2002 could complicate it still further.

This chapter explores the various connections between ESDI and ESDP on the one hand, and NATO enlargement on the other. It has r focus on the institutional and security issues raised by the ʒ but not always congruent memberships of the EU and NATO. These memberships have altered and will continue to alter as the twin enlargements of NATO and the EU proceed. There is thus an ebb and flow to the manner in which the relevant issues gain prominence and with which they are dealt.

NATO Enlargement and ESDI: The Missing Link?

Discussion of European defense has a long history, but its most recent phase can be traced to the reinvigoration of European integration inaugurated by the Single European Act of 1986 and the subsequent framing of the 1992 (Maastricht) Treaty on European Union. The latter declared "[a] common foreign and security policy [CFSP] is hereby established" and requested that the WEU "elaborate and implement decisions and actions of the Union which have defense implications."[1] Coincident with the Maastricht negotiations, the WEU issued a declaration in December 1991 that outlined the need to "develop a genuine European security and defense identity" via a strengthening of the WEU itself. This was with a view to creating "a common defense policy within the EU" that would remain "compatible with that of the Atlantic Alliance."[2] Consistent with this position, NATO, in the Rome Declaration of November 1991, welcomed "the further strengthening of the European pillar within the Alliance" and foresaw the development of complementarity and institutional links between the EU's then twelve members, the WEU and the Alliance.[3]

While these developments generated considerable debate, one ingredient largely missing from the discussions was the relationship between ESDI and the possible enlargement of NATO. This was not surprising insofar as consideration of the latter only began in earnest in late 1992. However, once that discussion was underway, very little explicit connection was drawn, and what connection there was tended to be general and imprecise. NATO's Brussels Declaration of January 1994 was significant for its support of ESDI ("as called for in the Maastricht Treaty") and "the strengthening of the European pillar of the Alliance" through the WEU. However, at this juncture no mention was made as to how these matters might impact upon any expansion of NATO's membership.[4] The final communiqué of NATO's NAC in December 1994 outlined what at that point was the most forthright statement in favor of enlargement. It also introduced a catchall formula whereby the opening up of the Alliance to new members was viewed in terms of the development of "a broad European security architecture" (i.e., which encompassed ESDI) and parallel with the enlargement of the EU.[5] NATO's 1995 *Study on Enlargement* outlined this formula in a little more detail. It also specified the desirability of maintaining an overlap of membership between the WEU and an enlarged NATO and even of achieving "[a]n eventual broad congruence of European membership in NATO, the EU and WEU."[6] The specific requirement of adapting NATO command structures to ESDI (by reference to the CJTFs) following enlargement was also noted. That said, both the political and military conditions for accession to NATO made no reference to either ESDI or the CJTF concept.[7] NATO's Berlin Declaration one year later, meanwhile, devoted considerable space to the NATO–WEU relationship and reaffirmed the commitment to enlargement. It spared, however, only a single sentence to an implied link between these twin processes, referring on this occasion to the fact that enlargement was consistent with the "wider process of cooperation and integration already underway in today's Europe involving the EU and the WEU. ..."[8] The 1997 Madrid summit Declaration, further, displayed a similar omission. Having commended the development of ESDI within NATO via *inter alia* the elaboration of the CJTF concept and, equally significant, having extended an invitation of membership to the Czech Republic, Hungary and Poland, there was no attention given to the possible consequences of the latter to the former.[9]

The under-articulation of any explicit official link between NATO enlargement and ESDI should be seen against the following four factors. First, it should be remembered that the debate within NATO on enlargement had proven to be highly charged. The contours of this debate centered around issues of membership (who and when), cost, integration and the massaging of relations with Russia.[10] The debate on the development of ESDI proved equally fraught and required the artful compromise of the CJTF concept in order to permit some conceptual clarity to the effect that ESDI should develop *within* NATO.[11] To have linked these two debates to a third concerning the place of ESDI within an enlarged NATO would have proven politically difficult and was, therefore, avoided.

Second, both NATO enlargement and ESDI were perceived by national governments as problematic in their own right and both harbored numerous imponderables. While those relating to enlargement were confronted head on (if not resolved) at Madrid, the range of technical complexities surrounding ESDI was still at an early stage of elaboration in 1997.[12] To have labored long on the link between the two would have required elaboration of a further set of modalities and thus the introduction of another layer of uncertainty.

Third, the push for NATO enlargement was, in large part, due to the efforts of the Clinton administration after 1994.[13] As one of the NATO member states least interested in ESDI, the United States consequently was not preoccupied with a need to make enlargement contingent upon any Europeanization of the Alliance. The French, who had held to this position, revised it once the Alliance had opted in principle for enlargement. From 1995, Paris sought rather to directly influence the enlargement debate by supporting (unsuccessfully as it turned out) its own favored candidates (Romania and Slovenia).

Fourth, the NATO applicant countries themselves had shown little interest in the ESDI issue even though they were simultaneously seeking membership of the EU, had entered (in May 1994) into "Associate Partner" status with the WEU and had been permitted (as NATO partners) the opportunity to participate in CJTFs. Some did accord an importance to cooperation with the WEU, seeing it as preparation for NATO membership, but the political, organizational and security issues relating to the WEU–ESDI–NATO triangle were hardly considered. This reflected a view that the shaping of the ESDI issue was beyond their influence and, in fact, outside of their immediate concerns. The fact that a commitment to ESDI was not posited as a condition of membership only encouraged such a position. The applicant states, further, were also increasingly of the view by the mid-1990s that the ESDI/WEU lacked credibility given the absence of the United States and the more obvious resolve being demonstrated by NATO proper at this juncture in Bosnia.[14]

Despite this lack of attention, NATO enlargement did nonetheless carry clear implications for ESDI given the manner in which it would impact upon the WEU and CJTFs. With regard to the former, one issue that enjoyed a temporary salience was that of security guarantees. The Maastricht Treaty (via an attached declaration of the WEU) had offered possible WEU membership to states within the EU.[15] On one reading, this declaration was made with an eye to *existing* EU members who were not then in the WEU (Ireland and Denmark) and not with a view to possible *future* EU members who were then outside it. That said, there was a theoretical possibility that new EU members might take the offer of WEU membership literally. Insofar as EU enlargement was at this point seen as moving ahead before that of NATO, a situation could now be foreseen in which new EU members would demand a WEU security guarantee (under Article V of the WEU's Modified Brussels Treaty)

without having obtained NATO membership first.[16] This woul
dict the so-called Cahen principles, according to which WEU
ship would only extend to existing NATO members, and tnus
potentially confront NATO (and the United States specifically) with
"backdoor commitments" to defend European states not yet in the
Alliance.[17] As it turned out, this proved to be something of a nonissue.
Upon entering the EU in 1995, non-NATO Austria, Finland and
Sweden were content—in line with their non-aligned foreign policies—
to accept observer status in the WEU only. After 1995, the issue receded
almost entirely as it became clear that the EU would not enlarge further
before NATO.

A second and related issue concerned the participation of East
European states in WEU activities; that was important given, first, the
WEU's designation as the institutional embodiment of the ESDI and,
second, an assumption that such cooperation offered practical experience of adapting military practice and decision-making procedures to
NATO standards. Involvement in practical operations, however, was
very small scale (reflecting, in part, the WEU's own limited operational
profile) and much less important than comparable activities under
NATO's PfP program. As Associate Partners, the East European states
were also allowed to play a participating role in the WEU's Permanent
Council (something, by contrast, they could not do as PfP states in relation to the NAC) and working groups and to maintain liaison with the
WEU Planning Cell and Military Staff. Importantly, however, they were
not permitted involvement in the WEU's institutional links to NATO.[18]

A third issue concerned the development of CJTFs. The IFOR/SFOR
deployment in post-Dayton Bosnia amounted to a CJTF even though it
was not always referred to as such. The participation of several NATO
applicant countries in this deployment thus meant their involvement in a
trial run of CJTF "as an interface in the evolutionary [development] of
both NATO and the EU/WEU in the framework of ESDI."[19] The CJTF
HQ trial of March 1998 ("Strong Resolve 98"), meanwhile, saw the
participation of eight applicant states.

NATO Enlargement and the Shift from ESDI to ESDP

In March 1999, the Czech Republic, Hungary and Poland acceded
formally to the Alliance and thus participated fully in NATO's
Washington summit the following month. This marked NATO's first
enlargement into formerly communist Eastern Europe. By taking such a
step, the organization was following an example already set by the

Council of Europe and the Organization for Security and Cooperation in Europe, but had acted before a comparable move on the part of the EU.

At Washington it was also affirmed that ESDI would continue to be developed within the Alliance and that this process would "require close cooperation between NATO, the WEU and, if and when appropriate the EU."[20] While this formulation recognized the possibility of a formal EU role, the WEU remained the official institution of choice for collaboration. Indeed, since the Berlin meeting of the NAC in June 1996, considerable energy had been devoted to consultations with the WEU over the modalities of cooperation and particularly the transfer of NATO assets in the event of a military operation in which NATO as a whole (minus the United States, in other words) was not engaged. Thus, the Washington summit communiqué noted that should the EU develop a military competence, any dealings with the Alliance would be built upon "mechanisms existing between NATO and the WEU."[21] Reflecting this position, NATO's three new members became involved in the processes of developing the (still incomplete) CJTF concept and enjoyed an upgrade in their status within the WEU to that of Associate Member (joining the other three non-EU NATO states of Iceland, Norway and Turkey), which afforded them the right to participate in activities of the WEU Planning Cell.

This affirmation of the WEU (and thus an ESDI within NATO) looked increasingly anachronistic, however, in light of the historic shift occurring at this same juncture toward the materialization of ESDP. The genesis of this development is considered elsewhere in this volume, but clearly the impotence of European efforts in Bosnia was crucial. It demonstrated an undesirable European deficiency in the face of an American-led intervention in the shape of NATO's Operation Deliberate Force. It also impressed upon the newly elected Blair government in the United Kingdom the need to shift some of the responsibility for security provision in Europe away from NATO (and thus Washington), thereby answering American criticisms that the United States was carrying too great a burden. This pragmatism also allowed the Blair administration to display its European credentials and was in accord with the long-held French desire to lessen European reliance upon the Americans.[22] It was against this background that the Saint-Malo initiative was launched in December 1998, with its call for a European "capacity for autonomous military action, backed by credible military forces."[23] The assumption at this point was that the WEU had failed to deliver such an instrument. The EU had, therefore, to adopt a more direct role that would build upon but also move beyond both the WEU and CFSP.

The events in Kosovo in the spring of 1999 seemingly confirmed these assumptions. The Europeans made only a paltry contribution to NATO's Operation Allied Force and this engagement once again demonstrated American leadership and superior military force. In June, the Cologne European Council established the institutional structures for the emerging ESDP and also announced the EU's absorption of the WEU pending "necessary decisions [to be taken] by the end of the year 2000."[24] The Helsinki Council that December outlined in greater detail the respective roles of these new institutions and set out "the headline goal" of desired force levels for the ERRF.[25] By this point Javier Solana, the former NATO Secretary-General, had been appointed the first High Representative for CFSP as well as Secretary General of the Council of the EU and WEU Secretary General.

The rhetoric surrounding these developments in the first half of 1999 often strove to match the sense of historic occasion. Statements of Western leaders were replete with presentiments of how the EU and NATO would, consequent upon ESDP and enlargement, be better equipped to meet the challenges of European security.[26] Meeting these aspirations, however, required paying attention to a whole host of troublesome issues. ESDP raised unanswered questions about capabilities and political commitment, while NATO enlargement, even after the first tranche of post-communist states was admitted, only deepened debate concerning NATO's strategic purpose, its relationship with Russia and how to go about any further enlargement rounds. Further, a number of immediate practical issues arose that mirrored matters related to the development of ESDI.

A significant bone of contention in this regard concerned the manner in which non-EU NATO states would be associated with ESDP. Given the obvious fact that the memberships of the EU and NATO were not the same, ESDP implied favorable treatment for those states that were simultaneously members of both organizations and discrimination against those who belonged only to the latter. This was of no small consequence given the likely operational dependence of the EU upon the Alliance,[27] the fact that the discriminated included military heavyweights such as Turkey, and also the fact that this group had enlarged by three with the entry of the Czech Republic, Hungary and Poland into NATO.

What made the issue of some political consequence, moreover, was the fact that it was taken up by the United States. From its very inception, Washington had a range of questions regarding ESDP. These were famously summed up by U.S. Secretary of State Madeleine Albright's reference in December 1998 to the "three Ds," the third of which—"discrimination"[28]—was formulated expressly with an eye to the six non-EU NATO states. One year after Albright's formulation, the third "D" still remained a worry to the United States. Speaking shortly after the Helsinki European Council, the U.S. Permanent Representative to NATO argued that inclusion of "the six" in some form in the ESDP was vital on two grounds. First, to ignore them would lower the chances of the EU obtaining access to NATO assets should these be required in any EU-led operation. The Six, he suggested, would most likely block any decision in the NAC to provide assets for the EU had they been excluded from EU policy making. And second, assuming that assent was given in the NAC, these six states as members of NATO have an Article V commitment under the North Atlantic Treaty to the eleven NATO members of the EU. Should an EU-led operation escalate or go awry this might require them to come to the assistance of their EU allies. Their willingness to do so would clearly be facilitated by some sense of having been involved in the policy making leading up to the operation in question.[29]

While remarks such as these need not be read as indicative of American opposition to the development of ESDP in principle, they did flag a significant political condition for its support. In the twelve months following Helsinki. the U.S. position was premised on the assumption that the European non-EU NATO states should be "players, not spectators" in the framing of EDSP.[30] Whether this reflected a genuine concern for the feelings of the six states concerned or a stalking horse for asserting the right in principle of *all* non-EU NATO states (including, of course, the United States) to have a greater say in ESDP is a moot point.

The importance of the discrimination issue was recognized early by the supporters of ESDP. The Saint-Malo Declaration noted "[t]he reinforcement of European solidarity must take into account the various positions of European states. The different situations of countries in relation to NATO must be respected."[31] The Helsinki European Council, in turn, referred to the desirability of "full consultation, cooperation and transparency between the EU and NATO" and, as a corollary, the need for the establishment of "appropriate arrangements" to allow for the participation of non-EU European NATO members in "EU military crisis management."[32]

As Sunniva Tofte demonstrates in chapter 7 of this volume, a tremendous amount of diplomatic energy was expended between 1999 and 2001 fashioning special arrangements for the Six, but these provisions have proved by no means entirely satisfactory. In this regard, the position of Turkey was most problematic, a state of affairs exacerbated by already strained relations with the EU over Cyprus and Ankara's longstanding and controversial bid for membership of the Union. Reflecting the strength of its feeling, Ankara effectively blocked, during 2000 and much of 2001, agreement within NATO on granting the EU guaranteed access to NATO planning capabilities and a presumption of availability to designated NATO assets and capabilities. A solution to this problem seemed to have been achieved in December 2001 with an agreement (known as "The Istanbul Document") brokered by the United States and the British. This compromise was not, however, the end of the matter, for the deal with Turkey prompted Greece to raise the objection that special arrangements had been made with Ankara.[33] It therefore blocked the deal and thus neither the Laeken European Council nor the ministerial meeting of the NAC (both held in December) were able to report the necessary breakthrough on EU access to NATO assets.

NATO Enlargement and ESDP after the Washington Summit

Enlargement Delayed

Following the formal accessions of 1999, NATO remained publicly committed to further enlargement on a seemingly open-ended basis. The Washington summit communiqué of April 1999, for instance, pledged that the Alliance would "continue to welcome new members" and that the three recently admitted states would by no means be the last.[34] If statements by the NATO Secretary General Lord Robertson were an accurate guide, even the strains of the Kosovo War did not seemingly lead to any revision of this position.[35]

At this point ongoing enlargement was a policy driven by a clear logic. In the first place, it was consistent with NATO's refashioned post–Cold War purpose—what the 1999 Alliance "Strategic Concept" referred to as the promotion of "a stable Euro-Atlantic security environment."[36] As NATO's interventions in Bosnia and Kosovo had demonstrated, there are ways other than an extension of Alliance membership by which stability (as NATO views it) can be promoted. However, enlargement was deemed to be important insofar as the commitments of membership encouraged both new and aspirant members to resolve potentially destabilizing territorial and ethnic-based conflicts as well as subjecting their militaries to democratic control.[37] Enlargement, moreover, was presented as demand led. Following the entry of the three East

Europeans in 1999, nine other former communist countries were formally committed to membership. In these circumstances, enlargement had to be seen as an ongoing process; to send out a signal that no new members were welcome would not only have institutionalized a new division in Europe and promoted a renationalization of defense policies, but would, in addition, have corroded NATO's credibility and undermined the PfP program (given that many aspirant states perceived it as a preparation for entry into the Alliance).[38]

Yet these advantages notwithstanding, ongoing NATO enlargement could not be regarded as a foregone conclusion. During 1999–2000 there was a strong case that the enlargement of 1999 was on its own costly enough—politically because it damaged relations with Russia and opened up disagreements within the Alliance, and militarily because it risked diluting NATO's military effectiveness and cohesion. Other considerations also applied. During 1999–2000, NATO was increasingly preoccupied with issues of greater priority, not least transatlantic discussions over National Missile Defense and the stabilization of the Balkans. Further, and Lord Robertson's judgment notwithstanding, NATO's campaign in Kosovo did hold implications for enlargement. The military deficiencies displayed there added to the case for improvements in capabilities among European NATO states. This, in effect, heightened the threshold of military competence that aspirant states needed to display in order to enter NATO while simultaneously lessening the enthusiasm with which existing members were prepared to greet the task of integrating them.[39]

On the basis of such considerations, the constituency in NATO in favor of enlargement appeared to have lost steam. The Clinton administration had championed the cause up to 1999, but tellingly neither of the two main contenders for the American presidency had expressed any real enthusiasm to take up the enlargement cause if elected in November 2000. Opinion in the U.S. Senate continued to be skeptical.[40] Exactly why the mood had dampened in the United States could be explained, in part, by the fact that political ambition on the scope of enlargement had (at least under Clinton) never realistically extended beyond the Czech Republic, Hungary and Poland. As for governments in Europe, the French, Germans and British were not pressing the case at this point and those in Greece and Turkey were even more skeptical.[41] The most vocal proponents of further enlargement were, in fact, the new members, Poland in particular.[42] Their view was, however, insufficient to detract from an unspoken near consensus among Alliance member states that the organization should pause, perhaps for a prolonged period, following the accessions of March 1999.[43]

A consolidation of this sort was, in fact, a not-so-hidden theme of official NATO documentation. Notwithstanding the "open door" rhetoric, high-level NATO communiqués and speeches were replete with all manner of qualifying conditions that added up to a pragmatic barrier against enlargement. The 1999 Strategic Concept, for instance, made it clear that enlargement was to be welcomed only if it "serve[d] the overall political and strategic interests of the Alliance, strengthen[ed] its effectiveness and cohesion, and enhance[ed] overall European security and stability"[44]—a phrase elastic enough to include almost any eventuality as a cause for delay.

This seeming becalming of NATO enlargement had a particular significance in light of developments within the EU. At the Helsinki European Council the EU suggested that it would "be in a position to welcome new Member States from the end of 2002."[45] In February 2000, Bulgaria, Latvia, Lithuania, Malta, Romania and Slovakia entered into bilateral negotiations with the EU on membership, thereby joining Cyprus, the Czech Republic, Estonia, Hungary, Poland and Slovenia, which had already opened talks with Brussels. During 2000 it looked likely, therefore, that an enlargement of the EU would occur before any further enlargement of NATO. This had both benefits and drawbacks for the EU–NATO relationship. On the positive side, the Czech Republic, Hungary and Poland were among the most likely next entrants to the EU, and their entry would eliminate at a stroke the issue of discrimination among three of the non-EU NATO Europeans.

An enlargement of the EU before that of NATO would thus have led to a reduction in the number of non-EU NATO states. By the same token, however, it would also have resulted in an expansion of another important group, that of non-NATO EU states. In light of doubts over NATO enlargement at this point, a situation could thus be envisaged in which a number of NATO aspirants (in particular Slovenia and the Baltic states) achieved membership of the EU well before that of the Alliance. In some respects, their position would then become akin to the already existing non-NATO EU states of Austria, Finland, Ireland and Sweden (the so-called "post-neutrals") with the important exception that these states (the Baltic states of Estonia, Latvia and Lithuania in particular) resided in a troubled security environment and were thus very conscious of maximizing access to forms of security protection. The obvious place to look for these was, of course, in NATO, but in the absence of the defense guarantee provided by Alliance membership, non-members had to rely on other less formal assurances.

Indeed, during the 1990s, NATO itself had had to face this issue and had, in fact, developed a number of methods by which non-members could receive security reassurance. Thus, Article 8 of the PfP Framework Document signed by all partner countries provided for consultation with NATO in the event of a direct threat.[46] A similar provision was also contained in NATO's South East Europe Initiative announced at the Washington summit. This had a very specific context, namely the threat of Serbian aggression against states hosting NATO forces during Operation Allied Force.[47]

Precedents such as these were welcomed, but for the Baltic states in particular were no substitute for full NATO membership. Entry into the Alliance, however, appeared unlikely at this point, not simply because of the pause in enlargement noted earlier, but because Baltic membership was especially sensitive owing to the fierce objections of Russia. And as relations with Moscow were being repaired after the Kosovo War, the leading NATO states were not prepared to risk opening up a new fracture by pressing the Baltic case.

At a time then when NATO membership appeared unlikely, but that of the EU a closer possibility, some consideration was given to how new EU entrants (and the Baltic states in particular) might be afforded security assurances within the Union. Indeed, the development of ESDP opened up the possibility that any and all non-NATO members of the EU, both present and future, might be afforded some sort of security guarantee. There was no assumption that this would be formal, comparable that is to an Article V guarantee within NATO. This was because ESDP was quite clearly geared to the Petersberg Tasks of crisis management and not with the territorial defense of EU members. Further, the non-NATO states within the EU did not enjoy full WEU membership and thus had no recourse to the collective defense provisions of Article V of the Modified Brussels Treaty (the WEU's equivalent to Article V of NATO's North Atlantic Treaty). There was no assumption, moreover, that the formal transfer of the WEU to the EU consequent upon the development of ESDP (and slated for the end of 2000) would lead to an incorporation of this Article into EU Treaties.[48]

Yet the absence of a formal guarantee did not preclude the suggestion that a less formal guarantee could follow simply by dint of obtaining EU membership. In the suggestive language of the Commission President Romani Prodi, "any attack or aggression against an EU member nation would be an attack or aggression against the whole EU."[49] Given that such a statement was made at a time when the prospect of an EU defense force was still out of the question, any commitment that would be forthcoming in response to such an attack would hold clear implications for NATO. As the British Defense Minister Geoffrey Hoon explained in February 2000: "I cannot imagine that NATO would stand idly by if there was an attack on a non-NATO EU member and simply say 'We are not . . . going to respond to this aggression to a country that was in the Western European sphere of influence.' "[50] This statement's allusion to a NATO response raised the issue of American participation and at least implied that the United States would come to the defense of an EU member, even though Washington had had no say in the entry of that state into the EU. As such, this would constitute a continuation of "backdoor commitments" even after the disappearance of the WEU. How far the United States would be willing to match up to this so far untested commitment was, however, a moot point.

These observations were of some significance as long as Russian–Baltic tensions were high and Estonia, Latvia and Lithuania resided outside of NATO. As we shall see below, by 2001–2002 both these conditions had changed. However, the premise that underlies them remains valid so long as the EU counts among its member states that do not belong to NATO.

Whatever the institutional trajectory of the Baltic states, it remains the case that the EU will continue to retain states falling into this category. Among the EU member states current at the time of writing, this includes the four "post-neutrals." In their case, some discussion has occurred over the possibility of NATO membership in elite circles, but entry into the Alliance does not enjoy the necessary political and public support to make it a credible plank of foreign policy. Among the EU candidate countries, meanwhile, Turkey is already a NATO member and the majority of the remainder are as likely to join NATO before or near simultaneous with the EU. The exceptions here are Cyprus and Malta, which are not NATO applicants.

Thus, by 2004–2005 a situation could be envisaged in which an enlarged EU contains six or more states who are outside of the Alliance. This is of more than theoretical interest in defense terms. A variety of scenarios could be envisaged. First, after the events of September 11 one could conceive of a situation where a major European city is subject to a catastrophic terrorist attack comparable in scale to the attacks on the Twin Towers in New York and the Pentagon in Washington. Should this occur, the question would be posed as to whether the invocation of Article V by NATO after September 11 to assist the defense of the U.S. sets a precedent for a similar action in Europe. In the case of summoning assistance for a European NATO state the case could be made that it clearly does. In the case of a non-NATO EU state, however, the issue is less clear-cut, and the issues posed by Prodi and Hoon noted earlier become relevant. Imagine, for instance, that Vienna fell victim to a large-scale attack; in such a situation, the question of an EU and hence a possible "backdoor" NATO response would be urgently posed.

Exactly what form this might take is an open question, but what is clear is that after September 11, ESDP has made no significant adjustments toward engaging in the "war against terrorism." Some in the EU did argue in the wake of the September 11 attacks that the Union should pay more attention to the protection of its own territory, rather than to an ESDP geared to conflict management outside its borders.[51] However, this was not the agreed or even the dominant position. In the words of Solana, ESDP and the ERRF remained earmarked for "peacekeeping and peacemaking" and not for military contributions toward "the fight against terrorism."[52] Hence, after September 11 there was no adjustment to the HG or the Petersberg Tasks. The EU does possess instruments for preventative measures against terrorism (through Justice and Home Affairs activities in the "Third Pillar") but the EU has not developed the means to take retaliatory military action. In this light, the type of attack noted above would require either some swift adjustments in the received wisdom on ESDP or a path-breaking step by NATO to assist militarily a nonmember within the EU.

A second scenario worth contemplating concerns Cyprus. Should this state join the EU in the face of Turkish objections and then become subject to destabilization from the unrecognized Turkish north of the divided island, the EU would be in truly uncharted waters. It would be faced with a situation in which an EU member state is confronted with the threat (or even the actuality) of territorial aggression and against which EU military instruments (the ERRF) had not been principally conceived to cope.

Enlargement Advanced

The previous section suggested that the prospect of an EU enlargement before any further enlargement of NATO seemed a real possibility in the period 1999–2000. After 2000, however, the situation was reversed. The likelihood of NATO extending further invitations of membership increased and with it the possibility that the Alliance would enlarge once more before the EU.

The reason for this change was not linked to any recognition that the "digestion" of potential new members had become any easier. Indeed, the task of militarily incorporating the 1999 entrants into the Alliance had proven far from easy.[53] What seems to have been crucial was a forthright advocacy of enlargement by the new Bush administration in Washington. Speaking in Warsaw in June 2001, the American president suggested "[a]ll of Europe's new democracies, from the Baltic to the Black Sea and all that lie between" should have the "same chance to join the institutions of Europe as Europe's old democracies." Thus, he implied, the approach toward enlargement at NATO's Prague summit would be ambitious rather than cautious and, moreover, would not be subject to "the agendas of others" (i.e., not hostage to Russian objections).[54]

At this juncture, the reasons for U.S. advocacy were in part the consequence of domestic political factors. Congressional opinion, while not unambiguously in favor of enlargement, began to articulate the case with increasing clarity during 2001.[55] So too did influential conservative commentators such as former Secretaries of State Henry Kissinger and Zbigniew Brzezinski.[56] Both these constituencies, moreover, were increasingly subject to the well-organized influence of pro-enlargement lobby groups, particularly those representing the case of the Baltic states. Transatlantic politics also had an impact. Enlargement was taken up as a cause by the Bush administration because it provided an opportunity for leadership within the Alliance, particularly at a time when none of the key European states were acting on the issue. Given also that EU enlargement was trundling on at its normal slow pace, the calculation in Washington appeared to be that NATO enlargement was the more expeditious means of promoting European stability. The fact that this could be done through an organization with entrenched American leadership was also no doubt attractive.[57] More direct calculations relating to ESDP were also important. By promoting NATO enlargement the United States was, in effect, promoting the centrality of the Alliance in European security and drawing the attentions of the European allies back to NATO proper (these states having spent two years of intense labor institutionalizing ESDP and the ESDP–NATO relationship).

American enthusiasm for a broad enlargement of NATO was boosted still further by the events following September 11. One unexpected effect in this regard was a sharp move by President Putin of Russia in favor of a strategic alignment with the West. This move was based upon deeper foundations than simply a pragmatic alliance against the Taliban. Economic dependence upon the United States and Western Europe, the problematic viability of a Eurasian foreign policy orientation and a simple recognition of the advantages of siding with the world's dominant power all played their part.[58] Part of this shift was a tacit acceptance of the next phase of NATO enlargement, even if this involved the Baltic states.[59]

As well as considerations regarding Russia, calculations pertaining more directly to NATO itself were important. The American military response to September 11 was conducted through national rather than NATO structures. However, the significance of the Alliance as a vehicle for American political and security interests was not in itself diminished by this. NATO provided political cover for the operation (through expressions of solidarity and the first ever invocation of Article V of the North Atlantic Treaty) and offered a "toolbox" of NATO and allied assets that the United States could select from in order to facilitate American operations.[60] The ability of American allies to conduct joint operations alongside the United States and subsequently to work together within the international peacekeeping force in Afghanistan was facilitated by decades of joint exercises within NATO, efforts within the Alliance to standardize equipment and procedures and peacekeeping experience built up in Bosnia and Kosovo. An enlarged Alliance, the argument ran, promoted still further American access to NATO and allied assets and experience along this model, as well as offering an extended coalition of political support.[61] Indeed, the assistance rendered to the United States in its operations in Afghanistan by NATO aspirants such as Bulgaria and Romania (continuing a pattern these states set in aiding NATO during Operation Allied Force in 1999) brought them more firmly into the frame as serious candidates than had been the case prior to September 11.

Statements on the part of the United States and its NATO allies continued to refer during 2001–2002 to the necessity of proper military and political readiness prior to membership. However, the sense of political and strategic expediency provided by September 11 implied a lowering of these thresholds and meant that by the spring of 2002, at least five and possibly seven countries were being given serious consideration. Further, while U.S. support of these candidates was crucial, at this juncture other important NATO states (France, Germany, Turkey and the United Kingdom) were issuing clearer statements on the enlargement issue. This was done both with an eye to the American position and out of a recognition that advocacy of candidates began to matter as the Prague summit approached.[62]

At the Prague summit this meant that invitations could be extended to the three Baltic states (Estonia, Latvia and Lithuania) as well as Slovenia, Slovakia, Bulgaria and Romania. On the basis of a comparable timetable to the previous enlargement, these states could hope to be admitted during late 2004–early 2005, thereby bringing the Alliance up to a total of some twenty-six members.

A development of this sort would raise the possibility of a sharp increase in the number of non-EU NATO European states and with it a revival of the "discrimination" issue within ESDP. The severity of this issue would depend on how long the new NATO states in question had to wait before a subsequent accession to the EU. Certainly in the cases of the Baltic states, Slovenia and possibly the Slovak Republic the expectation is that membership of the EU would occur by the time of the European parliamentary elections in 2004.[63] Accession to both the EU and NATO would consequently be almost simultaneous and the discrimination issue either nonexistent or short-lived.

The more problematic cases are Bulgaria and Romania, given that their prospects for entry into the EU are much more distant. The problem of discrimination could, therefore, linger that much longer. The experience of the Czech Republic, Hungary and Poland would seem to suggest that there is a political limit to the issue, however. Like these three states, Bulgaria and Romania would have an incentive not to make too much of the matter for the sake of smoothing their entry into the EU. That said, should EU accession negotiations proceed slowly, Sofia and Bucharest would have the example of Turkey on which to fall, using their newfound positions in the Alliance to complicate EU–NATO relations for the sake of winning concessions over ESDP or indeed over EU membership. Further, Turkey itself may wish to make alliances of convenience with these two states within NATO and thus an anti-ESDP caucus within the Alliance could take shape.

In light of such difficulties, the case has been made in favor of parallel enlargements of the EU and NATO. This argument is not new (see earlier). It did, however, fall away after 1996, something that reflected a growing American disillusionment with the slow pace of EU enlargement into post-communist Europe. Significantly, while EU–NATO dialogue has developed since 1999 consequent upon the development of ESDP, this has not extended to any formal discussions on the respective enlargements of the two institutions. The enlargements of NATO and the EU have, in other words, developed in a largely discrete fashion. The former has been driven by the United States and has been influenced by geostrategic and geopolitical considerations. The latter has not involved the United States, and the geopolitical vision that underlies it has been blurred by technical, largely economic, criteria of admission.[64]

A number of advantages have been claimed for parallel enlargements. As James Sperling has pointed out, membership of the EU and NATO generates, in each case, "positive externalities" that are beneficial to both organizations. The economic, financial and political integration provided by the EU helps promote regional stability and is thus a security gain to NATO. The sense of external security provided by NATO membership, meanwhile, enables governments to concentrate their political energies on issues of economic reform and trade and is thus a net gain for the EU.[65] More specifically, positive effects could also be generated with reference to ESDP. Parallel enlargements would minimize the problem of discrimination and would reduce the ambiguities surrounding security assurance to non-NATO EU members. As already noted, a parallelism of sorts is likely to occur by 2005–2006.

That said, the chances of synchronized enlargement after 2005–2006 are slim, owing to the obvious absence of the United States in the EU and thus of a hegemonic power that straddles both that organization and NATO. There is, therefore, plenty of scope for the two enlargements to remain "disconnected"[66] and for continued divergences in organizational memberships. This may be tempered by some movement across organizations (involving, hypothetically, the entry of Austria, Finland and Sweden into NATO) but there are other possibilities that would overshadow any institutional benefits that this might bring. Albania and Macedonia, for instance, have applications to NATO pending (and one from Croatia is a distinct possibility), which, following Bulgarian and Romanian entry would look credible. These might then be the subjects of an accession invitation at a NATO summit in 2004. The chances of any of these states joining the EU, however, are remote and not under consideration at present. Looking still further ahead, it is realistic to conceive of Russia and Ukraine in NATO as part of a grand strategic bargain between the Alliance and Moscow. This may be a long way off and subject to all manner of changes in Alliance operations, strategic thinking and decision-making practices. It is, however, a more likely prospect than these states joining the EU so long as the Union retains its strict accession criteria.[67] A situation could thus be envisaged by say 2015 in which a powerful quartet comprising Turkey, the United States, Russia and Ukraine is situated in NATO but outside the EU, with all the consequent problems that this would bring for ensuring a smooth institutional and operational interface between ESDP and the Alliance.

Conclusion

The enlargement of NATO's membership has been part of Alliance history. The Prague summit in November 2002 will see a continuation, indeed acceleration of this process, and enlargement will be a central Alliance preoccupation for years to come. The scale of recent and upcoming enlargements is path breaking. These have, moreover, occurred within a shifting strategic context characterized first by the end of the Cold War and second by the end of the "post–Cold War order" heralded by the terrorist attacks of September 2001. The upshot has been a NATO that has had to confront the question of purpose and rationale and which has had to make significant adjustments in practice and operation.[68]

One issue, however, which has received relatively little attention relates to the institutions and procedures of NATO decision making. In this regard, some have claimed that an enlarged NATO need not be a more complicated one politically. The difficulties of decision making do not increase relative to the number of states that an organization contains. In terms of adding to decision-making complexity, there is thus little difference between admitting say three, five or even seven states to an organization that already has nineteen members.[69] American leadership of the Alliance, moreover, and the fact that most of the new entrants can be expected to defer to the United States, moderates the problems of decision making still further.[70] However, no less a figure than the NATO Secretary-General Lord Robertson has noted the need to attend to a possible reform of decision-making structures in an enlarging Alliance.[71] Others within the organization have expressed somewhat stronger views, fearing that already cumbersome practices will become politically more problematic.[72]

The political configurations within the Alliance are made that much more difficult to manage because of the complicating factor of ESDP. As Stuart Croft has argued, there are four categories of state in NATO: the United States, EU members pursuing an ESDP that might or might not be compatible with NATO, new members who are outside the EU awaiting entry, and states capable of "causing great procedural complication" such as France and Turkey.[73] The problems of NATO decision making are compounded, when it comes to ESDP, by the complexity of decision-making structures within the EU. Knitting together NATO and the EU in service of ESDP has thus required considerable political effort and institutional crafting, and has not avoided controversy.

How far the NATO–EU/ESDP institutional interface matters ultimately depends upon whether the ESDP obtains real material substance. Although declared "operational" at the Laeken European Council in December 2001, doubts on the military capabilities that underpin ESDP have been voiced both before and since. In this connection, it has been suggested that ESDP will remain dependent upon NATO for all but the "lowest end operations" envisaged in the Petersberg Tasks.[74] Strategic thinking after September 11, however, has given some credence to the notion of a more autonomous and robust ESDP. This is because of debates over EU territorial defense and because the case has been strengthened for a U.S. disengagement in the Balkans in favor of global contingencies—something that will require a "further devolution of Balkan responsibilities from the United States to the European powers."[75]

Yet ESDP may falter. It is only one of four projects aimed at the generation of order in Europe, the others being EU enlargement, Economic and Monetary Union (EMU) and the reform of EU institutions. The EU, in other words, has an ambitious agenda. It is mutually reinforcing in the sense that it is increasingly led by a vision of European stabilization, but its various parts do not always sit comfortably together. EMU, for instance, places limits on European defense spending that inhibit the development of capabilities both within NATO and for ESDP.[76] ESDP may also be simply incapable of breaking free from the military and security primacy of NATO and thus it may be another chapter in the frustrating story of European defense autonomy that stretches back as far as the aborted European Defense Community of the 1950s.

NATO enlargement is part of this story. It has the potential to contribute to NATO's continuing relevance and its ongoing transformation, and to sustain American engagement in Europe. A NATO of this sort will be one that will conduct military operations such that ESDP does not need to. Should enlargement, however, dilute the Alliance's political and military effectiveness then it may well render the EU–NATO interface increasingly unworkable and access to NATO assets much more problematic. In a crisis situation this could well present the Europeans with a stark choice: to act alone or not to act at all.

Notes

1. Title V, Articles J and J.4.2. Reprinted in C. Hill and K.E. Smith, eds., *European Foreign Policy. Key Documents* (London and New York: Routledge, 2000), pp. 153–155.
2. "The Role of the Western European Union and Its Relations with the European Union and the Atlantic Alliance" reprinted in Hill and Smith, *European Foreign Policy*, pp. 202–205.
3. "Rome Declaration on Peace and Cooperation" issued by the North Atlantic Council, November 8, 1991, paragraph 6.

4. "Declaration of the Heads of State and Government" issued by the North Atlantic Council, January 11, 1994, paragraph 4.
5. Final communiqué issued at the ministerial meeting of the North Atlantic Council, Brussels, December 1, 1994, paragraph 5.
6. *Study on NATO Enlargement* (Brussels: NATO, 1995), paragraph 20.
7. Ibid., paragraphs 69–78.
8. Final communiqué issued at the ministerial meeting of the NAC, Berlin, June 3, 1996, paragraph 13, reprinted in *NATO Review* 44 (1996), p. 33.
9. "Madrid Declaration on Euro-Atlantic Security and Cooperation," reprinted in *NATO Review* 45 (1997).
10. S. Croft, J. Redmond, G. Wyn Rees and M. Webber, *The Enlargement of Europe* (Manchester and New York: Manchester University Press, 1999), pp. 27–46.
11. See S. Duke, "NATO and the CFSP: Help or Hindrance?" NATO Fellowship Report, 1995–1997 cycle, pp. 24–28.
12. J. Solana, "Preparing for the Madrid Summit," *NATO Review* 45 (1997), p. 6.
13. See J.M. Goldgeier, *Not Whether but When: The U.S. Decision to Enlarge NATO* (Washington D.C.: Brookings Institution Press, 1999).
14. Croft et al., *The Enlargement of Europe*, pp. 103–104.
15. Hill and Smith, *European Foreign Policy*, p. 205.
16. Such a situation would also have arisen had Ireland taken the unlikely step of seeking full WEU membership.
17. T. Taylor, "West European Security and Defense Cooperation: Maastricht and Beyond," *International Affairs* 70 (1994), p. 3; R.D. Asmus, R.L. Kugler and F.S. Larrabee, "NATO Expansion: The Next Steps," *Survival* 37 (1995), pp. 11–12.
18. M. Casan (rapporteur), "Security of the Associate Partners after the NATO Summit," Assembly of the Western EU, Document 1649, May 19, 1999, paragraph 10.
19. R. Estrella (general rapporteur), "CJTF and the Reform of NATO," NATO Parliamentary Assembly (International Secretariat) Committee Report, AN230DSC(96), October 24, 1996, paragraphs 15–18.
20. "The Alliance's Strategic Concept," paragraph 30, *NATO Review* 47 (1999), p. D9.
21. "Washington summit communiqué," *NATO Review* 47 (1999), p. D4.
22. J. Howorth, *European Integration and Defense: the Ultimate Challenge?* (Paris: Institute for Security Studies, 2000), Chaillot Paper 43, pp. 22–30.
23. The document is reprinted in Hill and Smith, *European Foreign Policy*, pp. 243–244.
24. "Declaration of the European Council on Strengthening the Common European Policy on Security and Defense" and "Presidency Report on Strengthening of the Common European Policy on Security and Defense," reprinted in M. Rutten, *From St-Malo to Nice; European Defense: Core*

Documents (Paris: Institute for Security Studies, 2001), Chaillot Paper 47, pp. 41–45.

25. "Presidency Report on Strengthening the Common European Policy on Security and Defense," reprinted in Rutten, *From St-Malo to Nice*, pp. 83–91.

26. See Deputy Secretary of State Strobe Talbott, Address to the German Society for Foreign Policy, Bonn, February 4, 1999, at http://www. state.gov; and Prime Minister Tony Blair, Speech to the Lord Mayor's Banquet, November 22, 1999, cited in A. Dorman, "Reconciling Britain to Europe in the Next Millennium: The Evolution of British Defense Policy in the Post-Cold War Era," *Defense Analysis* 17 (2001), p. 195.

27. See "Presidency Report on Strengthening the Common European Policy on Security and Defense," Presidency Conclusions, Cologne European Council, June 3–4, 1999, reprinted in M. Rutten, *From St-Malo to Nice*, pp. 42–45.

28. See M. Albright, "The Right Balance will Secure NATO's Future," *Financial Times*, December 7, 1998.

29. Ambassador A. Vershbow, "Next Steps on European Security and Defense: A US View," Berlin, December 17, 1999 at http://www.nato.int.

30. Speech of Secretary of Defense William S. Cohen, Willard Hotel, Washington, June 28, 2000, at http://www.defenselink.mil.

31. Reprinted in Hill and Smith, *European Foreign Policy*, pp. 243–244.

32. "Presidency Report on Strengthening the Common European Policy on Security and Defense," Presidency Conclusions, Helsinki European Council, December 10–11, 1999, in Rutten, *From St. Malo to Nice*, pp. 84, 88.

33. "FM Objects to US–British Proposals on Turkey–ESDP Relations," press release, Embassy of Greece, Press Office (Washington D.C.), December 11, 2001.

34. "Washington Summit Communiqué," April 24, 1999, paragraph 7 in *NATO Review* 47 (1999), p. D3.

35. Speech to the SACLANT Symposium, Reykjavik, Iceland (September 6, 2000), at http://www.nato.int.

36. "The Alliance's Strategic Concept," paragraph 10, *NATO Review* 47 (1999), p. D8.

37. NATO Secretary General Lord Robertson, "NATO in the 21st Century," Millennium Year Lord Mayor's Lecture, London, July 20, 2000.

38. Senator W.V. Roth, Jr., "NATO in the 21st Century," Special publication, NATO Parliamentary Assembly, October 2, 1999, paragraph 82.

39. B. Koenders (rapporteur), "NATO Enlargement" Draft Interim Report, Political Sub-Committee on Central and Eastern Europe, NATO Parliamentary Assembly, April 19, 2001, paragraph 8.

40. See C. Lockwood and T. Butcher, "NATO Plans for Eastward Enlargement Put on Hold," *The Daily Telegraph*, April 3, 2000.

41. For the French and German positions see Smith and Aldred, pp. 15–19; for the British see Foreign Secretary Robin Cook, evidence before the Foreign

Affairs Committee of the House of Commons, December 8, 1999, paragraph 327, at http://www.parliament.the-stationary-office.co.uk.

42. See Polish Foreign Minister Bronislaw Geremek as cited in Drozdiak.

43. Interviews, NATO HQ, Brussels, November 1999.

44. "The Alliance's Strategic Concept," paragraph 39, *NATO Review* 47 (1999), p. D10.

45. "Preparing for Enlargement" in "Presidency Conclusions, Helsinki European Council December 10–11, 1999," at http://ue.eu.int.

46. http://www.nato.int/docu/comm/49-95/c940110b.htm [July 12, 1999].

47. Emphasis added; "Chairman's Summary, Meeting of the NAC at the Level of Heads of Government with Countries in the Region of the Federal Republic of Yugoslavia" (April 25, 1999) in *The Reader's Guide to the NATO Summit in Washington, 23–25 April 1999* (Brussels: NATO Office of Information and Press, 1999), pp. 31–32.

48. J. Roper, "Two Cheers for Mr. Blair? The Political Realities of European Defense Cooperation," *Journal of Common Market Studies* 38 (2000), p. 21.

49. Prodi's statement cited in B. Koenders (rapportuer), "NATO Enlargement," Draft Report of the Political Sub-Committee on Central and Eastern Europe, NATO Parliamentary Assembly, August 23, 2001, paragraph 129, at http://www.naaa.be/publications.

50. House of Commons Select Committee on Defense, Eighth Report, "European Security and Defense" (London: the Stationary Office, 2000), p. 23.

51. French Prime Minister Lionel Jospin cited in Mr. Marshall (rapporteur), "Europe's Security and Defense Policy Confronted with International Terrorism—Reply to the Annual Report of the Council," Assembly of the Western EU, Document A/1764, December 3, 2001, p. 8.

52. Ibid.

53. "NATO's Newer Members Battle to Upgrade Their Military Punch," *Financial Times*, July 10, 2001.

54. F. Bruni, "President Urges Expansion of NATO to Russia's Border," *New York Times*, June 16, 2001.

55. The House of Representatives passed a resolution in November 2001, by 372 votes to 46 endorsing continued NATO enlargement. Opinion on the Senate Foreign Relations Committee was generally pro-enlargement in 2000–2001, but greater caution was in evidence on the Senate Armed Services Committee. See R. Wolffe, "Republicans Hit Out at NATO Expansion," *Financial Times*, February 28, 2001.

56. H. Kissinger, "What to Do with the New Russia," *Washington Post*, August 14, 2001; Z. Brzezinski, "NATO and EU Need to Grow Together," *International Herald Tribune*, May 17, 2001.

57. J. Demsey, " 'No Vetoes' on Bigger NATO," *Financial Times*, June 14, 2001.

58. A. Lieven, "The Secret Policeman's Ball: The United States, Russia and the International Order after 11 September," *International Affairs* 78 (2002), pp. 253–254.

59. M. Evans, "Baltic States 'are US Favorites' in Race to Join NATO," *The Times*, February 25, 2002.

60. For detail see P.H. Gordon, "NATO after 11 September," *Survival* 43 (2001–2002), p. 93.

61. J. Fitchett, "NATO Sees a 'Big Bang' Enlargement to the East," *International Herald Tribune*, February 26, 2002; T. Valasek, " 'Coalitions of the Willing' Ease Way for NATO Enlargement," *Defense Monitor* 6 (April 11), 2002.

62. T. Kuzio, "Western Support for Baltic Membership in NATO Increases," Radio Free Liberty/Radio Free Europe, *Newsline*, October 19, 2001.

63. "Presidency Conclusions, European Council, Laeken, December 14–15 2001," paragraph 8.

64. Croft et al., p. 59.

65. J. Sperling, "Enlarging the EU and NATO," in J. Sperling, ed., *Two Tiers or Two Speeds? The European Security Order and the Enlargement of the EU and NATO* (Manchester and New York: Manchester University Press, 1999), p. 3.

66. This phrase is taken from M. Rühle and N. Williams, "NATO Enlargement and the EU," *The World Today* 51 (1995).

67. O. Alexandrova, "Ukraine and Western Europe," in L.A. Hajda, ed., *Ukraine in the World* (Cambridge, Mass.: Harvard University Press, 1998), pp. 158–165.

68. A. Forster and W. Wallace, "What is NATO For?" *Survival* 43 (2001–2002), pp. 107–122.

69. Interviews, NATO HQ, Brussels, October 2001.

70. S.R. Schwenninger, "Bush's Globalized NATO," *The Nation*, December 24, 2001.

71. "NATO: Enlarging and Redefining Itself," speech at Chatham House, London, February 18, 2002.

72. See un-named NATO ambassadors cited in J. Kitfield, "NATO Metamorphosis," *National Journal*, February 9, 2002.

73. S. Croft, "Guaranteeing Europe's Security? Enlarging NATO Again," *International Affairs* 78 (2002), p. 109.

74. J. Woodbridge, "The Laeken Summit and ESDP: Much Ado about Nothing," *European Security Review*, No. 10, January 2002, p. 3.

75. Dessu and Whyte, p. 127.

76. M.J. Brenner, "Europe's New Security Vocation," *McNair Paper 66* (Washington, D.C.: Institute for National Strategic Studies, National Defense University, January 2002), pp. 8, 37, 57, 73–74.

CHAPTER 9

Dilemmas of NATO Enlargement

Julian Lindley-French

At NATO's Madrid Summit in July 1997, the Czech Republic, Hungary and Poland were invited to join the Alliance. The Alliance also committed itself to "extend further invitations in coming years to nations willing and able to assume the responsibilities and obligations of membership."[1] So far, so good. However, enlargement is, in many ways, an affliction, not just for the Alliance but also for the EU. Indeed, the two enlargements are intrinsically linked because the stabilization of the European security space is as much (if not more) about economic security, as military. Although they are linked they are not politically compatible, and because of the political complications they entail and the pressures they create enlargement undoubtedly destabilizes transatlantic relations at a time when the emphasis is on the search for a new political bargain between traditional members. This search is lent some urgency by the election of a new administration seemingly less predisposed toward Europe and the allies, and yet for whom enlargement, of both the EU and NATO, remains a sine qua non of the wider relationship.

There is, therefore, a certain degree of political incoherence between the allies as, on the one hand, NATO attempts to become a more political organization while, on the other, the EU endeavors to become more military. This takes place against the backdrop of Kosovo that demonstrated that NATO must be able to *act* in pursuit of security as well as *exist* in the interests of security. Deterrence must be backed up by credible conventional capability. Enlargement tests that balance because it redefines the political mission, complicates decision making, creates a diffuse security role for the Alliance, reduces the qualitative level of military-operational effectiveness and costs a lot of money—money that no one seems willing to spend.

Consequently, the internal and external pressures upon NATO as an organization are profound and becoming steadily more so as Europe and America drift into a dysfunctional strategic relationship in which there is little or no consensus over the risks and threats that must be confronted or the solutions that must be found. Missile defense, European defense, sanctions against Iraq are but three areas where a profound malaise in the relationship manifests itself. Moreover, NATO enlargement cannot be neatly packaged or quarantined from those tensions. Indeed, in many ways, the process will become a litmus test for the state of transatlantic relations as the debate over extending the security umbrella meets head on the need for greater military efficiency. Not surprisingly, the 2002 NATO Review Conference, which will assess the progress made on enlargement and decide who next will be offered full membership, is likely to prove an exacting and delicate affair.

In the fog of a peaceful but vaguely unstable European continent, what cannot be denied is that the political heart of the Alliance is changing radically and it is difficult to assess what the outcome will be. Unfortunately, such change seems poorly appreciated in the United States, particularly in a Congress that has driven much of the enlargement process. Consequently, the United States will doubtless react to this perceived drift in its now time-honored way by attempting to reassert U.S. leadership when the rhetoric of partnership would probably be more politically effective. This dichotomy in both the policy positions and perceptions of Americans and Europeans covers all the issues that cause contention in the transatlantic relationship, not just enlargement. In addition to the tensions over the strategic direction of the Alliance, there are a host of more immediate problems. NATO–EU relations, a redefinition of burden sharing in a complex security environment that requires holistic, civil–military approaches (including civilian aid programs), the policy toward Russia and, of course, U.S.–European disagreements over an extra-European role for NATO. Certainly, it is a challenge to see how further enlargement can take place without some sort of settlement between the United States and its allies over the future shape and role of the Alliance. There is also a degree of urgency because, as the EU is now finding to its cost, failed promises not only complicate relations with candidate countries but also create a climate of insecurity, which is precisely the outcome the process seeks to avoid.

Implications of Enlargement for NATO: The Legitimacy/Effectiveness Dilemma

NATO enlargement is paradoxical because while embracing states in a security regime is normally deemed to reinforce its strength this is by no means automatically the case, either in the wider context of European security or in the case of NATO. Indeed, enlargement brings as many complications to the Alliance, both political and functional, as security benefits. As early as January 1996, Gebhardt von Moltke, NATO's assistant secretary general for Political Affairs, wrote "Allies will want to know how possible new members intend to contribute to NATO's tasks . . ."[2] In this respect, an enlarged NATO is a leap in the dark because no one really knows how successive enlargements will change the political balance and/or the military efficiency of the Alliance.

At the military level there will certainly be no NATO standard of military capability. Indeed, there are already four levels of military capability in the Alliance—the United States, which is vanishing into the military-technical distance, the United Kingdom and France, which find themselves floating in the military mid-Atlantic, the other continental Western Europeans and, finally, the new members. Moreover, if the partner countries are added to this politico-military soup then the problem becomes even more complex. The most likely outcome, therefore, is that NATO will come to resemble a military "clearing house"— a kind of interoperability nexus in which asymmetrical capabilities are cobbled together in some form of (hopefully) working politico-military mechanism.

At best, an enlarged NATO could help to reinforce interlocking institutions, underpin NATO–EU relations and, in cooperation with the OSCE, establish a broad security guarantee in the European security space. At worst, an enlarged NATO could push Russia toward an aggressive posture, duplicate OSCE, reinforce the military role of the EU as juxtaposition to that of NATO and undermine the basic political consensus and military mission of the Alliance. NATO enlargement, therefore, is a risk—a cost-benefit exercise in which the Alliance must confront exactly the same "deepening" and "widening" dilemma that the EU faces. In the absence of a systemic threat American hegemony loses its ability to influence by cooptive means. Indeed, hegemony is not what it used to be. Consequently, at a time of supreme American power, the

United States will find leadership increasingly difficult to assert within an Alliance more fractious, more divided and more political than at any time in its history.

This will also lead progressively (irony of ironies) to a NATO that more resembles the political machinations of the EU. Thus, the position of the European members will be further reinforced because they have fifty years experience of playing the kind of games that are part and parcel of Brussels daily life across town from NATO. In such a situation the new members are likely to be disappointed because the NATO they join is unlikely to be the NATO they want. Moreover, they themselves are faced with a choice: spend limited resources on bringing their armed forces up to NATO standard or embark on the thoroughgoing economic reform required to prepare for EU membership.

The complexity of contemporary Alliance and European politics is already constraining the Alliance. First, the reform of the armed forces of both new members and aspirant countries is proving extremely slow and complex. Indeed, the mechanisms for "self-improvement," such as the Individual Partnership Programs (IPPs), Membership Action Plans (MAPs) and the Planning and Review Process (PARP) tend to underline the extent of problems, rather than offer any meaningful solutions. Second, as indicated earlier, NATO was built around a core political understanding and an asymmetric political and military partnership between North America and Western Europe, led by the United States. Enlargement takes place at a time when that balance is being disturbed not only by Western Europe's legitimate political ambitions but also by the demands of a new group of members who are not so much partners as clients. Third, enlargement transfers security risks from beyond NATO's borders to within them, which further complicates the nature of the Alliance and bifurcates its mission. Fourth, by creating the expectation of enlargement, NATO creates winners and losers with those "excluded," such as Ukraine, needing constant reassurance to avoid the overt reestablishment of the very dividing lines in Europe that NATO seeks to prevent. Fifth, the paraphernalia of enlargement have expanded over the past decade in inverse proportion to the political will necessary to make it happen. Indeed, the architecture of quasi-enlargement has become an industry: the Euro-Atlantic Partnership Council (EAPC), the PfP, the NATO–Russian Permanent Joint Council, the Committee of National Armaments Directors with Partners (CNAD with Partners). They place a disproportionate burden on a bureaucracy that is ill suited to the task, is badly underfunded and that still needs urgently to attend to existing core functions, such as ESDI and the DCI. NATO is in need of reform.

Not surprisingly, as a result of these many conflicting forces and inconsistent positions, NATO is going about enlargement in an almost ad hoc manner, with neither the political nor the practical implications being properly addressed. Indeed, in spite of the many declarations to the contrary, there is no political roadmap guiding the allies on the path to enlargement—no agreed timetable, no agreed order of prospective members, no plan of action. NATO is muddling through enlargement because the members lack sufficient political cohesion to will either its means or its ends.

Implications for the EU: The Asymmetric Membership Dilemma

The report of the French presidency of the EU to the Nice summit in December 2000 stated: "The Union will ensure the necessary dialogue, consultation and cooperation with NATO and its non-EU members, other countries who are candidates for accession to the EU as well as other prospective partners in EU-led crisis management, with full respect for the decision-making autonomy of the EU and the single institutional framework of the Union."[3] In EU-speak that means the great and the good have absolutely no idea how the relationship with the candidate/accession countries is going to work in practice.

Certainly, NATO enlargement creates problems for the EU. First, it increases the political pressure on the EU to enlarge itself. Second, it reinforces asymmetric memberships that further complicate interinstitutional relations between the EU and NATO. There are fifteen candidate countries seeking to "accede" to the EU, among them Turkey which, although a full member of the Alliance, finds its candidature for the EU perpetually on the back burner. The "word on the street" is that 2006 will be the earliest that the first wave of EU enlargement will take place, in spite of recent reassuring comments from British Prime Minister Tony Blair.[4] The Alliance is not much better. In 2002 NATO is, at best, likely only to offer full membership to Romania, Slovenia and possibly Lithuania. The complexity of their respective enlargements leaves NATO and the EU politically paralyzed with the result that everybody, member and candidate alike, find themselves in a kind of political no mans land. The recent Intergovernmental Conference (IGC) on reform of EU institutions in preparation for EU enlargement underlined the sheer complexity of the process, and served only to demonstrate that progress is by no means certain.

In practice it is very hard to separate the two enlargements in the minds of those who aspire to be members of the two organizations.

Previously, there was a trade-off between economic security and military security by which candidates sought a U.S. security guarantee alongside an EU economic "guarantee." Indeed, that was the implicit "deal" between the United States and its allies. However, the United States has become increasingly concerned that EU membership means a "back-door" security guarantee from NATO for EU members, thus implying an involuntary extension of U.S. commitments in Europe. To counter this, the debate in the early 1990s centered upon the need for parallel enlargements, but that goal proved to be politically and practically impossible. The United States had a point. The debate that took place in Finland in the run up to their accession to the EU was often heavily laced with references to the security that the country would gain from EU membership. Given the relative paucity of EU military capabilities and that Finland's main security concern has been and remains Russia, they were not voting for a EU security guarantee. Through ESDP a European guarantee may one day prove feasible, but not for the foreseeable future (and is hardly likely to enjoy U.S. support).

This interinstitutional imbroglio is further complicated by the pressure emanating from those in Washington who see EU enlargement as a commitment to what they regard as asymmetric burden-sharing, whereby the U.S. military commitment *to* Europe is offset by the EU's economic investment in Europe. Thus, there is a fine balance between the forces pushing the EU to enlarge (including NATO enlargement) and the many pressures from within it to delay. It is also a debate fraught with difficulty because there are undoubtedly some in the United States (and United Kingdom) who believe that a wider Europe will mean less Europe and those in Europe who believe that a wider Alliance will mean less America.

One solution could be for the EU member states to opt for a kind of "virtual enlargement" in which non-EU, NATO allies and, indeed, partners, are invited to formalize the decision-shaping formula through a kind of EU "Partnership for Peace." In effect, this would be an extension of Pillar Two of the Treaty on EU (i.e., the intergovernmental CFSP). There is already pressure from some EU accession states to "join" Pillar Two before they are fully admitted to the rest of the Treaty on European Union.[5] Certainly, if NATO embarks upon a second wave of enlargement before the EU has even reached the starting post, the problem of block-building within the Alliance will become more acute as *Western* European interests become increasingly distinct, by contrast to those of other members, irrespective of the final shape of NATO enlargement. This would also help ease the problem of EU-caucusing within the Alliance that NATO enlargement tends to reinforce because it further dilutes a single European position. EU-caucusing is not Euro-caucusing and so long as there is an imbalance between the two enlargements Western Europeans will tend to see their interests as being distinct from their Central and Eastern European neighbors. Moreover, in many ways EU-caucusing is as inevitable as it is desirable because of the need for a functioning mechanism that can adequately reflect the changing political balance of power in the Alliance. Indeed, it is simply a reflection of political reality. Ultimately, there will only be true symbiosis between the two enlargements if both sides to the transatlantic security bargain recognize that membership of either will afford the same security guarantee.

Implications for the "Neutrals": The Are We, Aren't We Dilemma

The debate over NATO and EU enlargement is also having a significant impact upon how the so-called "neutrals" see themselves. Neutrality is no longer really an option for any EU member state, at least in the strict sense of the term. Even that doyen of neutrality, Switzerland, has compromised itself to an extent by joining NATO's PfP. This is a reflection of geo-political change that is also encouraging a reevaluation in other "hard-line" neutrals, such as Sweden and Ireland. Having joined the EU they are now engaged in often-tortured debates about what is the purpose and, indeed, the benefit to be derived from neutrality in a postmodern world, including whether or not NATO membership is an option in the medium to long term. Moreover, although the EU's autonomous capacity is still more autonomous than capable, the fact that it exists exerts increased pressure upon them to come off the neutral fence. It is hard to imagine a scenario in which a NATO member is confronted with a major challenge to its security without the non-NATO "EU Four" (Austria, Finland, Ireland and Sweden) making some form of contribution. NATO enlargement will undoubtedly reinforce this tendency, which will, in turn, create not only pan-European mutually assured vulnerabilities but also the need for mutually reassuring commitments. Indeed, such commitments are already implicit in the EU's HG. Included in the planning framework for the EU's ERRF is a Committee of Contributors made up of non-EU European states. They will have what is termed a "decision-shaping" capability, although what that means exactly has yet to be defined. It is ironic that it is the foggy peace of post–Cold War Europe that is forcing an abandonment of traditional neutrality, rather than the ideologically charged atmosphere of the Cold War.

Implications for Russia: The Partner/Adversary Dilemma

Russia is an enigma for the Alliance. At a superficial level important steps have been taken to reassure the Russians that NATO is no longer an anti-Russian coalition. The 1997 NATO-Russia Founding Act and the creation of the NATO-Russian Joint Permanent Council, sought to frame a new relationship between the two former adversaries that committed the new partners to joint efforts to construct peace and stability in the Euro-Atlantic area. To that end, the Act stated: "NATO and Russia do not consider each other as adversaries. They share the goal of overcoming the vestiges of earlier confrontation and competition and of strengthening mutual trust and cooperation."[6] However, much of Russia's relationship with the West hinges on NATO enlargement and, not surprisingly, there is a very distinct Russian point of view. "To hold out the prospect of NATO expanding to include the ECE [Eastern and Central European countries] would require simultaneous attempts to address Russia's real and alleged concerns about the future of European security. Otherwise the stated assumptions of all Western security policies—that Russia is in some meaningful sense a partner and the substantial decisions affecting its security should therefore not be made without full consideration of Russian interests, including detailed consultations with Moscow—could be considered in Russia as meaningless."[7] This Russian view of NATO enlargement not only sums up the Russian attitude—it encapsulates the West's dilemma. All Western governments would like partnership with Moscow but not at the price of giving the Russians an enduring veto over the future expansion of the Alliance. Equally, NATO cannot pretend that Russia does not exist. Unfortunately, the very name "NATO" is replete with negative implications for a Russian people who labored under forty years of state propaganda. NATO was the enemy and now it wants to move its eastern border ever closer to Mother Russia. It is powerful and it is emotive.

NATO has made great efforts to convince the Russians that enlargement is not aimed at it and although it has been repeatedly stressed that Moscow has no veto it is clear that much still depends on the Russian attitude. Unfortunately, Russia continues to suffer from a form of "Versailles Syndrome," with NATO enlargement being only the most visible sign of Russian "defeat." This is a tragedy, not just for Russia, but for the whole of Europe, because Russia still sees the end of the

Cold War in terms of a defeat and any developments that come there-after as the imposing of terms by an arrogant victor. Thus, while the implications for Russia of NATO enlargement are not in themselves great, much depends on how Russia deals with it. Russian opposition will certainly have implications for the Alliance. As indicated earlier, the further east that NATO expands the more dilute Article V will become. Would the West go to war for the Baltics if Russia reinvaded? No. Would NATO go to war for Poland? Most certainly, yes. Therefore, it is a sad but inescapable conclusion that Russia's hostility to NATO enlargement continues to divide Europe and it is Russia who sets this particular agenda by choosing to see NATO enlargement in those terms. Consequently, it is also difficult to escape the conclusion that countries such as Estonia, Latvia and Lithuania will only join a meaningful NATO when they are no longer in need of it.

It would appear, therefore, that the best that can be hoped for from Russia is a reluctant and grudging acceptance. It is as yet unclear how President Putin will react to further NATO enlargements, but early signs suggest a "lucrative" pragmatism if the NMD debate is anything to go by. He will certainly exact a price, both political and financial, for each wave of enlargement that takes place. Moreover, given the somewhat anachronistic (hard-line realist) bent to current Russian thinking, it seems reasonable to assume that "linkage" could well raise its ugly head again as the Russians demand further alterations to NMD, the Conventional Forces Europe (CFE) Treaty or even European defense in return for grudging support for limited NATO enlargement. At the same time, it is certainly difficult to see how progressive NATO enlarge-ment can take place if Russian opposition is implacable, at least if it involves any of the Baltic states. Indeed, if NATO enlargement simply makes Russia ever more hostile how can it be said to serve European security. That is, after all, the object of the exercise.

There is also something ironic and illogical about Russian negativity. A stabilized border to the West, which is implicit in NATO enlarge-ment, would enable it to focus more effectively on dealing with the many zones of insecurity and instability to its south and east. However, that is the "charm" of Russia, a country whose painful history leads it perennially to confuse legitimate security concerns with those that are, frankly, illegitimate. One area of linkage that NATO must be careful to avoid is one in which enlargement is linked to domestic behavior. The West must not turn a blind eye to the manner by which Russia deals with its internal security concerns. Chechnya must not become an accepted norm. That said, it is impossible to overstate the psychological impact of NATO enlargement on the Russian mind and it is beholden upon the West to use every means at its disposal to put these historical concerns to rest. NATO must, therefore, be sensitive to Russia without ever allowing it any right of veto. By all means trade the tradable, but not the inalienable.

Implications for the Candidate Countries: The Article V Dilemma

"The door to NATO membership remains open to other European countries that are ready and willing to undertake the commitments and obligations stemming from NATO membership and contribute to security in the Euro-Atlantic area. The admission of new democratic members into NATO is itself part of a wider process of greater integration in Europe involving other European institutions."[8] The NATO enlargement debate all too often has an unfortunate tendency to be discussed within the Alliance as though the candidate countries are a theoretical device. There is always much talk about the interests and burdens of existing members and often little about the legitimate aspirations and security needs of candidate countries. Unfortunately, there are no quick solutions to this problem because, contrary to Joschka Fischer's now famous view, widening does affect deepening and it makes little sense to pretend otherwise. Indeed, a NATO of twenty-three, twenty-eight, or in the longer run, even thirty plus, would probably find unanimity of purpose in an ever more complex security environment only at the expense of democratic representation. Unfortunately, as the EU knows only too well, to be effective unanimity is not an option, whereas to be democratic, neither is effectiveness. NATO must get used to a world that is even more suboptimal than the one it currently occupies.

NATO must avoid becoming simply a more muscular OSCE. Consequently, NATO enlargement is a dilemma for the candidate countries. They want to join the Alliance because of what it *was*. Unfortunately, their very membership changes NATO making it less attractive as a military security "product." Radu Bogdan captures the problem succinctly by posing a couple of questions: "NATO has committed itself to reviewing the enlargement process in 2002. In the meantime there will of course be much debate. Could the Alliance remain functional if it were much further enlarged? How many new members should be invited to join, in what order and how fast?"[9] The problem is centered upon Article V of the Treaty of Washington, NATO's founding act. Indeed, it is Article V that candidate countries really want because it implies an automatic security guarantee. However, it is not. Compared, say, with Article V of the modified Brussels Treaty of the WEU, it is merely an agreement to consult in the event of an attack on a NATO member. In any case, what constitutes an attack in the modern age? Cyberwarfare?

Implications for NATO's Nuclear Policy: The Credible Deterrent Dilemma

During the Cold War the assumption (and it was thankfully only an untested assumption) was that Article V linked the U.S. nuclear arsenal to the territorial defense of Western Europe. Enlargement definitively breaks that link and denuclearizes the Alliance. There is no conceivable scenario in which NATO would use nuclear weapons in defense of Central and Eastern European members. Consequently, NATO enlargement further decouples the United States from its allies (it would be ironic if Lithuania achieved by default what Russia had been working so hard for over the past fifty years). Therefore, the NATO nuclear security guarantee is, by and large, a bluff. Actually, it was always thus, at least since the mid-1960s when the Soviets gained effective nuclear parity with the United States. What the candidate countries have to consider is whether a contemporary conventional "bluff" is worth having. Clearly, for the majority of them it is. Indeed, its very uncertainty and ambiguity lends it some deterrent value. However, any deterrent needs credible military capability and overt political will to reinforce its credibility. This is the central paradox of NATO enlargement because it adds responsibilities without adding capabilities. It is the *sense* of security and stability that Alliance membership affords candidate countries that seems to matter, rather than the reality.

Implications for Public Opinion: The Who Pays What Dilemma

The past decade has witnessed a new phenomenon in the shaping of security and defense policy: the direct and potent influence of public opinion. All Western governments are increasingly sensitive to public concerns about the cost of security, be it in human or financial terms. Unfortunately, the celebrations were just a little too long and too loud at the end of the Cold War, and convinced their respective publics that the days of extensive security commitments were over. As a result, Europe has one almighty security hangover and it is questionable whether Western Europeans and Americans are prepared to spend large amounts of money on extending either military or economic security to Central and Eastern European countries. Certainly, what passes for debate is hardly matched by enthusiasm. Indeed, much of the debate on this issue has been a quintessential exercise in transatlantic "buck-passing," primarily because public opinion in the West is otherwise engaged. Therefore, public opinion will have to be managed by governments more effectively than has hitherto been the case and that could have significant implications for NATO enlargement.

NATO enlargement will certainly have to be done on the cheap, if it is done at all. There are too many other competing interests in search of state funding for significant amounts to be invested on enlarging the Alliance. This is a problem that is exacerbated for many of the European allies by the strict budget constraints required by membership of the Eurozone. Unfortunately, today's politics are those of the immediate and sophisticated arguments about investing in the future of Europe that rarely get heard above the clamor for new hospitals and schools, or a further cut in income tax. This leaves two options. First, NATO enlarges within the framework of the existing bureaucracy. Second, the new members have to fund, more or less, the requisite reforms themselves.

There is another constituency that Americans and Western European all too readily forget: public opinion in the candidate countries. For many the promise of enlargement, be it that of NATO or the EU seems little like an Eastern Promise—always just over the horizon. The implications of dashed hopes and broken promises are replete with risks to stability. When does a delayed promise become a broken one? When is a broken promise an act of betrayal? These are very real issues for countries whose own histories have been consistently brutalized by a tragic combination of Great Power aggression and/or indifference. In such an environment security policy could be increasingly renationalized and in a region of weak and failing states this would be dangerous not just for the candidates themselves, but for all the NATO allies. Failure to export security to the East will only result in the East exporting problems to the West. Indeed, this is the reality that the West must confront. Crime, illegal migration and the destabilizing effects of poverty are ever more apparent on the streets of Western Europe.

Functional Implications of NATO Enlargement: The Who Does What Dilemma

There is a dangerous gulf opening between the United States and its allies about the purpose of the Alliance. This gulf is primarily the result of contending military-technical choices that the United States and its allies are making. Indeed, there is a military-technical dichotomy in the Alliance today. The United States, for all its military might, seems able only to escalate from the top end of the Petersberg Tasks/small-scale contingency threshold. The Europeans, on the other hand, seem able only to escalate from the bottom end of the Petersberg Tasks (humanitarian and rescue missions) to some point up that limited scale (peacekeeping and some forms of peacemaking). Thus, the fundamental premise upon which the Alliance is founded, the sharing of both risks and burdens, is being undermined.

Many Americans reading this will no doubt jump at this statement and assert (once again) that the problems result from low European defense spending and a lack of willingness to follow the American lead. They are wrong. Indeed, the problem is primarily American in its making and, sadly, will only be made worse by NATO enlargement. For a whole range of domestic reasons (such as the power of defense-industrial lobby groups) the United States is preparing for a war that is not going to happen. It is being seduced into a military-technical "paradise" that is largely irrelevant for today's security needs. Consequently, the unwillingness of Americans to commit their forces to the kind of "muddy boots" peacekeeping that represents 90 percent of the security "market" effectively negates American leadership within the Alliance. It also forces the allies into a corner. They will never close the military-technical gap with the United States. Frankly, they do not need to because they face threats/risks different from those facing the United States. At the same time, peacekeeping is not merely a subset of war fighting. It is a very complex set of skills at which several European states excel and at which the United States is poor. In effect, the U.S. drive toward the Revolution in Military Affairs (RMA) forces Europeans to make a choice between war fighting and peacekeeping—a choice most do not want to make. Therefore, in order to demonstrate that they are able to perform at least some relevant missions, European states will increasingly opt to spend their limited funds on peacekeeping capabilities at the expense of war fighting. For the new members and candidate countries this problem is magnified. Indeed, such is the parlous state of their finances that they have no alternative but to follow the lead of their Western European counterparts in opting for cheaper, less capable, but more relevant peacekeeping. Consequently, it is difficult to envisage how in five years time Force XXI could possibly "interoperate" with, say, a Hungarian infantry battalion unless technology is diverted from its current course as a force separator and turned into a force bridge.

This military-technical schism, more than any other development, carries with it the potential to tear NATO apart. Moreover, in an atmosphere where it is British, French, Italian and German troops doing the dirty work and who are taking the casualties (East Timor, Kosovo, Sierra Leone) European public opinion will simply not countenance American whining about burden sharing. Indeed, in such an environment European public opinion might decide that the EU is a better option for its security and defense than NATO. The burden-sharing debate is not a one-way street and the United States had better start getting its peacekeeping act together.

Implications for the United States: The Leadership/Partnership Dilemma

Finally, what are the implications for the United States? To many Europeans such is American power today that the United States no longer really constructs foreign policy in the classical sense; it simply exports domestic policy. Nowhere is this more apparent than over the protracted issue of NATO enlargement.[10] And yet it is not that simple. In a speech at NATO's Atlantic Fleet headquarters in Norfolk, Virginia on February 13, 2001 President Bush focused on both the enduring and changing qualities of the Alliance: "The security and welfare of each member of this [transatlantic] community depend upon the security and welfare of all. None of us alone can achieve economic prosperity or military security. None of us alone can assure the continuance of freedom. This is still true today. Our challenges have changed, and NATO is changing and growing to meet them. But the purpose of NATO remains permanent . . . together, united, we can deter the designs of aggression, and spare the continent from the effects of ethnic hatreds." In those sentences the president summed up America's dilemma: how to lead a process in an environment where leadership is not possible. In spite of its awesome power the United States no longer leads NATO. Indeed, at a time of unrivalled power it confronts allies who, themselves, have rediscovered their political authority. Hitherto, Americans were used to driving the agenda inside the Alliance in a way that would today be unthinkable.

In the run-up to the presidential elections the U.S. debate over NATO enlargement subsided, although this is likely to prove only a temporary respite and will undoubtedly increase in the run-up to the NATO Review Conference in 2002. Indeed, with such a delicate political balance existing between the Bush administration and Congress in the run-up to the 2002 mid-term elections, it is one of the foreign policy issues that could well get mired in what is likely to prove an acerbic battle. The Clinton administration took the view that, having reached a binding agreement with the Europeans at the Madrid summit in 1997, the process of enlargement was a done deal and it was now simply a question of who and when, not if. That is no longer the case. Moreover, it was a bipartisan position held by both Democrats and Republicans, not least because of the vocal constituencies in the United States that trace their roots back to the candidate countries. It is Congress, therefore, that is again likely to take the political lead if, as seems possible, the administration fails to push the Europeans with sufficient vigor toward an acceptance of both a U.S. timetable and meeting much of the cost.

Of course, underpinning these tensions are two sharply contrasting views of burden sharing. Indeed, enlargement has become a metaphor for burden sharing in the American political mind mainly because of the refusal of Congress to fund the process. This sense of injustice is fuelled by the prevailing sense in Congress that the United States was doing Europe a favor through its presence during the Cold War. This is not only plain wrong, but it is likely to do irreparable damage if the United States does not back away from it. Moreover, Europeans will increasingly demand a redefinition of burden sharing to take into account their extensive aid programs (alongside which the U.S. effort pales) and their willingness to put troops in harms way during dangerous Peace Support Operations (PSOs) in a way that the United States seems unwilling to countenance. Europeans are also suspicious that for some in the United States (both Republicans and Democrats) NATO enlargement is simply a way for America to further disengage from European security.

For many Europeans NATO enlargement is indicative of the lack of clear thinking in a United States that encourages Europe to pay more and do more without wishing to concede any real concomitant increase in its political influence. Two things are clear. First, the United States is in Europe in pursuit of its own interests. It was always thus. Second, the United States is not going to leave Europe. The sooner the debate moves beyond the implied threat of disengagement that informs a lot of American rhetoric the sooner the political problems that afflict the alliance can be tackled.

Eastern Promise? The Implications of NATO Enlargement

So, what is to be done? Throughout this piece the complexities and paradoxes of NATO enlargement have dominated. Indeed, NATO enlargement was a metaphor for the wider transatlantic relationship and, as such, has been trapped in a vicious circle of political posturing and maneuvering that is undermining the Alliance. This is a shame because a modern NATO remains a cornerstone of security relations, not just in the Euro-Atlantic area, but beyond. These are not just political niceties but observable fact. However, NATO must also be politically relevant and this means that the allies need to focus. It was Madeleine Albright who gave the Alliance the 3Ds (no discrimination, no decoupling and no duplication). What NATO needs today are the 5Cs: credibility, cohesion, convergence, commitment and candor. A *credible* security policy that does away with a vestigial Cold War doctrine that is progressively undermining the deterrent value of the Alliance. Policy *cohesion* with the EU to ensure that the negative, but unavoidable, implications of asymmetric enlargements are kept to a minimum. Planned *convergence* of the enlargement policies of the two organizations so that candidate/accession countries trying to fulfill what are essentially competing membership requirements from NATO and the EU do not lose valuable and limited resources. Political *commitment* from existing NATO members to ease the legitimate security concerns of Partner and Candidate countries through the use not only of the enlargement "tool," but other confidence and security-building measures. A *candid* statement on both the likely timetable for enlargement and the reality of the security "product" that new members can expect from the Alliance.

To assist in this process, several measures should be adopted:

- *A Euro-Atlantic security guarantee*: NATO should commit itself to a new Euro-Atlantic Security Guarantee to recognize and resolve the military dimension of asymmetric memberships and back-door security guarantees. The guarantee would commit the U.S., Canada and the fifteen EU member states and partner countries to support each other in times of crisis.
- *The reworking of Article V*: in light of the Euro-Atlantic security guarantee, the wording of Article V should be reworked to reinforce its political credibility. Ironically, this would involve recognizing the conditional nature of the security guarantee, that is, it is only an agreement only to consult in the event of a challenge to the security of a partner.
- *Flexible interoperability*: NATO needs to recognize and formalize the four basic levels of military capability within the Alliance

(it is not going to change) by creating a new doctrine entitled "Flexible Interoperability." This would enable NATO to reach a true interoperability nexus and assist new members by permitting them to aim at interoperability targets that include peacekeeping as a goal in itself. Full spectrum war fighting is not a serious option for candidate countries.

- *Breaking the nuclear link*: NATO enlargement breaks the link between the territorial defense of a member and the American nuclear arsenal. This should be recognized in a protocol to the Treaty of Washington. It is inconceivable that the United States would go to nuclear war over, say, Lithuania and yet, in spite of all the doctrinal adjustments of the past decade, this remains implicit in the core mission of the Alliance. It is frankly ridiculous and undermines the wider credibility of the Alliance as a security and defense mechanism.

- *Denuclearizing the NATO–Russian relationship*: NATO's claim that it no longer considers Russia as an adversary is undermined by the presence of nuclear doctrine at the heart of the Alliance. Breaking the nuclear link would not only serve to reinforce the NATO–Russian Founding Act with little or no cost to the "reality" of Alliance capability, but help Russia accept progressive enlargement of NATO.

- *New Euro-Atlantic nuclear command*: a new autonomous nuclear command should be created by the United States, the United Kingdom and France that preserves a Western nuclear identity and the role of nuclear weapons as a deterrent of last resort.

- *NATO–EU membership coordination*: European security is as much a function of economic security as military security. NATO and EU enlargements must be coordinated where possible by including the force improvements necessary for NATO membership as part of the overall economic package required to prepare European countries for accession to the EU. At present, NATO and EU enlargements effectively compete for scare resources.

- *Joint membership criteria*: in addition, membership performance criteria should be created that link improvements in economic capability required by the EU with the achievement of NATO standards. This would assist in the "sequencing" of economic and military development.

- *Joint membership funding*: funding for NATO candidate and EU accession states should be linked to their performance under the joint membership criteria.

- *New Euro-Atlantic security contract*: The United States and its allies have certain rights and obligations implicit in the contemporary relationship that need to be made explicit. These include recognition that: (1) burden sharing cannot be defined only by expenditure on high spectrum war-fighting capability; peacekeeping efforts and "security investments," such as aid, must also be factored into the equation (this will require a mind-set change in Washington); (2) recognition by the Europeans that the United States has the right to expect from its allies constructive support in extra-European security management without carte blanche agreement; to underpin this commitment the Europeans should create a register of forces (like the mechanism that governs forces answerable to the ARRC and ERRC) that are constantly in a high state of readiness and able to support U.S. forces in extra-European, out-of-area operations; and (3) in what is an extraordinarily fluid security environment in which any number of coalitions could confront any number of challenges, the West needs a new force and operational planning nexus that can work up possible coalition formats (both through virtual and real-time exercising) for operations worldwide.

Ultimately, true European security (and that is the end state of NATO enlargement) will only be achieved through a security settlement to which all agree and from which all benefit, including Russia. For the time being, however, the need for NATO to remain a European military security agency is compelling. This reinforces the need for a balanced approach to enlargement that matches expansion of members with improvements in capabilities, which militates against the "big-bang" approach to enlargement favored by some in the United States. NATO, therefore, is in the insurance business, offering different policies to different members. And, of course, like all insurance companies, hoping that disaster does not strike each and every member at one and the same time.

Notes

1. NATO, *The NATO Handbook* (Brussels: NATO Office of Information and Press, 1999), p. 83.
2. Gebhardt Von Moltke, "NATO Moves Towards Enlargement," *NATO Review* (January 1996), p. 6.
3. "Arrangements Concerning Non-EU European NATO Members and Other Countries which are Candidates for Accession to the EU," from "The Presidency Report on the European Security and Defense Policy," December 4, 2000, p. 22.

4. Speech by U.K. Prime Minister Tony Blair to the Polish Stock Exchange, October 6, 2000, at www.number-10.gov.uk.
5. This is effectively what happened to Norway, Spain and Portugal in the year prior to their accession. They were treated as full members for all aspects of foreign policy coordination under the EPC formula. Norway then withdrew following a referendum that rejected EU membership.
6. "The Founding Act on Mutual Relations, Co-operation and Security between the North Atlantic Treaty Organisation and the Russian Federation" (Brussels: NATO Office of Press and Information, 1997), p. 2.
7. Yuriy Davydov, "Russian Security and East-Central Europe," in V. Baranovsky, ed., *Russia and Europe—The Emerging Security Agenda* (Stockholm: SIPRI, 1997), pp. 382–383.
8. "NATO's Open Door," in *The Reader's Guide to the NATO Summit in Washington* (Brussels: NATO Office of Information and Press, 1999), p. 82.
9. Radu Bogdan, "Romanian Reflections," in *NATO Review* (Spring/Summer 2000), p. 25.
10. "Remarks by the President to the Troops and Personnel," February 13, 2001, at www.whitehouse.gov.

Two Contrary Conclusions

CHAPTER 10

Why ESDP is Misguided and Dangerous for the Alliance

Anand Menon

Despite the impact of September 11, the EU has, since that date, continued doggedly in its attempts to equip itself with a defense policy. Whatever the outcome of these efforts, the progress made recently toward that end has been impressive. No longer can critics (the current author included) simply dismiss as mere rhetoric the stated ambitions of Europeans to do more in the military sphere. Space constraints preclude a description of the process of negotiation and bargaining that led from a northern French coastal resort to a southern one, and which has been examined in some detail elsewhere.[1] Between the Anglo-French summit at Saint-Malo in December 1998 and the European Council meeting at Nice in December 2000, a series of practical steps were taken to equip the EU with the structures and military capacities to implement a defense policy of its own. The organization now incorporates structures specifically designed to take decisions relating to defense. Uniformed officers now stroll through the corridors of the Council building, and provide military advice to decision makers occupied with the EU's defense dimension. In addition, the member states have committed themselves to creating, by 2003, a European intervention force of at least 60,000 troops.

Yet all is not as rosy as the above may suggest. This chapter questions some of the prevalent claims and assumptions about the EU's security and defense policy, arguing that the implications of ESDP are far from benign. It highlights in particular the many ways in which ESDP threatens to weaken rather than strengthen Europe's ability to confront threats to its security. More specifically, at least four potential problems can be identified as inherent in the ESDP undertaking: the risk it poses to transatlantic relations; the possibility that the EU will not manage to act effectively in the defense sphere and, even if it does, that its new competence will slow institutional reactions to security crises; the fear that ESDP represents a dangerous politically inspired initiative that might serve to divert attention from the central question of military resources; and, finally, the real danger that the development of ESDP represents something of a threat to the development of an effective, functioning partnership between NATO and the EU.

Financial Considerations

The first criticism that can be leveled at the ESDP concerns money and, more particularly, the inability, or, rather unwillingness, of the member states adequately to fund their European defense ambitions. In November 2000, the so-called capabilities conference produced a "Headline Goal," which committed EU leaders to creating an intervention force of 60,000 troops deployable within a month for up to a year. The creation of this rapid reaction force in fact remains the major military capability of the EU.

On one reading, such an ambition is hardly excessive, in that the numbers involved are not dissimilar to those announced by President Chirac for France alone.[2] Yet arming and equipping such a force would not be cheap. The harsh reality is that European defense budgets have been in decline for some time, and there seems little prospect of significant short-term increases. A truly "autonomous" ESDP—that is, one that is not reliant on American military hardware—would necessitate the West Europeans equipping themselves not only with the requisite forces, but also with the means to transport them and provide them with accurate intelligence. A RAND study carried out in 1993 estimated that a force of 50,000 would cost between 18 and 49 billion dollars to equip over twenty-five years, with an additional bill of 9–25 billion dollars for the creation of a satellite intelligence capability.[3]

ESDP has been portrayed by its supporters as a way of increasing the military preparedness of West European states. There are some for whom this involves more effective use of existing resources.[4] For most proponents of ESDP, however, its real appeal lies in its alleged potential for legitimizing higher defense spending. Their argument is simple: ESDP will finally put to rest the long-running debate about burden sharing within NATO because it will impel the Europeans to contribute more to transatlantic security by legitimizing, under the cloak of European integration, higher levels of defense spending in Europe.[5]

Such arguments proved effective in leading to perhaps one of the most striking aspects of ESDP to date—the apparent conversion of traditionally conservative defense ministries, wedded for over fifty years to the principle of the primacy of NATO, into EU enthusiasts. However, there are several reasons to be skeptical about the claim that ESDP will prove as effective in convincing the general public of the need for higher defense budgets. First, with fears of recession growing, with serious fiscal problems affecting both the provision of public services and the payment of pension debts in Europe, and with defense simply not being a high political priority given the absence of any clear threat to West European territories, it is hard to see, in political terms, how such increases can be achieved. More specifically, the validity of the argument that the need for an EU defense capability will help to legitimize increased defense expenditure is highly contingent on national circumstance. While such reasoning may work in more pro-EU states such as Italy, the notion that the EU will make defense more sellable than NATO already does in Britain is, at best, open to doubt. Moreover, given both the rising signs of French Euro-skepticism and the increasing sensitivity of the question of contributions to the EU budget in Berlin and elsewhere, there seems little reason to suppose that national politicians will be anxious to ask electorates to pay more in the way of taxes to support the Union's defense policy ambitions.

Transatlantic Relations

There has always been anxiety in Washington when the Europeans show a desire to increase their own autonomy, or institutional capacities, in the defense sphere. Some of this is unavoidable. There are those, both within and outside the U.S. administration, who, almost instinctively, shy away from the notion of Europe as an equal partner of (and therefore, as they see it, a threat to) the United States. They will never be reconciled to the idea that a strong Europe would be a better ally of the United States than a weak one. If Europeans aspire, as they should, to become stronger, they can do little to win the approval of such people.

The real problems for transatlantic relations[6] that may result from the ESDP lie elsewhere. First, since the terrorist attacks of

September 11, and dating from dissatisfaction within the Pentagon about the constraints imposed by NATO upon American military strategy in the Balkans, Washington has been reassessing its attitude toward NATO. A fundamental question is whether ESDP will stymie or reinforce such trends. On the one hand, attempts to create alternative structures to perform—apparently—very similar tasks, might encourage opponents of NATO in Washington to feel that, if even the Europeans do not value that institution, it really has no purpose. On the other, in the (unlikely) event that ESDP serves as a means of increasing European contribution to the collective Western defense effort, this might have the consequence of reassuring those in Washington who see the transatlantic relationship as a form of European exploitation of American military spending.

Macedonia will represent an interesting test case as to how the Americans will react to the practical—as opposed to notional—idea of ESDP. The Balkans is increasingly seen as a sideshow by a Bush administration preoccupied, not to say obsessed, by the "war on (Islamic) terrorism." Should the EU manage to implement its objective of taking over the leading role within Macedonia from the United States, it will become much clearer as to whether ESDP is merely serving to hasten American disengagement or, by illustrating greater European commitment to contributing directly to Western security, simply facilitating a more equitable division of responsibilities within the Western Alliance that, in turn, will serve to strengthen American commitment to it.

Here the financial doubts about ESDP come together with concerns about its implications for transatlantic relations. Unlike previous instances when Europeans have revitalized their own collaborative security efforts—such as the non-event that was the supposed relaunch of the WEU in 1984—the development of the ESDP has been taken seriously in Washington. Having raised expectations so high with their ambitious rhetoric, and at a time when the Americans are, more than ever, looking for military support from their partners and allies, European leaders risk spawning tremendous dissatisfaction across the Atlantic should they fail to deliver, strengthening the hand of those who see the Europeans as selfish, self-interested free riders on American military might. Ironically, therefore, the real danger of ESDP is that it threatens to antagonize and disillusion even those American officials who are generally supportive of European efforts to develop into an effective partner of America, and who have attempted to convince skeptical colleagues that this time Europe really means business.

Defense Decision-Making and the EU

Quite apart from whether the EU will mange to fund ESDP, or whether its defense policies will improve or further strain relations with the United States, is the fundamental issue as to whether the Union will manage to take defense decisions effectively. There are at least three good reasons to suspect that it will prove unable to do so.

The Member States

Process
The member states dominate the decision-making structures created for the ESDP. In contrast to the first pillar of the EU, the European Commission, the European Court of Justice, and the European Parliament enjoy no formal prerogatives over defense. Not only do member states predominate, but decision making between them is based on a system of unanimity, ensuring that each of the fifteen enjoys a veto. Clearly, this is hardly a recipe for decision-making efficiency. Procedural problems, moreover, are compounded by significant and cross-cutting differences of opinion between the member states over matters of substantive importance.

Substantive Issues
France and Britain, the two states who have been at the heart of the drive to create the ESDP, appear to have significantly different ideas on the crucial question of the appropriate relationship between NATO and the EU. Some of these concern only the longer term—the French are keen to see Europe develop one day into a global player that can rival the United States. However, even as far as the short term is concerned, French officials are prone to stress the notion of European autonomy more than their British counterparts, and to argue in favor of the EU being able to carry out missions independently of NATO. London, in contrast, emphasizes the need for the EU to work with NATO in the security sphere. The French went to great lengths to stress the separation between the two institutions during their presidency at the end of last year, insisting that meetings between the EU and NATO be carried out on a "fifteen plus nine" basis, rather than at twenty-three in order to stress the institutional separation between the two (see later). Such divergences of opinion are not of course limited to France and Britain but, rather, permeate the EU, with the various member states allying—implicitly or explicitly—with either camp. Moreover, the fact that divergences still exist over the single most important institutional question in

the area of European defense hardly inspires confidence about the ability of the member states to arrive at consensual opinions concerning the most appropriate form for the EU–NATO relationship.

Defense Policy

A further cleavage dividing the member states stems from the fact that — they have very different ideas about what defense policy is actually for. The fifteen have historically adopted very different attitudes toward the concept of defense, ranging from neutrality (Sweden fought its last war in 1813) to an acceptance of military engagement, often far from home, as an integral part of a nation's "mission." Differences of emphasis characterize discussions over, for instance, whether a putative ESDP should be a tool to stabilize Europe's periphery or, rather, something used globally as a means of increasing Europe's political weight. Similarly, there seems to be no consensus over whether priority should be placed on the "soft" or "hard" end of the Petersberg spectrum. Thus, on the one hand, Sweden has insisted on greater priority being given to including a significant police element in any EU reaction force, while Finland will not participate in peace enforcement missions. On the other, Britain and France have focused on the "harder," more military end of the Petersberg spectrum. Such differences will almost certainly complicate future bargaining, not least because the rotation of the presidency of the Council of Ministers every six months allows different states to set the agenda of the institution as they see fit (see later).

The lack of consensus over core issues related to ESDP, along with the unanimity requirement in the Council, do not bode well for the ability of the EU to take defense decisions effectively. More worrying still, the EU, when discussing defense policy, lacks either of the following core elements of any effective decision-making system.

Leadership

Hegemonic Leadership

While one should not exaggerate the influence of the United States, the fact remains that it is, within NATO, the first among equals. This enables it to push decisions through in the face of reluctance, or even opposition from member states which all, on paper at least, enjoy a right of veto. Debates about enlargement or the strategy to be used in the Kosovo conflict are cases in point.

Having a clear leader is clearly one obvious way to overcome potential problems associated with a decision-making system characterized by reliance upon unanimity. Unlike NATO, the EU contains no single leader. Moreover, the problem of achieving an appropriate balance between the relative weight in decision-making terms between the large and small member states has become particularly acute in recent times. The area of defense policy is one of the most sensitive in this regard, not least because officials from the three largest EU member states—Britain, Germany and France—have on occasion implied that there is a need for them to enjoy special decision-making privileges in the defense sphere given their overriding military superiority over their smaller partners.

The arguments put forward by the larger EU member states for some kind of reweighting of formal influence in their favor are intuitively reasonable: how can Luxembourg, for instance, be allowed to veto decisions about military operations in which it may not even participate? However, unlike NATO, the EU is a law-based system founded upon the principle of equality between its members. The Commission, absent from ESDP, has traditionally been seen as defender of the rights of the small member states who, consequently, feel all the more exposed in this sector because of its absence. And insofar as voting rules do not accurately reflect size, they have traditionally erred on the size of giving undue weight to the smaller states. The smalls are wedded to the notion of formal equality in voting situations based on unanimity. It is hard to see a way in which they can be persuaded to go along with what would, in effect, represent the creation of some kind of formal or informal *directoire* within the Union to manage defense policy. Unlike within NATO, the logic of hegemony is simply not acceptable to them in the context of the EU.

All this raises a stark question: if formal equality is demanded by the smaller member states, while rejected as impractical and unacceptable by the larger ones, and if unanimity is required for any decision to alter current arrangements, is a workable compromise possible? If not, we face the real possibility of deadlock in the Council—particularly as the EU member states remain profoundly divided over the ultimate goals and purpose of the ESDP.

Institutional Leadership

Within pillar one of the EU, the European Commission plays a crucial role not only in its exclusive spheres of competence (such as competition policy), but also via its ability to foster agreement and compromise between the member states, or, in other words, to act as an honest broker and agenda setter. The Commission, however, enjoys no such role in matters pertaining to the ESDP. All ESDP related negotiations take place between the member states, with the Commission confined to observer status.

In contrast, NATO possesses, in the form of its civilian and military staff, and the office of the secretary-general, important organizational resources able to provide neutral expertise, promote consensus between allies and steer discussions of potentially divisive subjects toward successful conclusions. Their role is in some ways similar to that of the European Commission in traditional areas of EC competence; indeed in some respects it even surpasses that of the Commission, in that the secretary-general is responsible for chairing NATO meetings—a task performed in the EU by the presidency.

Insofar as leadership exists over the overall direction of the ESDP, it is exercised by the member state holding the presidency of the Council. This, however, causes three problems—of weight, consistency and expertise. By weight is meant the ability of particular states to assume the mantle of leader of the external policies of the EU. Officials in Brussels acknowledge that it was hardly a source of profound international influence that the EU was led by Belgium at the time of the attacks on the United States.

In terms of consistency, the fact that the presidency rotates every six months is a cause of profound instability. It is no surprise that, in its dealings with the external world, the EU flits effortlessly from pursuing a northern dimension (Finnish presidency) to agonizing about a Mediterranean strategy (several French presidencies). In defense policy per se, similar inconsistencies are obvious, with the Swedes prioritizing conflict prevention, while the French were more interested in their own hobbyhorse of ensuring a strict separation between NATO and the EU (see later). There is a real possibility that the consistency question will be addressed during the forthcoming IGC. The large member states in particular have expressed dissatisfaction with the six-month rotating mandate. British officials propose an elected head of European Council to provide real strategic direction.

No such solutions are forthcoming however for the final problem— that of expertise. Problems here take two forms. First, some member states have a tendency to rely almost exclusively on national administrative resources when running the presidency. The case of Britain is the most marked in this respect. Commenting on one British presidency, Ludlow remarks:

> A self-sufficient [United Kingdom] bureaucracy prepared their ministers as meticulously as ever in an entirely British environment, and on the basis of exclusively British advice about what would or would not work.

As a result, the tendency to parochialism and inflexibility to which many ministers were already too prone was actually exacerbated by the efficiency of the British civil service. As one well-placed player put it. . . . we all sing out of tune form time to time. The trouble with the British is that when they sing out of tune, they do so with such conviction and authority that the dissonance reverberates around the Community.

London, therefore, eschewed drawing upon the resources of the Council secretariat, therefore potentially undermining coherence and consistency in EU action. The flip side of this is that smaller member states find that they lack the resources effectively to run the presidency. France and Britain submitted papers to the Finnish presidency which it submitted in its own name, because the Finns lacked the necessary expertise. Within NATO, by contrast, papers for discussion in NATO meetings are drafted by the international secretariat.

Cultures of Decision Making

Formal decision-making structures aside, there is a third reason to believe that the EU will struggle to take rapid decisions. NATO members have traditionally shared a common belief in the enduring utility of the organization and all are agreed that it provides the only effective tool for carrying out territorial defense functions. This is crucial in that it impels member states to seek consensus in order to preserve an organization whose value none of them questions. The EU, in contrast, does not possess the "glue" that, in NATO, is provided by common recognition of the residual importance of the territorial defense function enshrined in Article V. Indeed, European opinions are divided as to exactly how worthwhile an undertaking the ESDP really is (the traditionally Atlanticist Dutch, to take but one example, have gone along with it only reluctantly). In NATO, there is a sense that, when difficult issues are on the table, compromises must be made as the continued efficiency of the institution—and particularly the continued engagement of the Americans—takes precedence over virtually all other considerations. The fate of the ESDP is simply not considered as fundamentally important, and hence member states will prove more reluctant to compromise.

The Problems of Institutional Complexity

Moreover, even should the EU prove more effective than the above suggests, the very existence of a further institutional layer could serve to slow responses to security crises. The fact that both NATO and the EU may need to consider the nature and appropriate response to security challenges is hardly a move toward more efficient decision-making. And it raises the question, as to whether the EU and NATO decisions-making systems can be effectively and neatly meshed. This problem is made all the more acute by the fact that the two institutions have different memberships. The inclusion of neutral states in the EU will certainly have some influence over its ability to take defense-related decisions.

Less esoterically, the development of ESDP may well either divert attention from, or fail to address, the question of the military capabilities of the West. European construction has involved more than its fair share of semantic, quasi-theological disputes on matters of post structure and substance. The danger is that discussions about security will fall prey to similar tendencies. And this has already occurred. During the latter part of 2000, capabilities took a back seat in discussions of Western security. Debates have focused on the institutional structures that are most appropriate for guaranteeing that security. At one stage, during the French presidency of the EU at the end of last year, the situation became almost farcical, with bitter disputes separating the allies on questions as crucial to our security as whether the EU and NATO could meet as 23 states, or should, rather, meet as 15 plus 19 and, in the event of this being decided, where the NATO and EU chairmen should sit in relation to each other. This represents a serious distraction from the crucial issue of how to improve the capacities of NATO and the EU to deal with military crises.

It should, however, come as no surprise. For some people at least, ESDP is not primarily about enhancing the defensive military capabilities of Western Europe but, rather, about building a European political union. Indeed, the commander-in-chief of Europe's putative rapid intervention force commented that ESDP is as much a part of creating a European political identity as EMU or the EU flag. More recently, the heated political debates over possible EU intervention in Macedonia have illustrated the curious, and debilitating inversion of priorities that leads at least some European leaders to focus their attention on how best to ensure that ESDP at least looks successful, rather than the optimal way of ensuring security.

Given these extraneous political agendas, it is easy to understand why the rather mundane issue of military capabilities may be forgotten.

Relations with NATO

This brings us to perhaps the most important and simultaneously confusing questions of all: what is the ESDP meant to be, and what will be its relationship with NATO? There are two aspects to this issue: structures and tasks.

As far as the former is concerned, the institutional relationship between NATO and the EU is clearly of utmost importance given that both aspire to play a role in defense policy. A series of working groups was created to discuss specific aspects of the NATO–EU relationship and discussions within these has been ongoing. A close relationship is increasingly being created between the two institutions—not least because of close and amicable working relationship between George Robertson and Javier Solana. Some tricky institutional problems have also been resolved—thus during the Swedish presidency, Sweden was represented on the North Atlantic Council by Belgium.

However, major stumbling blocks remain because of a lack of clarity concerning the division of labor between the two institutions. For those interested in seeing ESDP as a way of enhancing the overall defensive capabilities of the West, it is not an undertaking that should lead to the Europeans duplicating military competence that NATO (or the Americans) already possess. This seems to be very much the British view, but there are those—including the French—who see ESDP as a way of giving Europe a political and military clout independent of NATO.

Broadly speaking, three kinds of military mission are foreseen by European policy makers. First, normal NATO missions; second, so-called Berlin plus missions, or those undertaken by Europeans in the way foreseen by the Berlin summit, using NATO assets and command structures; finally, European-only missions, separate from NATO and not drawing on any NATO assets. The fundamental uncertainty enshrouding ESDP concerns what kinds of tasks fit into each of the above categories. For those who view ESDP as a way of allowing Europeans to act independently of NATO, the third category will include missions that are now handled solely by NATO and, if some French rhetoric is to be believed, far more ambitious undertakings than the minor peacekeeping and humanitarian missions that most member states see as appropriate tasks for the EU. Interviews in the French defense ministry, for instance, revealed a strong belief that the EU should not be content to deal solely with low intensity conflict, while leaving "sexier," high-tech tasks to NATO.[7]

Yet the more that the EU, pushed by proponents of European "autonomy," goes down the road toward creating its own planning capabilities, thereby circumventing the need for reliance on NATO, the more the idea of the European pillar of NATO is being sacrificed, and the more immediate the danger of duplication. As the ESDP process takes on a momentum of its own, states like Britain, which had promoted it as something to reinforce rather than compete with NATO, seem increasingly to be led down a path that they did not and do not wish to tread. The situation in Macedonia is indicative of this. British officials are more than ever convinced that the EU simply lacks the wherewithal to intervene even in this modest conflict. The logical solution would be to allow NATO to stay and indeed London has increasingly sought to delay a decision about EU involvement in the country. But the foreign office has insisted that, if the EU were to take over responsibility in Macedonia, it is imperative, for political reasons, for the United Kingdom to participate even if it has reservations about the security of its forces. Not only is this a strange way to plan military intervention, but it also, in the event that something goes wrong, is not a method calculated to endear ESDP to European publics.[8]

An EU that competes with NATO is not merely harmful in terms of the duplication and unnecessary competition it implies. It also risks undermining what could have been a highly effective institutional partnership and division of responsibilities between the two institutions. Whatever its shortcoming as a defense institution, the EU is actually quite well adapted to carrying out "soft" security tasks such as crisis prevention and management. It possesses both economic and diplomatic resources and expertise, and has a proven track record of undertaking tasks such as post-crisis rebuilding and policing. NATO has no expertise in such matters (despite the obvious attraction of such a role for the United States, keen to see NATO, and hence their own influence, extend into areas where, among other things, lucrative rebuilding and reconstruction contracts may be on offer). Moreover, one can well imagine areas—such as the former Soviet Union—where an EU role would be politically more palatable than NATO involvement.

In contrast, NATO, despite its obvious flaws, is a relatively effective military organization. It is hard to envisage a purely European force managing the military dimension of the Kosovo affair as effectively as did NATO, not only because the enormous majority of the hardware was American (as were the enabling assets underlying the tangible military effort), but because NATO has systems and procedures in place to deal effectively with crisis situations. A clear division of responsibilities between "hard" and "soft" security between the EU and NATO, therefore, seems an eminently sensible one. It was seen in action in December 2000 when George Robertson wrote to Javier Solana requesting that the EU take action to deal with border skirmishes on the Serbian–Kosovan border with which KFOR was simply not equipped to cope.

The problem now is that, as the EU comes to focus more and more of its attention on developing a military role, not only might the relationship between the two institutions possibly deteriorate, but the EU will fail to devote sufficient time and resources to developing those aspects of its security policy where it enjoys real competence and a real comparative advantage.

Conclusion

Ill-judged and insensitive leadership wielded on one side of the Atlantic has therefore spawned an ill-thought out, precipitative initiative on the other. Indeed, the speed at which ESDP has been developed is no coincidence. The more ambitious European states are coming to realize that, once EU enlargement takes place, the development of ESDP will be made infinitely more difficult as a result of the inclusion of states such as Poland that value NATO above all else.

Whatever the explanation for its rapid development, ESDP carries within it the potential to undermine the ability of the West to respond to security threats. It threatens to cause disillusionment with the EU in the United States, to encumber the EU with a defense capability it may never manage to use effectively, to distract attention away from the crucial issue of Western military capabilities, and possibly to foster competition rather than mutually beneficial collaboration between NATO and the EU. It therefore represents a highly risky undertaking.

The EU's defense policy has placed both the Americans and Europeans in difficult situations. On the one hand, there is a genuine need for Europeans to be able to do more for themselves in the security sphere. Not only will this help reduce the burden on the United States, but there are areas in which Europeans can (because they must) be more effective and act more decisively than the United States—witness the Balkan conflicts. Moreover, a European counterweight to American global predominance is desirable, not only to act as a check on excessive American power and influence but also to reduce the burden that leadership clearly places on American shoulders. Increasing the political and military weight of Europe is, therefore, a commendable objective. On the other hand, no one doubts the crucial role of NATO not only for Article V purposes but also as the obvious institution to carry out more militarily intensive operations. This being the case, effective cooperation between the two sides of the Atlantic remains crucial, and the question of transatlantic military capabilities remains every bit as important—if not more so—than that of European aspirations in the defense sphere.

Therefore, European attempts to increase their own potential must take place within a cooperative, transatlantic framework.

The most obvious way of mitigating the potential problems that ESDP will pose is to attempt to incorporate it as completely as possible within NATO, thereby effectively foreclosing the possibility of European-only missions except in cases of very low intensity conflict where NATO is not involved. This would both minimize the risk of unnecessary duplication of military competence, and also allow the two institutions to play complementary rather than competing roles. As far as the implications for American policy are concerned, Washington must ensure that NATO is as generous as possible with its European members in order to reduce the incentives they face to go it alone. There are signs that the Americans have finally come to understand this. Since the late spring of 2000, Washington has agreed that Europe's Deputy SACEUR can be double-hatted with the approval of the North Atlantic Council and that the Europeans can enjoy assured access to NATO's operational planning capabilities (something that, of course, could have been achieved immediately after Berlin, without the complication of an EU decision-making role). A softening of the American stance on any kind of European caucusing within NATO would also act as a further incentive for its European allies to concentrate on the Berlin plus agenda as the means of implementing their defense ambitions. In practical terms, the Europeans must ensure that their new intervention force—potentially a highly laudable development if it actually increases Western military capabilities—be closely tied to NATO, and, if possible, developed in such a way as to complement existing NATO capabilities. By contributing more, they would only be strengthening the case for the Americans to accede to a greater European role within the Alliance. In addition, EU member states should not, in their desperation to gain a military capability, forget other, nonmilitary aspects of security. In particular, the expertise of the Commission should be fostered in areas such as crisis management and confidence building. The EU should be encouraged to find a role that complements the purely military capacities of NATO.

The Europeans should not see this course of action as an admission of defeat. The fact is that they are now in a far stronger bargaining position than they were at Berlin in 1996. The Americans believed at the time that what happened at Berlin was the stuff of nightmares. They have subsequently realized that the EU alternative is even worse. Washington, therefore, is more than willing to negotiate on issues it refused to discuss openly in 1996, and to be more forthcoming on ensuring an effective European pillar within NATO. Moreover, having had the experience of the last few years, the Americans are highly unlikely to attempt to block the launching of European missions from within NATO for fear of undermining the European pillar once again and causing Europeans to look elsewhere for an institutional basis for their military aspirations. ESDP has at least made it clear to the Americans that Berlin was a far more desirable outcome than they thought at the time. In this sense at least, it provides an opportunity for Europe to assert itself in the defense sphere. The EU may, paradoxically, provide the key to Europeanizing NATO.

Notes

1. See in particular, Jolyon Howorth, *European Integration and Defence: The Ultimate Challenge?* (Paris: WEU Institute for Security Studies, 2000), Chaillot Paper 43.
2. See David Yost, chapter 5 in this volume.
3. M.B. Berman and G.M. Carter, *The Independent European Force: Costs of Independence* (Santa Monica, California: RAND, 1993); Philip Gordon, "Europe's Uncommon Foreign Policy," *International Security* 22 (Winter 1997–1998), pp. 93–94; Michael O'Hanlon, "Transforming NATO: The Role of European Forces," *Survival* 39 (Autumn 1997).
4. François Heisbourg, "European Defence takes a Leap Forward," *NATO Review* (Spring/Summer 2000).
5. Interviews, Brussels, June 2000, July 2001.
6. For a full discussion of how the United States has reacted to ESDP, see Stanley R. Sloan, *The United States and European Defence* (Paris: WEU Institute for Security Studies, 2000), Chaillot Paper 39.
7. Interviews, French Ministry of Defence, October 2001.
8. Interviews, FCO, April 2002.

CHAPTER 11

Why ESDP is Necessary and Beneficial for the Alliance

Jolyon Howorth

Current developments in ESDP have arisen out of powerful historical forces arising on both sides of the Atlantic. There are major problems in making the ESDP project a success, but the resolution of those problems is a historico-political necessity that will have positive consequences not only for the EU itself but also, eventually, for its relations both with NATO and with the United States. One must thus reject the approach that, through focusing on the difficulties, concludes from the outset that the project itself is ill conceived. Attempts to forge a common ESDP are not the product of an aberration on the part of misguided politicians unwittingly putting at risk the delicate framework of the European integration process, or, even more seriously, that of the Atlantic Alliance itself.[1]

Let us first rehearse some of the arguments deployed against ESDP by those who fear its deleterious impact. Many of these arguments contain more than a kernel of truth. However, it is the conclusions deriving from them that need close examination.

It is true that the EU–U.S. strategic balance since 1945 has been massively weighted in favor of the United States, in terms of leadership, military capacity and willingness to engage. The EU has indeed proved rather good at delivering what is inappropriately referred to as "soft" security.[2] But that is not necessarily a reason to conclude that such an imbalance is desirable—or that it should be preserved indefinitely. There are good reasons to believe that a more balanced Alliance would be a healthier Alliance.

It is also true that the EU-15 includes many different security cultures, informed by very different historical and military experiences, different relations with NATO and different attitudes to European integration, and that these cleavages are often crosscutting. Nicole Gnesotto has defined a common security culture in a relatively straightforward way as "the aim and the means to incite common thinking, compatible reactions, coherent analysis—in short, a strategic culture that is increasingly European, one that transcends the different national security cultures and interests."[3] It will be a major challenge to bring the existing cultures together into something approaching a workable synthesis. But the forging of a common European security culture—highly desirable in its own right—is not impossible, indeed some progress has already been made in a positive direction.[4]

Another argument used against the project is that institutional crosspillar coherence in the delivery of an ESDP mobilizing instruments from the entire range of EU resources will be highly problematic. Turf battles between many different agencies—national capitals, the European Council, the Commission, the High Representative and various military establishments—are real and ongoing. But that is also true in Washington, D.C. and such turf battles, while complex and regrettable, do not preclude the delivery of a viable U.S. policy. A great deal of institutional engineering will be required in order to optimize defense and security decision-making procedures in an organism which, hitherto, has been exclusively civilian. Everybody is agreed on that. For the moment there is little agreement on how to achieve it.[5] But as Alexander Moens stressed in chapter 2, it is early days yet. The ESDP is an infant in diapers. The bath water may need changing regularly. But the infant will mature and is certainly worth hanging onto. The United States also began life with an overwhelmingly civilian constitution. Adaptation to the decision-making constraints of military power was slow and laborious, a point to which I shall return.

Another problem raised by critics is that relations with a number of key allies, including Turkey and the United States, have been rendered complex by the development of ESDP. Yet the real problem with Turkey, as Sunniva Tofte has demonstrated, is a Greco-Turkish problem that predates both ESDP and indeed the EU. Finding an institutional arrangement that will satisfy Ankara and Athens is not impossible—indeed the EU came within a whisper of just such an agreement at the Seville European Council in June 2002. And relations with the United States are at the very heart of the project—and ongoing. There is a huge range of opinion within the United States about ESDP, including (as Kori Schake makes clear in chapter 6) an important constituency that is favorably disposed. The EU is, in any case, a mature international actor and the problem of upsetting one or two individuals within the D.C. beltway should not weigh heavily on the minds of European statesmen. None of these problems is insuperable. Even collectively, they do not amount to a case against the development of ESDP, but rather constitute so many hurdles whose successful clearance will enormously strengthen it. Two more serious problems that are often cited as evidence that ESDP is unlikely to work are finances and leadership. These I shall address at greater length below.

European Security Capacity: Answering the Call of History?

As John Keeler and I argued in chapter 1, ESDP is not a temporary aberration, misguidedly entered into at Saint-Malo by ambitious or reckless politicians, but a project that has been in gestation for some fifty years. Despite the difficulties in finding the magic formula for making ESDP work, the very fact that each succeeding decade since 1945 has seen a renewal of the effort to succeed is eloquent testimony to the urgency and legitimacy of the task. What is ESDP? Notwithstanding differences of interpretation, approach and ambition among the EU-15, most European leaders would subscribe to the following broad definition: *a project to confer upon the EU the ability to take collective decisions relating to regional security and to deploy a range of instruments, including military instruments, in operations of crisis management, peacekeeping and, if necessary, peace-enforcement (preferably with a legal mandate), as a distinctive European contribution to the overall objectives of the Atlantic Alliance and in consultation with both European members of NATO and non-allied EU accession candidates.* Clearly, there are differences of opinion as to the eventual scale and ambition of the project. Most Nordic countries and Green-leaning politicians would prefer it to remain geared to low-intensity Petersberg Tasks, while more traditional interventionist countries such as France and the United Kingdom might see it eventually assuming more ambitious missions. But nobody questions the necessity of the project.

This is first and foremost because ESDP arises naturally from both endogenous and exogenous historical forces. In the first category can be found the inner dynamics of the European integration process.

Whatever the precise intentions of the various founding fathers, the project of "ever closer union" was always, in essence, a political project. It has seen the community progress from a common market to a single market (the largest in the world) with a single currency (already holding its own with the dollar). It has also made significant progress in the harmonization of elements of justice and home affairs, including the abolition of most internal frontiers. It now aspires—perfectly logically, given the intense interdependence of its economic, industrial and commercial interests—to develop a common foreign and security policy and to speak to the outside world with a single voice. That such a body should also seek to provide for its own security—defined largely in terms of regional stability—is eminently logical. It is all the more logical in that exogenous forces have pushed strongly in the same direction. Even while the Cold War was at its most intense, the United States, which had hegemonic leadership grudgingly thrust upon it in the late 1940s and early 1950s, grumbled constantly about burdensharing. Transatlantic tensions were so frequent that U.S. Defense Secretary Harold Brown once remarked: "They tell me the Alliance is in disarray. When has it ever been in array?"[6] Given the nature of the threat, the Alliance held together, despite considerable "free-riding" on the part of some European members.[7] In 1982, Lawrence Freedman noted that "the strains facing the Alliance reflect fundamental changes in the international system and cannot be eased simply by a reassertion of the Atlantic spirit. [...] In these conditions, it is not surprising if the United States and the Europeans develop alternative perspectives on the international system and their positions within it."[8] Those "fundamental changes" included the INF crisis of the early 1980s, the rise of Gorbachev and the end of the Cold War. Clearly some new transatlantic bargain would have to be struck.

The U.S. taxpayer—quite reasonably—baulked at continuing to underwrite security across a Continent with a GDP equivalent to that of the United States and a population 50 percent greater, especially in the absence of any obvious threat. Throughout the 1990s, the United States proposed to its allies a "global deal" whereby the Europeans should take care of their own backyard and the Americans (with European political support) should concentrate on the rest of the world.[9] With the Maastricht project for CFSP, the Europeans seemed eager to concentrate on their part of this deal, but the severe security problems immediately thrown up by the collapse of Yugoslavia proved beyond their capacity and the United States was yet again called to the rescue, not once (Bosnia) but twice (Kosovo). Under these circumstances, it was imperative that the EU do something far more serious to shore up its own military capacity. As argued in chapter 1, various schemes involving the WEU simply did not work out. The Alliance was in deep—and growing—trouble. That is why Saint-Malo "happened."[10] The rest has been a question of making it work.

ESDP: Making It Work

The challenge facing the EU in moving beyond the WEU "solution" was essentially threefold. First, to introduce new institutions into the Union allowing its member states collectively to address issues of security and defense efficiently and expeditiously. Second, to develop significant military capacity by new approaches both to procurement and to budgets. Third, to ensure that the new arrangements were conducted in harmony with NATO and with the United States. None of these challenges has proved easy. But there has been significant—albeit to date inadequate—progress in all three. It is not my intention in this chapter to *describe* the developments that have taken place on these three fronts. That has been done in various ways in the preceding chapters of this volume. My aim in the remainder of this chapter is to address the *nature* of the problems that have been faced and the extent to which they have been resolved.

Institutional Engineering

The development of new institutions has often been criticized as having absorbed a disproportionate amount of the EU's energy since 1999. The charge is linked to the suggestion that what really matters is military capacity.[11] There is much truth in this. But without institutions, military capacity is undeployable and an important underlying principle of ESDP is that it should be led by foreign policy. Therefore, I shall begin the discussion of making ESDP work with an assessment of three institutional problems, two of which were relatively minor and were rather successfully resolved, the third being a major problem that remains complex.

The first problem had to do with the establishment and bedding in of the two key new agencies: the *Political and Security Committee* (COPS) and the *High Representative-CFSP*. Given the considerable responsibilities accruing to the COPS under Article 25 of the Treaty of Nice (2000),[12] and given that, inevitably, this body would have to be grafted onto an already intricate policy-making structure including agencies in the national capitals, in the Council, in the Commission and in NATO, the challenge of bedding it in was not insignificant. A number of issues had to be addressed immediately. What was to be the rank and level of representation of the ambassadors serving on COPS? Clearly, they had to be sufficiently senior to discharge their duties effectively, but not so senior as to risk breaking free of the control of national foreign ministries. What should be the nature of the relationship between COPS and its equivalent body in NATO, the NAC? Establishing a formal relationship too early would risk allowing NATO too great an influence over the development of the embryonic EU body. Excessive delay in engaging in discussions with the NAC could be prejudicial not only to European security but also to transatlantic relations. How should the COPS relate to other key security actors such as the six non-EU members of NATO or the nine EU applicant states, to Russia, to Canada and even to the United States? Again, it was important to balance the necessary autonomy of EU decision making against the wisdom of widespread consultation. On these and other issues, the development of COPS has been a clear success story. Analysts have agreed that the COPS has succeeded remarkably well in striking precisely the right balance in its relations with other agencies and particularly in treading a fine line between representation of national interest and collective pro-activism. All think-tank blueprints for the future of ESDP's institutional nexus call for the upgrading and reinforcing of COPS.

Equally successful has been the story of the HR-CFSP. Javier Solana (in addition to actually *doing* the foreign and security policy job) faced massive turf battles in writing his own job description, as well as a budgetary problem that frequently required him to go to the Council with a begging bowl. It is widely recognized that—in large measure as a result of his own personal skills—he succeeded remarkably well in establishing the position as the fulcrum of the EU's CFSP. In June 2002, *Newsweek* concluded that "quietly and almost unnoticed, Javier Solana has done the unthinkable. He has created a common European foreign policy."[13] This might be considered by some to be hyperbole, but it captures the sense of how Solana is viewed on both sides of the Atlantic. The post has not yet become the apocryphal EU telephone number called for by Henry Kissinger, but it is a fact that the American Secretary of State speaks to the High Representative almost every day.[14] One potential problem here is that Solana's achievement will be a hard act to follow. Will the post survive the moving on of the founding post-holder?

The second institutional problem had to do with the cultural shock to the EU's system sparked by the appearance of military uniforms in the hitherto exclusively civilian bastion of the Council building (Justus Lipsius) in Brussels. The need to inculcate into the Council apparatus a minimum sense of security consciousness produced an EU–NATO working party on the issue. The Justus Lipsius building was likened by military specialists to Swiss cheese. A clash between Solana and Green MEPs over access to classified information generated recourse to the European Court. In January 2001, a classified internal report by Solana critical of EU procedures for Common Strategies was leaked to the press. The main thrust of the HR's criticism was precisely that the EU's civilian culture had ensured that the strategies be produced with total transparency, all documents being transferred to the public domain. This, he argued, effectively prevented the development of a strategic approach worth the name. The Pentagon's strategic policy on Russia is not made public, nor is that of the U.K. Ministry of Defense. Pressure from the European Parliament for far greater oversight of ESDP drew attention to the birth pangs that the delivery of this new infant was generating.

Some suggest that the absorption by the EU of this new policy area need not necessarily threaten or even fundamentally change its essentially civilian base.[15] Others see the very different methods and processes of defense policy decision-making as profoundly threatening to the open bargaining culture that obtains in other policy areas.[16] I believe that the advent of ESDP *will*—eventually—change the preponderant culture of the EU, but in a positive way. There is no direct reason why decision making in the field of security policy need have an impact on policy making in other areas. But *indirectly*, assuming ESDP can be made to work, the example of nation states reaching common decisions without engaging in pork-barrel politics, trade-offs or logrolling could have a knock-on effect in other areas. The decision in 2001 to move the Military Staff from the Council building to new secure premises in the nearby Rue de Cortenberg took much of the sting out of this early clash of institutional culture. Interviews with officers on both the Military Committee and the Military Staff suggest a smooth transition to a cooperative working environment. The interaction between the civil and military dimensions of ESDP—in a state of constant evolution—is likely to be one of the most interesting but also one of the most constructive of the EU's features.[17]

It is important to note in this regard that the United States itself went through a long process of institutional adaptation to military superpower status. The institutions originally designed by the founding fathers were not designed for a military power, let alone a superpower.

Congress had considerable control over the executive, which constantly complained of its lack of ability to act swiftly and efficiently in international crises. As Arthur Schlesinger, Jr. has brilliantly demonstrated,[18] the U.S. presidential system was forced to adjust to its status as a military superpower throughout the twentieth century, but especially after 1945. And the institutional tug-of-war continued after Vietnam as Congress won back some of its influence, the CIA was defanged and transparency flowed back again into the security arena. These are developments inherent to politics and to the exercise of power. The EU will find its own balance between civilian and military imperatives—in its own time.

The biggest problem area for the institutional dimension of ESDP, still unresolved, is the rationalization of the many overlapping and occasionally competing agencies involved in decision making. This is an issue that has been widely discussed in a range of publications[19] and there is little point in entering into further detail here. There are two fundamental problems: the tension between national capitals and "Brussels," and the issue of cross-pillar coherence. The former involves the interaction between entrenched national practices and preferences and a strangely unfamiliar new collective ethos slowly emerging out of the dialectical process itself. This interaction is healthy. The fundamental reasons why EU states agreed to pool their resources and deliver security collectively (single state defense incapacity, indivisibility of security, interdependence through European integration and the need for coherence of response) are strong guarantees that the process will continue to evolve.

Having embarked on the long and difficult road toward a new security order, EU states know that there will have to be some tradeoffs if the whole process is not to implode. It is those tradeoffs that will progressively flesh out the contours of the new baby delivered in Brussels. This will be complemented by the deliberations in the European Convention that, in July 2002, began discussion of external and security policy. The EU is deploying considerable energy in the task of maximizing institutional efficiency. Short of pulling the plug on the whole exercise, which no state could afford to do, they are all going to have to learn to live with compromises that everyone recognizes to be essential if the EU is truly to emerge as a viable international actor. The consequences of failure, having embarked—even so far—on this particular course, are too serious even to contemplate. Cross-pillar coherence is another matter. The issue here is one of political pragmatics. Nobody is suggesting the complete elimination of the Commission from the ESDP process, the more so in that the most important aspect of ESDP is likely to be those very peacekeeping and nation-building exercises that are the domain of the Charlemagne building. Few go along with the suggestions of Romano Prodi that the Council's dominance of security and defense issues should be called in to question.[20] All the evidence suggests that, despite inbuilt institutional tensions over "turf," the Commissioner for External Relations (Chris Patten) and the High Representative (Solana) have cooperated well, although that in itself is no guarantee that their eventual successors would prove to be as amenable. Most blueprints for institutional reform include the merging of these two posts to create a European foreign and security policy supremo with one foot in the Council and one foot in the Commission. Such a development seems increasingly plausible. Even the U.K. government is favorably disposed toward the upgrading of the Solana post, although in the summer of 2002 London was concealing its cards on the question of merger.

An alternative course might be the spring 2002 Franco-British suggestion of a European president elected by the Council for a five-year mandate. This proposal gained the support of Spain and Italy as well as of the president of the Convention, Valéry Giscard d'Estaing. It would seem to imply the "presidentialization" of the HR-CFSP post and it is widely assumed that the job would be tailor-made for a young former prime minister such as Aznar or Blair.[21] However, all of this is a matter of political pragmatics and intelligent institutional bargaining. If the need to make ESDP work is as strong as history suggests—and as most member states insist—it is, then the institutional conundrum will one day find the solution that so many are currently demanding. Several viable options are currently on the table. One will be selected.

The Franco-British proposal for a Council-based president raises the issue of leadership that is indeed one of the more serious problems for ESDP. It is clear that U.S. leadership in NATO derives both from the enormous military superiority enjoyed by Washington and from the fact that the United States is a non-European power, acceptable as leader to a number of small countries in ways in which no European lead country or even group of countries could be. Attempts, overt or covert, to create an informal *Directoire* have, as several chapters have noted, usually been counterproductive, fuelling irritation among the smaller member states. Since the Council works (under CFSP) by unanimity, this gives any one member state a theoretical power of veto. Greece has wielded that veto on several occasions, notably in refusing to accept a U.K.-brokered "non-paper" agreement with Turkey over assured access to NATO assets.

However, predictions of immobilism over the leadership issue are premature. So far, the EU itself has succeeded remarkably well in adapting to the exigencies of collective decision-making. And in matters of collective security, policy choices are not unlimited. There is likely to be consensus on "lower end Petersberg" missions and the deployment of "soft" instruments to attain agreed policy goals. Even at the higher end of the Petersberg scale, it is unlikely that any significant EU action in favor of regional security would be opposed by a single member state, particularly since, under the HG procedures, each nation retains sovereign control over the deployment of its own forces. The French president has proposed adopting procedures of "enhanced cooperation" under ESDP to circumvent possible opposition to military intervention, particularly in the absence of a UN or OSCE mandate. But all European peacekeeping and peace-enforcement missions since the end of the Cold War have been "coalitions of the willing" and if the willing are willing, the unwilling are unlikely to be able to stop them. This leads us to the question of military capacity.

Military Capacity

There is a strange irony in the fact that the immediate U.S. reaction to the Saint-Malo Declaration was concern that the EU would, through duplication of military capacity, become a rival to NATO or even to the United States. Within a year, however, U.S. officials were voicing the opposite fear: that the putative ERRF would turn out to be a paper tiger. As Kori Schake's chapter demonstrates, the truth lies elsewhere. The HG "Force Catalogue," which has been painstakingly assembled through the two Capabilities Conferences (November 2000 and 2001), was never intended to constitute an ERRF as such. It was intended as a "ball-park" target that would allow the EU member states to assemble a reasonably sizeable force, which would gradually be rendered "operational" through iterations involving the military staffs of both the EU and NATO. Care was always taken to avoid discussion of operational specifics or "scenarios" under which forces drawn from this Catalogue might be used—other than to speak in the vaguest of terms of "low," "medium" and "high" levels of intensity. What the EU had put together on the eve of 2003 corresponded fairly accurately to the target set in the Helsinki Headline Goal. The problem lay not so much in the *generation* of this Force Catalogue. That was never going to be difficult. Everything that was eventually pledged already existed at the time of Helsinki: all that was really required was to earmark it.

There is universal agreement that the EU is not yet in a position to engage in a high-intensity combat mission, but opinions differ as to what such eventual readiness would entail. Those who compare the EU force to U.S. military capacity suggest that the ERRF may need ten more years before being ready for high-intensity combat.[22] Others argue that the European force could engage in high-intensity combat much sooner by choosing to engage hostilities in a different way. For instance, one of the much-discussed "gaps" which the EU is currently aiming to fill is in SEAD (suppression of enemy air defenses). The U.S. system is high-tech and very expensive. But the EU could choose not to use such a system and to rely on pilot skills and risk-taking to achieve the same results. In other words, the *significant* questions about military capacity have to do with *the style* of military engagement envisaged. On this, there has been all too little discussion. It has become a truism to suggest that, whereas after Vietnam the United States vowed to fight wars at a distance with high-technology weapons and, ideally, "zero deaths," the Europeans were more prepared to settle for lower-technology equipment—and to take casualties. Toward the end of the Kosovo Crisis, as Frédéric Bozo had noted, it was the European allies who pressed for the introduction of ground troops and the Americans who resisted. But this difference of approach to and style of warfare remains highly theoretical. How many casualties would European publics be prepared to accept in order to carry out high-intensity Petersberg missions of the Kosovo type? We simply do not know.

Moreover, much has changed as a result of September 11. One huge problem for the Europeans is that the United States, via the 2001 *Quadrennial Defense Review*, is set to increase the EU–U.S. capabilities gap in ways that will make it difficult for European forces to remain interoperable with U.S. forces. The gaps discussed by Yost and Schake as being virtually unbridgeable are now bound to become even wider. In the fall of 2001, the United States chose to engage more or less alone in the Afghan campaign in part because of the painful experiences of fighting with less well-equipped allies in Kosovo. It is not clear under what circumstances—or indeed whether—the United States will, in future, decide to associate European forces with any large-scale American military campaign.

Robert Kagan stoked controversy in the summer of 2002 by arguing that "on major strategic and international questions today, [Americans and Europeans] agree on little and understand one another less and less."[23] The United States and Europe, he concludes, "have parted ways." Moreover, as the Afghan campaign showed unequivocally (and as Kori Schake warned), the EU would be unwise to make any assumptions about the availability of U.S. assets in the new strategic climate.

This leaves the EU facing major decisions about the future of its own procurement, which it would have faced anyway, irrespective of the existence of the ERRF. The prospect of military autonomy thus ceases to be a simple political aspiration and becomes, more and more, a functional necessity.

However, a second problem is that of knowing how to combine pursuit of the classic procurement objectives of the HG with the requirements of the EU's new priority focus on the "war on terrorism." On the positive side of the equation is the fact that most EU member states (with the notable exception of Germany) have either completed or are well on the way to completing professionalization of their armed forces. The Seville European Council in June 2002 published a "Draft Declaration on the Contribution of CFSP, including ESDP, in the Fight against Terrorism"[24] that, although so far extremely tentative, is a necessary first step in establishing procedures to examine the issue. Unfortunately the EU finds itself in a situation similar to that of 1991, when the Yugoslav wars broke out just as the CFSP seedlings were being sown. ESDP, while still in diapers, finds itself confronted since September 11, 2001 with the twin challenges of both a widening technology gap and a new—and lethal—adversary. Much time will be necessary in order to adjust to the new situation.

About the *urgency* of adjustment, however, there can be no question. A lively debate is already under way about the new military requirements of the new geo-strategic context. On one side of the debate are those who suggest that, while thinking through the *military* requirements for combating terrorism (which are not immediately obvious[25]), the EU should concentrate on delivery of the HG since there will, it is argued, continue to be a need for conventional intervention capabilities in the medium term (scenarios usually conjured up involve Africa, the Maghreb or even the Middle East). On the other side are those who suggest that the sort of military campaign witnessed in Kosovo (which greatly informed thinking on the HG) could well prove to be the first and the last of that type that will ever be fought in the European theater. In any case, the types of procurement systems necessary for that style of warfare are being pursued within NATO through the DCI. Seventy percent of the DCI improvements are relevant to ESDP. What the EU per se is more likely to require, according to this analysis, is small, high intensity, elite combat units to carry out limited missions such as those engaged by British commandos and special forces in Afghanistan in early 2002. This debate was really just beginning in the summer of 2002 and it is too soon to draw even provisional conclusions. But the key factor in the debate is the growing attempt to think through the necessary division of *military* labor between future EU-led NATO missions and EU-only missions. It is inadequate simply to assert that, for the latter, the EU should concentrate on "soft" security policy instruments. Few would go so far as to argue that the EU does not need and should not seek to possess its own autonomous military capacity. It is incumbent on the many who believe that it *should* have such a capacity to pay proper attention to the type and shape of that capacity.

A frequently voiced concern is that of money—of declining defense budgets. As table 1.1 shows, the EU-15 are currently spending approximately 50 percent of what the United States spends for defense and, according to most experts, getting about 10 percent of the U.S. combat capacity. Everybody agrees that that the EU can—and must—spend *better*. The debate revolves around whether or not it needs actually to spend *more*. Here again, there are two camps. Some analysts argue that the EU does not need more money: it is enough to spend more wisely.[26] Others insist that this will not be adequate and that the EU may need to ratchet up its collective defense spending by as much as an additional 1 percent of GDP. But who really knows? Deciding *how much* the Union needs is something of a theological discussion since nobody knows for sure what it might be used *for*.

This—essentially military—uncertainty is joined by another—political—conundrum. Most critics insist that there is little likelihood of an increase in EU defense spending, pointing to the contradiction within the Union between the constraints of economic convergence criteria, stability pacts and EU enlargement on the one hand, and defense spending needs on the other. But it is extremely hard to say with any precision (assuming a prior trans-European procurement and budgetary rationalization exercise had been conducted) how much *additional* cash would be required to meet the EU's military objectives. If it is true (as all EU governments insist) that there is no longer any real meaning to the notion of national defense; if it is true that the EU-15 genuinely believe in collective security; and if it indeed proves to be the case that the EU can no longer rely in any meaningful way on major U.S. assets, then the EU has no alternative but to develop autonomous capacity. Governments will then have no alternative but to explain this to their publics and to engage in political debate. Currently, as some claim, there may well be no sign of EU governments making the case for defense expenditure hikes. But that is largely because the definition of military need has not yet been finalized. When it is, the associated issue of raising the cash will not be beyond the ability of today's political communicators. The EU will require autonomous military capacity. It will acquire it.[27]

EU–NATO Relations

The acquisition of such capacity will then pose in its most direct form the associated question of the EU's ongoing and future relations with NATO. There are a number of straightforward issues here, and a few tricky ones. In the first category are the following assertions, which no mainstream EU statesman or strategic analyst would contest. ESDP is not intended as and should not become a rival or competitor to NATO. To the greatest extent possible, it should—and will—work in harmony with NATO. However, there may arise situations in which "NATO as a whole" (meaning, almost certainly, the United States) does not wish to engage in a particular operation and the EU does. In such circumstances, the EU should have the ability to do so. NATO is undergoing a process of transition and it was not clear in the summer of 2002 quite where the Alliance would wind up in 2012 and beyond. Under these circumstances, it is logical for the EU to continue to develop its own autonomous capacity, in consultation with NATO and avoiding *unnecessary* duplication of NATO assets. Since there will only be in Europe one set of forces and one set of equipment, much of each will be double-hatted, available for deployment under either an EU or a NATO command.

This raises the first of the tricky issues: NATO's "right of first refusal." This highly controversial notion is seen by many of ESDP's American friends as the first US "red line."[28] Since all Americans see NATO as the first port of call for any hypothetical military operation in Europe, this principle seems to them to be self-evident. In principle, European actors can also see the practical strategic logic of turning first to NATO. Empirically, that is almost certainly what would happen. However, it is the explicit and almost provocatively overt statement of the principle that some Europeans find difficult—rather like the earlier strictures on "no EU caucus" and "no decoupling," each of which posits a "nanny knows best" attitude on the part of the Americans which is all the more offensive to some Europeans in that it is unnecessary. It is highly unlikely that the EU would wish to keep the United States out of any mission in which the latter wished to be involved. And there are perfectly adequate channels for the rapid communication of individual national positions. In 2002, when the EU decided it was prepared to take over from NATO the *Amber Fox* mission in Macedonia, it was humiliating for the Union to have to wait months while NATO (meaning, in practice, the United States) decided whether or not it wished to transfer its remit. As the EU grows in stature and confidence, this issue, if left unresolved, could become a major bone of contention within the

Alliance. However, in practice, it is likely that a small number of judiciously placed telephone calls can resolve the issue of command before it actually becomes a problem.

Another contentious issue, as Terry Terriff's chapter has demonstrated, is the Europeanization of SHAPE and/or the development of some autonomous European planning capacity. The more cautious U.S. line on this tends to be that *all* planning should be done via SHAPE in order to avoid running the risk of an EU-planned mission getting out of control, with subsequent recourse to NATO firefighting under chaotic planning circumstances. There is no doubt that the EU will have to factor carefully potential crisis-escalation scenarios into its strategic analysis. But it remains a fact that the U.S. army is suspicious of any proposals to "Europeanize" SHAPE and, despite the pledge in the April 1999 Washington Communiqué of "assured EU access" to NATO planning capabilities, reality still lags far behind (see Schake's analysis of this issue in chapter 6). This situation needs very careful management since too resistant a stance on the part of the United States would almost certainly fuel cries (and not just in France) for the EU to develop its own autonomous joint service multinational planning capabilities. These European HQs (mainly based on British and French permanent joint HQs) will in any case progressively be put in place as a necessary fallback facility in the context of future EU-only missions. Such a prescription is written into the "Presidency Conclusions on ESDP" of the Nice Council meeting in December 2000, even though in the following two years little was being done to implement it.

A third—and more serious—bone of contention is the final form that will emerge for a new "division of labor" between the EU and the United States. I have already suggested that traditional notions of military interoperability might already be beyond reach. Julian Lindley-French has argued cogently for the establishment of an "escalation continuum" whereby the United States would occupy the top two-thirds and the EU the bottom two-thirds of a spectrum going from low-level humanitarian operations to all-out warfighting.[29] The important point here is to avoid an *absolute* division of labor involving no overlap at all. Robert Hunter, while noting that the United States seeks above all EU *political* support for its *global* ambitions, also insists that, inside the Alliance, a clear-cut division of labor runs directly counter to the "task and risk sharing" ethos on which NATO was founded.[30] Robert Kagan, on the other hand, suggests that it is already too late—a *de facto* division of labor now exists that involves an increasingly incompatible tension between the exercise of U.S. "hard" power and European attempts to rein in that power in the name of alternative "soft" instruments.[31] Most analysts agree that an *absolute* division of labor would eventually lead to the collapse of the Alliance. If the United States *only* did warfighting and the EU *only* did nationbuilding, synergy and complementarity would become impossible and the two activities would end up at cross-purposes. The United States, therefore, needs to take more seriously the softer policy instruments, just as the EU must put more effort into the acquisition of hard power. The same arguments hold within the EU. There cannot be a situation in which some nations do the fighting and others simply pay the bill. "One in all in" is the only acceptable—and the only workable—basis on which to manage an Alliance, whether transatlantic or intra-European.

One final problem area is the defense industry. The *de facto* creation of a European defense industrial base—at least in the key aerospace and electronics sectors—poses directly the question of subsequent trends in transatlantic defense relations. As Gordon Adams has argued,[32] governments on both sides of the Atlantic are keen, for political, technological and bureaucratic reasons, to protect their industries and their markets; while at the same time the demands of NATO interoperability, of technology research and of industrial strategy point to the likelihood of more cooperative global relationships. European firms, unable to rely on the domestic market to fill their order books, are keen to break into the American market, which is underpinned by an annual defense budget rising above $300 billion. American firms, for more *strategic* reasons, are open to deals with their European partners. But governments on both sides of the Atlantic are keen to forestall such cross-market penetration. In 2002, it was by no means clear which way the dice would eventually fall. The creation of two defense "fortresses" would be a body blow to Alliance solidarity. But the conditions under which significant transatlantic mergers would take place remained difficult to perceive. If significant missile defense projects are given the green light, then it is likely that U.S.–EU industry cooperation will increase.[33] But U.S. regulations on technology transfer and export licenses will need drastic liberalization for the cooperation to flourish.

Conclusions

It must never be forgotten that, for ESDP, it is still "early days." It is unrealistic to expect the EU to have solved, in three short years, a whole range of problems that remained latent but unaddressed for the previous fifty. After all, it took the EU fourteen years to harmonize policy on jam![34] The problems of security and defense policy are real and solutions must be found. But the world is changing fast and both the EU and NATO are changing with it. The broader forces of globalization, the shifting nature of strategic threat in the post-Soviet era, the new strategic challenges facing the United States, the rapid development of an increasingly confident EU, the inevitable evolution of NATO toward an organization for the delivery of collective security (rather than collective defense)—these and other reasons all militate in favor of the inevitability, and desirability, of some measure of European security autonomy.

U.S. strategists have argued for thirty years that a European pillar inside the Alliance is a necessary public good. Yet so long as the United States was prepared to take the lead in (and to foot the bill for) European security, some European nations saw no real need to pay much attention to these issues. French strictures on NATO proved in this respect to be remarkably prescient.[35] The Europeans are now finding themselves face to face with an entirely new strategic reality. The United States is simply not going to continue to ride to the rescue whenever the EU gets itself into a spot of regional bother. The Alliance will continue to exist, but the United States is likely to play a decreasing military role within it, reserving its unprecedented firepower for high-intensity high-technology U.S.-only operations.

Some form of European military capacity will be needed and the EU is going to have to pay for it. That capacity will be deployed in pursuit of the Union's CFSP whose cohesion and consistency is increasing constantly. The Union should not be afraid of its own ambition, but it will have to develop institutional capacity to cope with executive decisions, which will have to be taken rapidly and effectively. A more robust, lucid, confident and effective EU will be in its own interests, in the interests of both NATO and the United States, and in the interests of all of the EU's regional partners, which share its genuine commitment to collective security. If ESDP did not exist at this point, it would have to be invented.

Notes

1. As several speakers argued in the debate on ESDP that took place at the *New Europe* seminar at Chatham House in January 2001: *New Europe Seminar on the Future of the European Union* (London: New Europe Research Trust, 2001), pp. 63–69.

2. "Soft" security is much more difficult to deliver than a short, sharp military campaign. It requires the mobilization of many more resources and is usually a very long-term project.

3. Nicole Gnesotto, "For a Common European Security Culture," *WEU-ISS Newsletter* No. 31, October 2000, p. 1.

4. Jolyon Howorth, "The CESDP and the Forging of a European Security Culture," *Politique Européenne* 8 (Summer 2002).

5. Stephen Everts, *Shaping a Credible EU Foreign Policy* (London: Centre for European Reform, 2002); Jolyon Howorth, "European Defense and the Changing Politics of the European Union: Hanging Together or Hanging Separately?" *Journal of Common Market Studies* 39 (2001), pp. 765–789; Jolyon Howorth,"The European Security Conundrum: Prospects for ESDP after 11 September 2001," Policy Paper on-line at www.notre-europe. asso.fr. (March 2002).

6. Quoted in François Heisbourg, "Can the Atlantic Alliance Last out the Century?," *International Affairs* 63 (Summer 1987).

7. Stanley R. Sloan, *The US and Trans-Atlantic Burdensharing* Vol. 2 in Nicole Gnesotto, ed., *Burdensharing in NATO*, Paris, "Les Notes de l'IFRI," no. 12, 1999.

8. Freedman, Lawrence, "The Atlantic Crisis," *International Affairs* 58 (1982), p. 398.

9. David C. Gombert and F. Stephen Larrabee, *America and Europe: A Partnership for a New Era* (Cambridge: Cambridge University Press, 1997); Jennifer Medcalf, "Going Global? NATO and the Extra-European Challenge," Ph.D. dissertation, University of Bath, 2002.

10. The author was told in May 2000 by a senior official in Whitehall that the United Kingdom went to Saint-Malo because it was convinced that, otherwise, the Alliance's days were severely numbered.

11. It is best epitomized by George Robertson's quip that "You can't send a wiring diagram to a crisis."

12. To "monitor the international situation in the areas covered by the CFSP and contribute to the definition of policies by delivering opinions to the Council [...] monitor the implementation of agreed policies [...] exercise, under the responsibility of the Council, political control and strategic direction of crisis management operations."

13. Carla Power, "Europe's Mr. Fix-It," *Newsweek*, June 17, 2002, pp. 22–24.

14. Interviews in Brussels, June 2002.

15. Paul Cornish and Geoffrey Edwards, "Beyond the EU/NATO Dichotomy: The Beginnings of a European Strategic Culture," *International Affairs* 77 (2001), p. 579.

16. See Anand Menon's arguments in chapter 10.

17. Hanna Ojanen, *Theories at a Loss. EU–NATO Fusion and the "Low Politicisation" of Security and Defense in European Integration* (Helsinki: Finnish Institute of International Affairs, 2002), UPI Working Papers 35.

18. Arthur M. Schlesinger Jr., *The Imperial Presidency* (Boston: Houghton Mifflin, 1973).

19. See note 5; Gilles Andréani, Christoph Bertram and Charles Grant, *Europe's Military Revolution* (London: CER, 2001); Venusberg Group, *Enhancing*

the European Union as an International Actor (Gütersloh: Bertelsmann Foundation, 2000).

20. In a speech to the Conference of Presidents at the European Parliament on May 22, 2002, Prodi suggested that the three-pillar structure of Maastricht be abandoned in favor of communitarization of all policy areas. There is virtually no chance of this suggestion being accepted by all member states.

21. George Parker, "France and UK Call for New Force at Top of EU," *Financial Times*, May 15, 2002.

22. [IISS, 2001], International Institute for Strategic Studies, London, "The European Rapid Reaction Force," *The Military Balance 2001–2002* (Oxford: Oxford University Press, 2001), pp. 283–289.

23. Robert Kagan, "Power and Weakness," *Policy Review*, No. 113, June 2002, p. 1.

24. Annexed to the *Presidency Conclusions* (Annex V, pp. 31–34). This document can be found on the Council website at www.europa.eu.int.

25. See the cautionary essay by Lawrence Freedman, "The Coming War on Terrorism" in Lawrence Freedman, ed., *Superterrorism* (Oxford: Blackwell, 2002).

26. François Heisbourg, "European Defense Takes a Leap Forward," *NATO Review* (Spring/Summer 2000), p. 9.

27. On July 14, 2002, President Chirac of France, recently reelected on a platform of tax cuts, announced significant new spending for the defense budget . . . in an effort to bring France's military capacity up to the standard of the British. He presented this move as an example for other EU member states to follow; *Le Monde*, July 16, 2002, p. 6.

28. Robert E. Hunter, *The European Security and Defense Policy: NATO's Companion—or Competitor?* (Santa Monica: Rand, 2002), p. 149.

29. Julian Lindley-French, *Terms of Engagement. The Paradox of American Power and the Trans-Atlantic Dilemma Post-11 September* (Paris: EU-ISS, 2002). Chaillot Paper 52, p. 67.

30. Hunter, *The European Security and Defense Policy*, note 29, pp. 149–151.

31. Kagan, "power and Weakness," p. 13: "Europe does not see a mission for itself that requires power. Its mission is to oppose power."

32. Gordon Adams, "Fortress America in a Changing Trans-Atlantic Defense Market," in Burkard Schmitt, ed., *Between Cooperation and Competition: The Trans-Atlantic Defense Market* (Paris: WEU-ISS, 2001), Chaillot Paper 44, pp. 3–49. An earlier version of Adams' paper was given at the Seattle Conference in May 2000.

33. One positive sign came at the UK's Farnborough air show in July 2003 when Boeing signed a cooperation agreement with its arch-rival the European Aeronautic Defense and Space Company (EADS) as well as with BAE Systems for technology sharing in ballistic missile defense projects: Alexander Nicoll, "Defense Deal to Encourage Collaboration," *Financial Times*, July 23, 2002.

34. See Diana Welch, "From 'Euro Beer' to 'Newcastle Brown': A Review of European Community Action to Dismantle Divergent 'Food Laws,'"

Journal of Common Market Studies 22 (September 1983). On the broader issue of time frames, see James A. Caporaso and John T.S. Keeler, "The European Union and Regional Integration Theory," in Carolyn Rhodes and Sonia Mazey, eds., *The State of the European Union: Building a European Polity?* (Boulder: Lynne Rienner, 1995), p. 41.

35. De Gaulle, in 1949, was one of those who called energetically for the creation of the Alliance—but for an Alliance of rough equals as a basis for genuine health and strength. France has always believed in the compatibility of European capacity and Alliance enhancement. It was the French who refused to accept the strategic credibility of "extended deterrence," which has now been revealed as a bluff by its own architects. It was the French in the 1960s who said that Europeans had become so dependent on the Americans that they were incapable of properly coming to terms with the *European* requirements of security. Yet France has remained, throughout, a staunch member of the Atlantic Alliance. In many ways, France's positions throughout the history of NATO are those on which all EU countries are currently aligning themselves (with greater and lesser degrees of enthusiasm). The one exception to this rule (about which France can actually do little) is the aspiration to play a global strategic role. The United Kingdom may possibly share that aspiration (although patchily), but no other EU member state is really interested. It therefore remains a distant Gallic dream.

Index

135x175

Printed in the United States
78352LV00002B/212

9 781403 966902